A Desire Called America

A Desire Called America

Biopolitics, Utopia, and the Literary Commons

Christian P. Haines

FORDHAM UNIVERSITY PRESS

New York 2019

Fordham University Press gratefully acknowledges financial assistance and support provided for the publication of this book by Penn State University.

Copyright © 2019 Fordham University Press

All rights reserved. No part of this publication may be reproduced, stored in a retrieval system, or transmitted in any form or by any means—electronic, mechanical, photocopy, recording, or any other—except for brief quotations in printed reviews, without the prior permission of the publisher.

Fordham University Press has no responsibility for the persistence or accuracy of URLs for external or third-party Internet websites referred to in this publication and does not guarantee that any content on such websites is, or will remain, accurate or appropriate.

Fordham University Press also publishes its books in a variety of electronic formats. Some content that appears in print may not be available in electronic books.

Visit us online at www.fordhampress.com.

Library of Congress Control Number: 2019939349

Printed in the United States of America
21 20 19   5 4 3 2 1
First edition

For my mother, Donna M. Haines:
To the moon and back.

CONTENTS

Introduction: Impossibly American   1

1. A Revolutionary Haunt: Utopian Frontiers in William S. Burroughs's Late Trilogy   33
2. The People and the People: Democracy and Vitalism in Walt Whitman's 1855 *Leaves of Grass*   74
3. Nobody's Wife: Affective Economies of Marriage in Emily Dickinson   114
4. Idle Power: The Riot, the Commune, and Capitalist Time in Thomas Pynchon's *Against the Day*   157

Coda: Assembling the Future   205

Acknowledgments   209
Notes   213
Index   241

INTRODUCTION

Impossibly American

"Make America Great Again." The short-term history of this phrase speaks to Donald Trump's strange combination of anti-establishment rhetoric, political and financial corruption, verbal and physical violence, and popular appeal. It conjures up images of rallies in which racist, ableist, and xenophobic cries are delivered with religious fervor. These rallies are a postmodern tent revival in which violent intensity promises to accelerate providence, though a providence that has as much to do with entrepreneurial success as anything spiritual.[1] Trump and his supporters are winners; the rest of the world are losers; and America will return to its appointed position of greatness only if it gives itself over to this fundamental truth.

It's tempting to see Trump's rise from businessman to candidate to president as unprecedented, and certainly the zeal he inspires in a large portion of the U.S. electorate is quite distinct. That being said, the Trump phenomenon conforms to Stuart Hall's articulation of authoritarian populism as "an exceptional form of the capitalist state—which, unlike classical fascism, has retained most (though not all) of the formal representative institution in place, and which at the same time has been able to construct around itself an active popular consent."[2] Hall was analyzing Thatcherism in Great Britain in the 1970s, which might be understood as the inauguration of neoliberalism. Despite Trump's tendency to break the norms of liberal democracy, his administration is less an unprecedented deviation from the U.S. status quo than an intensification of a tendency that has belonged to neoliberalism from its beginning. If one usually associates neoliberalism with policies designed to privatize public services, deregulate the financial sector, and transform every kind of social relation into a market good—notably, the Trump administration has only intensified such measures—neoliberalism has equally relied on social conservatism and authoritarianism to destroy the power of organized labor, turn immigrants and racialized others into scapegoats for economic slumps, and recruit large swaths of the U.S. electorate regardless of their economic interests.[3] In short, Trump represents a difference in degree rather than kind—an intensification of the right-wing swing in U.S. politics that has been ongoing since the 1970s. It should come as little surprise, then, that "Make America Great Again" first appeared as a slogan during Ronald Reagan's 1980 presidential campaign ("Let's Make America Great Again").

"Make America Great Again" speaks to a failure of political imagination. It is an anti-utopian slogan—a reactionary call to respond to declining socioeconomic conditions through racism, misogyny, homophobia, transphobia, and xenophobia—but it is also symptomatic of an inability on the part of liberals and the left to mobilize a popular alternative to neoliberalism. In terms of U.S. party politics, this failure has to do with the way in which the New Democrat program of triangulation, or the turn to centrism, has narrowed the gap between the politics of Democrats and Republicans; it is this neoliberal convergence that helped to ensure the relative success not only of Trump but also of Bernie Sanders during the 2016 presidential campaign season. More generally, with the exception of some notable social movements (for example, Occupy and Black Lives Matter), left-wing political aspirations have increasingly shifted toward norms of inclusion, representation, and equal opportunity, marginalizing efforts at systemic social change. The war on poverty has been replaced by a mission to diversify the ranks of the upwardly mobile, as antiracist, anticapitalist, feminist, and queer politics increasingly accommodate neoliberal models of governance.

This failure of political imagination should be understood in terms of the American left's abandonment of its utopian impulse. The U.S. left hasn't simply been outflanked by the right. It has surrendered its utopian vocation to it. Put differently, it has given up on the desire to fundamentally change society—a desire embodied, for example, in nineteenth-century Populism and the antisystemic movements of the 1960s—in favor of fragmentary efforts to ameliorate the worst social pathologies. This claim shouldn't be conflated with the notion that the rise of identity politics has led to a fragmentation of the left. To the contrary, what remains of American utopianism is most evident in movements such as Black Lives Matter, which not only reckon with injustice and inequality but also propose expansive visions of the future. Instead, the failure has to do with the abandonment of systemic change, or the substitution of piecemeal reform for efforts to construct another world. This book argues that the utopian impulse has lingered on in U.S. literature and that it has done so in the form of a strange reversal of American exceptionalism, that is, a reversal of those practices that elevate the United States to the position of model nation, immunizing it from critique through narratives of global salvation. Literature has become a place in which that desire called America—the belief that the United States is a land of unique social, political, and cultural vitality—comes to be imagined against the grain of exceptionalism. In other words, there is a tradition of U.S. literature, going back to at least the nineteenth century, that pushes the revolutionary potential of American exceptionalism to the point where its nationalist-capitalist frame breaks. This literature invents what I call a singular America—a counter-nation in which statist and capitalist social structures give way to the commons (an egalitarian and radically democratic form of social solidarity). Although literature certainly cannot fix the United States, it can offer an education in a desire called America, a lesson not in what America is but in what it might become.

A Singular America: Between Exceptionalism and Its Critique

There is no redeeming America—no act of transcendence capable of expunging the histories of empire and genocide, slavery and internment, that compose "America." At the same time, that desire called America persists. It persists not only as an ideological appeal but also as an impulse to experiment with new forms of political life. This impulse is recognizable in colonial and postcolonial myths of a new American "race." Thomas Paine writes of the American Revolution:

> We have it in our power to begin the world over again. A situation, similar to the present, hath not happened since the days of Noah until now. The birthday of a new world is at hand and a race of men, perhaps as numerous as all Europe contains, are to receive their portion of freedom from the event of a few months.[4]

It's tempting to read these sentences as nothing more than the political corollary of those philosophies of history—Locke's, Hegel's—in which America is simultaneously a prehistorical wilderness (state of nature) and a historical endpoint (the aim of Eurocentric history).[5] The revolutionary impulse of America repeats, even as it displaces, European narratives of the New World as exceptional space: It consecrates violence against indigenous peoples in the name of "Man." In this anthropology of conquest, "Man" signifies a subject whose self-sameness requires not only the constitutive exclusion of otherness but also its assimilation: It is not simply that Man erects itself through the relegation of non-European peoples to subhuman status but also that it maintains itself, vampire-like, through the incorporation of non-European traits, customs, goods, and lands.[6] In this view, Paine's revolutionary zeal is but the ruse of imperial reason.

There is, however, a surplus of social potentiality immanent in the long arc of American exceptionalism—a singular America that doesn't transcend exceptionalism but lives within and against it. This singular, though not single, America exposes the United States to a threshold through which it becomes other than itself; it makes good on the exception in exceptionalism to such a degree that the normative model of America bursts apart. In this context, Paine's "birthday of a new world" no longer entails the reiteration of Man's empire over earth but the interruption of Man—the suspension of the *anthropos* and the advent of a "new race." Race ceases to designate the self-transparency of a universal subject ("the human race") but instead serves as a placeholder for that which comes after Man, for a new being whose *logos* (or mode of speaking and reasoning) no longer coincides with the *anthropos* of settler colonialism, slavery, and capitalism.[7] That this language cannot help but recall the political anthropology from which it breaks doesn't mean that it fails to bring something new into the world. The "birthday of a new world" gives rise to a singular America in the midst of exceptionalism. A singular America names that figure through which America becomes unrecognizable even to itself. It is the reversal of American exceptionalism, the moment when, in taking exception to itself, exceptionalism gives birth to another world.

American studies, American literary history, and American cultural studies have founded themselves, in the post–Vietnam War period, on a critique of American exceptionalism. The critical possibilities of these fields depend on an oppositional stance from whose perspective "America" names a nationalist project of empire—an apparatus of conquest, domination, exclusion, and exploitation. This oppositional stance has been immensely productive, not only because of its critical powers but also because of the way it converts practices of dissent into affirmations of political possibility. Americanist critique does not simply desubjectify or denationalize; it also gives rise to transnational or postnational subjectivities. However, this oppositional stance involves the disavowal of a certain ambiguity. Its crucial premise is the division of the world into two, or the rearticulation of "America" as a series of oppositions: exceptionalism/critique, imperial/anti-imperial, majoritarian/minoritarian, normative/antinormative, and so on. The condition of possibility of this division is the willful forgetting of a place—what one might call the excluded middle between American exceptionalism and its critique—in which these extremes mingle. American studies maintains its oppositional status through a disavowal of its own complicities with exceptionalism, or, as Robyn Wiegman articulates it, the New American studies of the post–Vietnam War period "establish[es] a critical subjectivity dedicated to the pursuit of noncomplicity with the object of study."[8]

This disciplinary pursuit of noncomplicity has led to an atrophy of the imaginative capacities of American studies. Chris Castiglia has described this condition as a kind of disciplinary embarrassment over expressions of hope: The affective or libidinal sources that invigorate practices of worldmaking appear trivial or wrongheaded from the perspective of a form of critique—what Castiglia calls "critiquiness"—dedicated to sniffing out political complicities.[9] It's not so much that American studies avoids positive identifications but that it assigns value to these identifications largely on the basis of their distance from the status quo. What's positive in these affirmations is first and foremost their negativity in respect to the dominant political order, rather than the futures they imagine or the alternative values they embody. Even in regard to those social movements with which oppositional intellectuals identify, the dominant intellectual orientation seems to be toward calling out shortcomings instead of building on the positive potential of these movements. In short, it's become easier to criticize the status quo than to imagine alternatives.

The biopolitical turn in American studies offers a way of overcoming this impasse. It emphasizes the need to positively articulate alternative forms of life, even as it maintains the importance of critique, including the critique of American exceptionalism. It concerns itself with the diverse array of power relations structuring social life, but it understands power not only as power *over* life but also as the power *of* life. The biopolitical turn in American studies derives, in part, from a general turn toward biopolitics in critical theory and the humanities. Associated with European intellectuals such as Michel Foucault, Giorgio Agamben, and Antonio Negri, this critical discourse has offered a means for the humanities to grapple with modern forms of power and to develop positive political alternatives. It would be a mistake, however, to suggest that American studies simply assimilates or accommodates biopolitical theory. The biopolitical turn in American studies is a productive transposition of biopolitical thought, one that not only adapts concepts but also reinvents biopolitics in response to the material situation of the Americas. Although it's difficult to date this turn precisely, it occurs sometime during the late 1990s and mid-2000s, in the wake of the counterglobalization struggles of the preceding century and in the midst of George W. Bush's so-called War on Terror.[10] This period sees the beginning of a reorientation of American studies away from ideology, discourse, and representation toward material assemblages and life itself. Priscilla Wald's 2011 presidential address to the American Studies Association (ASA), "American Studies and the Politics of Life," is the closest thing to an official announcement of this turn. Wald describes "an increasing turn in American studies from the familiar grounding terms of the citizen and the nation to the human and networks."[11] Of course, this shift doesn't encompass the entirety of the field, nor does it eliminate traditional practices of ideology critique, but it does move the center of gravity of American studies toward the twin conceptual registers of the power over life and the power of life.

The biopolitical turn in American studies might be understood as a belated reckoning with the ontological question of America. The productivity of the new American studies has depended on shelving the question of *what* America is in favor of asking *how* and *where* America is. Put differently, post–Vietnam War American studies abandoned the search for the cultural essence of America, replacing it with a diagnostic inquiry into the ideological mechanisms and material conditions of the United States and the Americas. Janice Radway's 1998 presidential address to the ASA, "What's in a Name?"—which suggests the field might abandon "America" in favor of less loaded terminology—is the logical conclusion of this methodological tendency: It imagines a way of achieving noncomplicity by disentangling the field of American studies from that desire called America.[12] In doing so, however, it disavows the ontological dimension of America— America as a speculative and libidinal object inextricable from (but also irreducible to) the empirical realities of the United States or the Americas. As William V. Spanos puts it, the New Americanists' critique of exceptionalism "has all too hastily rejected theory for practice, or, rather, has reduced them to a binary opposition that privileges practice over theory."[13] The biopolitical turn in American studies certainly doesn't try to return to a precritical version of American studies, as if what were needed was the recovery of some true America. It does, however, break with a field-imaginary in which critical value is premised on the division between the (false) speculative appeal of America and the (true) empirical reality of the United States/Americas. Instead of demystifying the appeal of America, this emergent field formation thinks through the discrepant forms of life inhabiting the Americas, including those whose desires are caught between American exceptionalism and its critique.

A Desire Called America calls attention to a strange form of literary praxis that inhabits the excluded middle between American exceptionalism and its critique. This praxis draws on the energies of American exceptionalism only to overturn its ideological structures. Examining texts from two periods—the "American Renaissance" (the mid-nineteenth-century moment of literary production that has come to assume the status of "classical" American literature) and the post-Vietnam era—I show how they develop utopian figures through which a singular America emerges as a reversal of the exceptionalist paradigm. For instance, the critical power of Emily Dickinson's marriage poems (examined in Chapter 3) does not simply derive from their overturning of nineteenth-century exceptionalism's constitutive exclusion of women. It also stems from the way that Dickinson redirects exceptionalism's project of reinventing humanity toward queer, antipatriarchal, and anticapitalist ends. A singular America is thus less anti- or postnationalist than counter-nationalist, a term I use to suggest a refunctioning of nationality: a nation without nationalism, a people without the exclusionary logic of citizenship, a collective bond without the mediation of the state. The form that this counter-nationality takes is the commons, or modes of cooperation that exceed the constraints of private and public forms of property, as well as liberal and socialist forms of the state. The commons is the social substance of a singular America, that which prevents it from being reducible to a mere regulative ideal. If a singular America emerges through the reversal of American exceptionalism, it is because exceptionalism includes—as the repressed alterity at its heart—an idea of the commons.

Thinking the concept of a singular America means risking a philosophical approach to America. The danger involved may seem obvious: the idealization of the social and political content of U.S. literature and culture. Less obvious, because of the anti-exceptionalist field-imaginary of American studies, is that there is also danger involved in avoiding speculation. Insofar as America names a desire as much as a place, it always already includes a speculative element. For desire, in a psychoanalytic sense, is never desire for this or that empirical object but always desire for an idea: the idea of an object that would realize a subject, that would make up for some fundamental lack. I follow Jacques Lacan in understanding the productivity of desire in terms of a strange identity between lack (of satisfaction) and surplus (of libido).[14] In the formula "a desire called America," America relates to desire in the same way that what Lacan terms the *objet petit a* relates to desire: It is not the goal or aim of desire but rather the (object-)cause of desire, that constitutive absence around which desire revolves.[15] No matter the teleology to which desire finds itself hitched, the *objet petit a* introduces a gap that is also a kind of stasis—a movement in place that is productive in the sense that it maintains the libidinal status quo. In the case of a desire called America, desire organizes subjectivity through the appeal of nationalist fervor or, just as often, through the "realistic" insistence on the limits of liberal democracy.

There is, however, that which in the desire called America is more than America, a jouissance that this desire simultaneously shelters and denies, feeds on and represses. Paine recognizes this surplus when he writes of the birthday of a new world, suggesting that the project of U.S. Independence means something more than the creation of yet another nation-state. Lacan distinguishes jouissance in a relatively consistent manner in his seminars and essays. He articulates it as a pleasure that exceeds the economy of the pleasure principle, a pleasure that is painful because it breaks with the regulation of libidinal energy or transgresses the symbolic order. Antigone (Lacan's exemplary figure of jouissance) experiences it when she refuses to obey the commands of the state, insisting on the sacredness of familial bonds to such a degree that it explodes the political order.[16] There is likewise a jouissance at the heart of a desire called America—a revolutionary commitment to the painful pleasure of ushering in a new world. American exceptionalism reproduces itself by deploying this surplus pleasure without allowing it to become an autonomous social figure. In other words, exceptionalism tames the jouissance of America, converting it into a docile patriotism or a knowing cynicism. Conversely, a singular America names the moment when the jouissance sheltered in that desire called America becomes autonomous. There are instances in literary, cultural, social, and political practice in which America realizes itself only by abolishing itself, moments when it lives up to its name only by becoming unrecognizable to itself. A singular America is thus not the opposite of a desire called America but rather its ecstatic consummation in the advent of another world.

My intention is not to suggest that American exceptionalism is unique, that it defies comparison to the nationalisms of other countries—certainly, other countries exercise power through claims to an exceptional status. There is, however, something singular in that desire called America, something irreducible to the empirical content of the capitalist world-system, even as its conditions and effects are resolutely material. A desire called America is speculative, which is to say that it requires philosophical engagement. Such engagement doesn't imply the transcendence of social and political matters but the recuperation of that which in a given state of affairs exceeds its actual dimensions. Gilles Deleuze and Félix Guattari describe philosophy as the creation of concepts, proposing that concepts do not designate things in the world but introduce events in the midst of things: Philosophy opens up new possibilities by reconfiguring the relationship between what is virtual and what is actual.[17] Deleuze and Guattari associate this creation of concepts with philosophy proper, relegating literature to the "plane" of affect, but they nevertheless make room for zones of interference between these practices or planes.[18] Philosophy and literature are irreducible to one another, but this doesn't mean they fail to meet. Cesare Casarino elaborates the interference between literature and philosophy as philopoesis:

> Philopoesis is the love of the potentiality that cuts across philosophy and literature—and this is a potentiality that makes itself manifest specifically in writing.... If philopoesis is the love of poiesis—that is, the making of words—it is above all the love of that which remains unmade in such a making, the love of words as unspent potentials.[19]

This book considers the unspent potentiality of America. It focuses on the literature of a singular America as so many instances in which exceptionalism's failure to discipline jouissance enables the remaking of America. This speculative wager on another world is resolutely utopian, without for all that being idealist. It doesn't indulge in the fantasy of making America great again; it dreams of other worlds.

The literature of a singular America is a literature of militant life, of life that refuses the status quo and invents another world. It is also a literature of exceptionalism's reversal into a utopianism whose force it cannot bear. These reversals appear as utopian figures, or dynamic representational forms whose relation to flesh is not merely mimetic but reflexive and anticipatory: a thinking of and through the possibilities of bodies.[20] The literary works on which I focus—writings by Walt Whitman, Emily Dickinson, William S. Burroughs, and Thomas Pynchon—propose utopian figures as self-destruct sequences of exceptionalism: They make good on the exceptional potentiality of America to the point at which America is no longer America. In this book, I ask what might happen if these fleeting sparks of the utopian imagination were fanned, turned into flames that set ablaze the political imaginary of the United States: What kinds of social relations and political institutions might emerge if we abandoned the identification of America with capitalism and the nation-state? What would happen if we scrapped the empty promises of the "American Dream" in favor of imagining another world in which to live?

Before moving on to a discussion of biopolitics and utopianism, allow me to offer a concise summation of the book's theses. These are meant not as final words but as openings onto vistas of critical reflection and political imagination. First thesis: *A desire called America is characterized by an irreducible ambiguity*. It is exceptionalist, and undeniably so. It links a rebirth of the subject to the coming of another world through the positing of America as exception. At the same time, there is an irrepressible singularity at the heart of this exceptionalism, a seed of radical alterity, of jouissance. Insofar as America is desire, it exceeds itself, it cannot help but exceed itself, because desire is not desire for this or that object but desire to have it all. Lacan's dictum that "from an analytical point of view, the only thing of which one can be guilty is of having given ground relative to one's desire" makes sense in this regard, not because it suggests some final satisfaction—"At last, America!"—but because it calls for a refusal of mere goods (exceptionalism's libidinal bribes) in favor of a commitment to jouissance: "America, we're through!"[21] Second thesis: *A singular America names the positive articulation of the impossibility at the heart of exceptionalism*. It is utopian because it is no place—that which is incommensurable with exceptionalism—and because it is the good place—not in moral terms but in the sense that it redefines value as such. A singular America doesn't dissolve desire's ambiguity, but it does signal an impossibility irreducible to it: impossibility as the redefinition of what is possible in the world, as the renewal of politics through the finding of another world within this world. There is no satisfying a singular America—it wants the world, and more. Third thesis: *The impossibility of a singular America makes its appearance not as place but as form of life*. A singular America has no home. To say that it has no home is not to say that it doesn't take place. It takes place in the flesh. This embodied life cannot be defined solely in terms of pleasure or pain, for there is that in life which is more than life, that which Freud termed the death drive but which also deserves to be called militancy (commitment to jouissance). The utopian praxis of a singular America is the refusal of this life not for the sake of a beyond but for the sake of an upheaval that brings into being something unrecognizable. To live a singular America is to live America's impossibility. It is to become impossibly American.

An Other Life, an Other World: On Biopolitics and Utopia

In the second volume of *The History of Sexuality*, Foucault identifies the motivation behind his research as "curiosity," "the only kind of curiosity worth acting upon with a degree of obstinacy: not the curiosity that seeks to assimilate what is proper for one to know, but that which enables one to get free of oneself."[22] True curiosity, Foucault suggests, has an air of impropriety to it. The curious researcher departs from certainty in favor of a refusal of disciplinary subjection—a disidentification with the self that is also an experience of freedom. In a contemporaneous article, "The Subject and Power," Foucault reaffirms this commitment to practices of disidentification, arguing "that the target nowadays is not to discover what we are but to refuse what we are. . . . We have to promote new forms of subjectivity through the refusal of this kind of individuality which has been imposed on us for several centuries."[23] To get free of oneself doesn't mean dispensing with selfhood altogether. Instead, it involves imagining forms of life that break with modern forms of subjectivity. It means learning to live otherwise.

Reading Foucault with this sense of curiosity in mind allows one to retrieve the emancipatory potential of his theory of biopolitics. It challenges the dominant interpretation of Foucault as an anti-utopian thinker by showing how his work is oriented toward utopian horizons. Foucault's conceptualization of power as an intricate network of forces generative of subjectivity may seem to leave little room for utopia, but that is only because Foucault redirects the energies of utopia toward practices that transform embodied subjects. Utopia becomes less a question of geography than of forms of life. Foucault has, of course, been an important touchstone for Americanists. Although the biopolitical turn in American studies certainly exceeds Foucault, it is difficult to imagine what the turn would look like without his contributions.[24] His work has not only set many of the terms of the biopolitical turn. It's also helped push the political desire of critics beyond emancipation in the narrow sense—emancipation as freedom *from* power—and toward the jouissance involved in inventing new forms of life. The proper name "Foucault" marks the possibility of a liberation immanent in, but in excess of, contemporary arrangements of power. It also indicates the theoretical coherence of a singular America, understood as the surplus of that desire called America in respect to American exceptionalism.

As a term, *biopolitics* is best known from the first volume of Foucault's *The History of Sexuality*, where it designates "nothing less than the entry of life into history, that is, the entry of phenomena peculiar to the life of the human species into the order of knowledge and power, into the sphere of political techniques."[25] In this "era of 'biopower'"—which, Foucault argues, is constitutive of modernity—politics stretches its fabric between two poles, an "anatomo-politics of the human body" and a "biopolitics of the population," or between the disciplines that compose and administer individual bodies and the techniques that regulate species or populations.[26] This biopolar apparatus (*dispositif*) serves as a productive point of departure for analyses of power, because it indicates that power operates at discrepant scales, for instance, at the level of national population, as well as of the imprisoned body. What frequently goes unnoted, however, is that these two poles do not constitute an exhaustive description of the political technologies of subject-production belonging to biopolitics. Foucault explicitly makes this point, writing that "these forms [the administration of bodies and the regulation of populations] were not antithetical, however; they constituted rather two poles of development linked together by a whole intermediary cluster of relations."[27] Indeed, what makes sexuality such an important object of inquiry, as well as the occasion for which Foucault formulates a theory of biopolitics, is that it serves as a "means of access both to the life of the body and the life of the species"—it is, in other words, a point of mediation between body and population. For Foucault, biopolitics cannot be reduced to the governance of populations, as some scholars suggest, but instead names the different processes through which life individuates itself as a series of political objects (*homo economicus*, the people, the bourgeoisie, etc.).[28] In sum, biopolitics concerns the individuation of life as a political object in modern times.

This approach clarifies what might be called the fundamental lexeme of biopolitics: "life itself." Critics have deployed this term in a number of ways. It sometimes names a zero-degree of biological existence, as in Giorgio Agamben's concept of bare life, whereas at other times it suggests the opposite, a surplus of fleshy potentiality, as in Antonio Negri's theorization of the multitude. Although refocusing the critical discourse of biopolitics on processes of individuation doesn't eliminate the polysemy of "life itself," it does provide more secure footing for this conceptual plurality: The multiplicity conjured up by this biopolitical lexeme is itself an effect of the discrepant processes through which life individuates itself. This perspective eschews the temptation of positivism—the axiomatic division of knowledge into proper and improper objects of study—acknowledging that what counts as biopolitical is itself an effect of struggle. Foucault presupposes this processual orientation, which explains why his analyses of political matters have less to do with empirical instances arranged in strict chronological order than with the nonsynchronous emergence of generic forms of life. Foucault cares less about specific empirical cases than what he terms the "historical *a priori*" enabling such cases. This is not to say that Foucault disregards the material conditions of history. To the contrary, his "genealogical" approach to history "attempts to restore the conditions for the appearance of a singularity born out of multiple determining elements of which it is not the product, but rather the effect."[29] The genealogist replaces assumptions regarding the subjective unity of historical agents with analyses of how such agents come into existence. When the genealogist "listens to history, he finds that there is 'something altogether different' behind things: not a timeless and essential secret, but the secret that they have no essence or that their essence was fabricated in a piecemeal fashion from alien forms."[30] The critical discourse of biopolitics exposes the fact that "life itself" is cobbled together from diverse discourses, knowledges, and practices.

Ruptures and breaks do not a utopia make, however. There needs to be not only radical discontinuity but also subjectivization—the production of forms of life that transform radical negativity (the refusal of modern subjection) into concrete positivity (an alternative to the status quo). Foucault, supposedly, is no friend of utopia, preferring the concept of heterotopia because of its nontotalizing localization of alterity. He characterizes utopia as a kind of "consolation: although they have no real locality there is nevertheless a fantastic, untroubled region in which they are able to unfold." In contrast, heterotopias "are disturbing . . . because they destroy 'syntax' in advance, and not only the syntax with which we construct sentences but also that less apparent syntax which causes words and things (next to and also opposite one another) to 'hold together.'"[31] Elsewhere, however, Foucault blurs the distinction between heterotopia and utopia, classifying heterotopia as a subgenre of utopia. He refers to heterotopia as "localized utopias," "situated utopias, these real places outside of all places."[32] Heterotopia is less the negation of utopia than its partner in crime; it names a praxis that replaces the "consolation" of a distant island or a hazy future with the troubling nearness of the "absolutely other." Heterotopia is, one might say, the becoming-immanent of utopia.

What is utopian in Foucault is not so much another place but the possibility of another life. Foucault argues this point explicitly in a 1966 radio address, "The Utopian Body." Foucault begins the address by positing the body as the "contrary of utopia": "It [the body] is irreparably here, never elsewhere."[33] The body epitomizes the here and now, and, as such, it bars the otherworldly. From this perspective, utopia can only be a way of "erasing the body."[34] However, Foucault reverses course only moments later, contending that if utopia is the contrary of the body, it is nonetheless immanent in the body:

> All these utopias through which I was sidestepping my body, they really had their model and first point of application, their place of origin, in my body itself. I was very wrong earlier to say that utopias were turned against the body and meant to efface it: they are born of the body itself and are perhaps subsequently turned against it.[35]

Foucault's distinction between a utopia of the body and a utopia that elides the body corresponds to Ernst Bloch's distinction between concrete utopia and abstract utopia: One is a matter of the real possibilities embodied in subjects and their material conditions; the other is a flight into fantasy—a daydream in which all the world's problems disappear into thin air.[36] Foucault elaborates on this point through a series of examples, including tattooing, spiritual possession, and dance. What these examples have in common is the way in which they generate a chiasmus, or crossing, in which the body "is *always* elsewhere, it is linked to all the elsewheres of the world, and to tell the truth it is elsewhere than in the world."[37] In the dancer's pirouette, the body doesn't merely twirl in physical space; it becomes absorbed in a revolution, transported outside of itself in a process of enfolding and unfolding: The body folds the world into itself, and, in doing so, it makes the world otherwise—it exposes the world to the singular difference of this body in this dance at this instant. This is what one might call utopian figuration: a mode of expression that transforms the body into the figure of another world. The concept of the utopian body thus offers a way of thinking utopianism less as a place or space than as the living embodiment of radical alterity.

Foucault's account of the Cynics in his final lectures at the Collège de France extends this vision of the body as utopian figure. Foucault frames the Cynic as a figure who refuses the current value system of a world; his motto is "change the currency," which implies "changing the custom, breaking with it, breaking up the rules, habits, conventions, and laws."[38] The Cynic lives philosophy by attempting to incarnate the true life, but, in contrast to Socrates, for whom the true life could at least theoretically belong to the present order of things, for the Cynic, "the true life is an other life."[39] The Cynic reduces himself to a state of utter destitution in order to go beyond the constraints of convention. This destitution isn't salvation. Instead, the Cynic's life is a "militant life, the life of battle and struggle against and for self, against and for others."⁴⁰ This militant life is singular and divisive, but it is also universal, addressed to everyone. It is a form of concrete universality predicated on the destruction and reconstruction of the world. Foucault sums up this ethos as follows:

> Not only has Cynicism pushed the theme of the true life to the extreme point of its reversal into the theme of the life which is scandalously other, but it has laid down this otherness of an *other* life, not simply as the choice of a different, happy, and sovereign life, but as the practice of a combativeness on the horizon of which is an other world.⁴¹

This account of militancy articulates the conceptual grammar of biopolitical utopianism, for it makes utopia the embodied struggle for another world. "An *other* life for an *other* world"—this could be the slogan of a singular America.

This kind of biopolitical utopianism is already at work in the field of American studies. It sometimes goes under the name of utopia, as in José Esteban Muñoz's work, but it also goes under other names, including "assemblages," "queer asynchronies," and "the commons."⁴² Muñoz, for instance, writes that it is "important not to hand over futurity to normative white reproductive futurity. The dominant mode of futurity is indeed 'winning' but that is all the more reason to call on a utopian political imagination that will enable us to glimpse another time and place: a 'not-yet' where queer youths of color actually get to grow up."⁴³ Jasbir Puar suggests that we consider queer assemblages "as spaces and moments of resistance, resistance that is not primarily characterized by oppositional stances, but includes frictional forces, discomfiting encounters, and spurts of unsynchronized delinquency."⁴⁴ Although differing a great deal from one another, what such approaches share is a shift from oppositional modes of critique toward the cultivation of nonnormative forms of life (or the positive articulation of social and political alternatives to the status quo). The lesson to be drawn from this shift is threefold. First, it suggests that antinormativity is not synonymous with pure negativity. The swerve from normativity has its own consistency, its own procedures for inventing life. Indeed, the blurring of positivity and negativity is constitutive of utopia—it is the phenomenology proper to a praxis that converts what has no place in this world into the possibility of another world. Second, radical alterity is irreducible to extrinsic determination. The elsewhere springs up in the midst of things, just as new forms of life often arise from residual social forms. A singular America begins with the terms of exceptionalism only to overturn them. Finally, the immanence of utopia—its location in the here and now—implies endurance, or the ongoing practice of insisting on deviation despite the pressure of normative regimes. One can call this endurance *militance*, for it implies not only the punctual break with the status quo but also the quotidian reproduction of nonnormative forms of life in the face of overwhelming adversity. A singular America, then, names the plurality of practices, forms, and events through which life not only breaks with exceptionalism but also endures as the embodied possibility of another world.

American Literary Commons

A singular America is the unbearable pleasure that exceptionalism denies and jealously guards. It is a ferment of utopian energy, a jouissance of political invention. It is within America and against it, for it but also beyond it. It's a utopian nexus through which the negativity of critique becomes the positivity of militance. A singular America troubles the conceptual geography underpinning exceptionalism and anti-exceptionalism alike, for, instead of framing resistance in oppositional terms, it locates alternatives to the status quo in the belly of the beast. It is not that America saves itself from itself—there is no redeeming America—but rather that escaping from exceptionalism means tarrying with the libidinal energies that fall under the name of America. If literature has a special role in thinking a singular America, it's because it doesn't need to abide by the ideological procedures through which one tends to separate reality and fiction, or history and the imagination. It enjoys the freedom to speculate. The concept of a literary commons suggests that what's at stake in a singular America is the development of the commons, or the production of forms of social life that are characterized by cooperation on egalitarian terms and democratic self-management. Literature, in this context, potentializes social reality, fracturing the self-evident qualities of historical existence to reveal the possibilities of living together otherwise. The American literary commons is akin to an aquifer: Just as an aquifer stores and circulates groundwater, so too does the literary commons harbor the energies of a singular America, transmitting them to the future as resources for political struggle.

Literature isn't the only the medium through which a singular America expresses itself. Recent social movements—such as Occupy and Black Lives Matter—and nineteenth-century social movements—such as abolitionism and first-wave feminism—can be read as expressions of a singular America. Their demands for justice exceed what is possible within the constraints of the dominant social order. Moreover, as much as these movements position themselves against the state and/or capitalism, they tend to do so in the name of America, in the name of fulfilling a revolutionary promise that has been betrayed. They are counter-national more than post- or anti-national. They want that which in America is more than America—the birthday of a new world. At the same time, the utopian dimension of these political projects implies a constitutive inadequacy, an inevitable sense of dissatisfaction with respect to particular instances of struggle. These movements prefigure a better world, but they also demonstrate a searching quality—an incompletion that is less teleological than organizational. They are still trying to invent the institutions that would sustain a radically different world. I want to suggest that this sense of incompletion can be understood as a problem of form, specifically, a problem of how to formalize the political potentiality of social movements in institutions capable of sustaining a different kind of social system.

The literature of a singular America experiments with social and political form. In Caroline Levine's words, "Forms are organizations or arrangements that afford repetition and portability across materials and contexts."[45] Forms travel across the differences between ontological modalities, enabling one to compare, for instance, an Emily Dickinson poem to nineteenth-century domestic architecture. Levine emphasizes the "collision" between forms, rather than their correspondence, so as to avoid falling prey to the trap of assuming an indexical, homological, or mimetic relationship between literary forms and social or political forms. Instead of tracking the ways in which literary form mirrors social and political realities, Levine suggests that critics consider "the strange encounter between two or more forms that sometimes reroutes intention and ideology."[46] From this perspective, the literature of a singular America is defined by those moments when the forms of American exceptionalism clash with the forms of the commons: Whitman assumes the citizens of the United States as his audience only to arrange a pattern of communion/communication whose anonymity and ecstasy defies the constraints of nationalism; William Burroughs cultivates the desire for the Frontier, a staple of Manifest Destiny, but he transforms it into a queer and egalitarian form of solidarity. In these instances, forms intersect and diverge, so that what's generative about this poetry and fiction is not how adequately they represent reality but their ability to test out different arrangements of life.

Such methodological formalism only partially accounts for the literary expression of a singular America, however. It doesn't reckon with the surplus of potentiality that inhabits and exceeds form—the jouissance that traverses and disrupts the symbolic order. A biopolitical approach to literature thinks through the dialectic between form and potentiality, or the symbolic and the real, considering the excess of social power immanent in, yet irreducible to, the literary. Gilles Deleuze gestures toward such an approach when he describes literature as "an enterprise of health: not that the writer would necessarily be in good health . . . , but he possesses an irresistible and delicate health that stems from what he has seen and heard of things whose passage exhausts him, while nonetheless giving him the becomings that a dominant and substantial health would render impossible."[47] At first glance, this view of literature appears little more than a reiteration of the Romantic ideology of genius, according to which the writer is a kind of seer—a melancholic creature whose courage consists in staring unflinchingly into the abyss. Deleuze complicates this view, however, by introducing an antagonism between a normative model of health and another health: Literature doesn't realize the human; it "exhausts" it, and, in doing so, it generates other modes of existence ("becomings"). "The ultimate aim of literature," Deleuze elaborates, "is to set free, in the delirium, this creation of health or this invention of a people, that is, a possibility of life. To write for this people who are missing . . . ('for' means less 'in the place of' than 'for the benefit of')."[48] From this perspective, the biopolitics of literature has more to do with inventing new forms of life than with representing power's hold over life. Literary texts redefine the kinds of subjectivity available under the rubric of the human. They expand the register of what counts as vital or animate beyond the normative regimes governing human and nonhuman life.

Deleuze attributes to American literature an "exceptional power" for biopolitical invention. In the company of Stanley Cavell, Sharon Cameron, and Branka Arsić, among others, he identifies a counter-Romantic current in American literature: practices, styles, and affects that crack open individualistic forms of expression to reveal an impersonal force of existence. For Deleuze, the impersonal power that seeps out of American literature is collective in nature, defined by "companionship" and "conviviality," rather than the individualism of the so-called American Dream. "The society of comrades," Deleuze writes, "is the revolutionary American dream—a dream . . . which was disappointed and betrayed long before the dream of the Soviet society. But it is also the reality of American literature."[49] Deleuze locates a singular America within and against the individualistic, possessive, and hierarchical terms of exceptionalist America. The American literary commons is a dream whose betrayal doesn't spell its end but only its beginning again and otherwise.

Deleuze belongs to a lineage of European philosophers for whom America is a concept and a libidinal object as much as a territory. For Locke and Hegel, to name two prominent examples, America is simultaneously a land of futurity and prehistory. It is a prehistorical state of nature not because it is devoid of people but because Enlightenment philosophy refuses to recognize the people that inhabit the land as anything other than savages. What defines America is the promise of renewing history, of taking a leap into the future, by drawing on the untamed energies of the wilderness. Emptiness and plenitude, prehistory and progress, annihilation and discovery become indistinguishable in that desire called America. This is the logic of conquest, the power of which lies not in its claims of epistemological novelty but in its staging of an ontological event: the opening of an epoch defined by a new sense of planetarity—colonial-capitalist modernity—along with a slew of biopolitical imperatives—proletarianization, racialization, and the invention of modern sexuality.

Jared Hickman describes this ontological event as a "mythography," "dividing reality into discrete powers that can be managed, the difference being that, within the echo chamber of the human created by global finitude [or "planetary immanence"], these powers now manifest ambiguously as divinized humans and humanized divinities most fully captured in discourses of race and peoplehood."[50] Hickman argues that the secular deconstruction of the myth of America—the critique of exceptionalism—neither exhausts America's capacity to take hold of subjects, nor takes into account the "black Prometheus": "an anarchic rebel, an anti-absolute who embodies a genuinely *other* and novel cosmic alternative," one which "becomes possible only in the context of what, from a certain standpoint, it is politically vital to perceive as a *pseudo*-ontological distinction between raced bodies and spaces."[51] In line with the work of Sylvia Wynter and Fred Moten, among others, Hickman demonstrates that the institutional and discursive construction of racial divisions within historical time doesn't suspend ontology. Instead, it constitutes a (non-)place through which ontology becomes radically transformed. A singular America, I contend, overlaps with the black Prometheus, without of course being identical to it. If the black Prometheus is the *anti*-absolute—the irrepressible underside of colonial-capitalist modernity—a singular America is the *post*-absolute: the absolute pushed to its breaking point. It's what happens when exceptionalism is forced to reckon with the explosive force at the heart of its own eschatological promise.

Visions of America as the destiny of the planetary absolute find themselves plagued by the very thing that sustains them, namely, the commons. Exceptionalism feeds on fantasies of the North American continent as a vast commons—a *terra nullius* of immeasurable riches. In Hegel's words, "For those who are ready to work hard, and have not found the opportunity in Europe, America has opened a new theater of action."[52] The labor of the negative, to use the dialectical terminology, transforms the supposed emptiness of the American landscape into the motor of progress. The presupposition of non-property is the condition of possibility of capitalist accumulation. This is, of course, a well-documented ideological fantasy—an instance of settler colonial rationality, transferring the agency of indigenous peoples to European colonists and justifying genocide in the name of "progress." In other words, it is little more than an alibi for conquest. At the same time, there is a rich legacy of the commons that stands in an antagonistic relationship to the colonial-capitalist matrix of exceptionalism: a history of struggle, custom, and culture defined by egalitarian modes of cooperation, democratic self-management, and social autonomy. This is the tradition in which a singular America participates, standing the possessive individualism of the American dream right-side up to reveal the social power of the commons.

Peter Linebaugh traces this social power back to the Magna Carta, though it would be more accurate to say that he shows how it codifies already existing customs involving the communal sharing of resources. Indeed, the commons distances itself from the legal structures of the state, so that "common rights" should be understood not as privileges granted by sovereign institutions but as "perpetuities" whose roots descend "deep into human history."[53] The state may try to protect, exploit, or destroy the commons, but it can never entirely abolish the gap between sovereignty and custom. This isn't to say that sovereignty does not try to do so. Exceptionalism, in one of its guises, is precisely the fantasy of an identity between the state and the commons: It is a dream of fusion in which "the people" (in the form of the mass of property owners) would recognize state sovereignty as the consummation of their collective will.[54] American exceptionalism's commitment to private property, Linebaugh explains, rests on a distortion of the commons—"a whitewash [of] the tale of a Magna Carta extolling individualism, private property, laissez-faire and English civilization."[55] The American Dream's promise of opportunity passes off restrictive forms of upward mobility as if they were a heritage accessible to everyone. Behind this "whitewash," however, there persists the historical legacy of commoning practices in the United States—the memory of pre- and noncapitalist social formations, constituting a resource for political imagination and struggle. Linebaugh draws attention to a subterranean history of the commons, an alternative itinerary through American politics and culture.

Dana Nelson elaborates on "the culture of the commons," describing it as a "practice of self-provisioning and mutual support." Nelson continues: "Above all, the culture of the commons is both distributive *and* productive. And this productive dimension is significant. Functioning optimally, commoning produces a specific good, nurturing practical experiences of communal, self-determining power.... In other words, commoning cultivates a political sensibility, one specifically grounded in use-value, in face-to-face community and negotiation."[56] The culture of the commons calls into question liberalism's belief in the autonomy of politics—the premise that politics belongs to a distinct sphere of formal government—by articulating politics as coextensive with social activity: Producing in common is an education in governing in common; it entails a process of deciding on and managing the common good in an immediately collective manner. Nelson's articulation of the culture of the commons as "vernacular democracy" offers compelling grounds for revising our political vocabulary to include activities of resistance and institution-building that fall below the state's purview. Cultivating the commons is an egalitarian project, not only because it has social equality as its content but also because it scrambles the hierarchical construction of politics as an activity reserved for the elite. It proposes politics as an activity for anyone and everyone.

The American literary commons participates in this practical utopian imagination by renewing our political vocabulary through aesthetic means. In a manner akin to Elizabeth Maddock Dillon's performative commons, the literary commons contests dominant political sensibilities by disrupting the hierarchical division of the social and by establishing relations of mutual support and collective self-determination.[57] The literary commons mobilizes aesthetic form as a milieu for developing social potentiality; it traces paths of social mediation outside of state and capitalist modes of relation. Crucially, the literary commons doesn't presuppose a notion of aesthetic autonomy but, to the contrary, opens up a zone of indistinction between artistic and social/political practice. It sets into motion a dialectic between form and potentiality that traverses ontological, social, economic, and political domains. It is, to recall Levine and Deleuze, a (non)place in which different patterns of existence are exposed to their potentiality for becoming otherwise. The literary commons makes a virtue of impropriety; it exchanges the autonomy of politics and literature for the promiscuity of form and potentiality.

A singular America institutes itself as a literary commons. Deleuze defines institutionality in terms of "procedures of satisfaction": Institutions are means through which we satisfy our needs and desires.[58] They function as means, however, only insofar as they shape the subjects who rely on them. They are less instruments than milieux, less tools than schools. "Every institution imposes a series of models on our bodies, even in its involuntary structures, and offers our intelligence a sort of knowledge, a possibility of foresight as project."[59] To say that a singular America institutes itself as a literary commons is to say that it actualizes itself as specific means for satisfying that desire called America. It differs from the institutions of American exceptionalism, contesting the latter's hierarchical distribution of goods and opportunities by proposing an alternative social form—a mixture of egalitarian cooperation, democratic participation, and self-governance. It is a utopian institute, because rather than educating subjects to accept the conditions of the present, it teaches them to demand the impossible, to imagine a world without property or states. If it expresses itself as literature, it is not simply because of the difficulty of translating the energies of social movements into enduring institutions. It is also because of literature's capacity for experimenting with form, for testing out new arrangements of existence, for developing new kinds of knowledge and intelligence.

"Times Like These"

Published in the wake of the first Gulf War, Adrienne Rich's poem "What Kind of Times Are These" lingers over the remnants of that desire called America: "There's a place between two stands of trees where the grass grows uphill/ and the old revolutionary road breaks off into shadows/ near a meeting-house abandoned by the persecuted who disappeared into those shadows."[60] Rich describes a secret place, where hope manages to survive—a "ghost-ridden crossroads, leaf-mold paradise"—but the ghosts that linger, here, are also the disappeared, lives extinguished by political violence. One finds oneself caught between different hauntings: on the one hand, the specter of a revolution that might have been—the revolution that would have realized the potential for another world—and, on the other, the ghosts of indigenous peoples, slaves, the exploited, and the oppressed. The present teems with futures past, with the potentiality of lives cut short and projects left unfulfilled. "I won't tell you where the place is, the dark mesh of wood/ meeting the unmarked strip of light," Rich worries, "I already know who wants to buy it, sell it, make it disappear." Rich's poetry bears witness to a sliver of utopian light in the ruins of the neoliberal present, but it does not give away its location. This is literature as counter-jeremiad: a warning, a lament, a call to arms, which, instead of reaching for national consensus, transforms dissent into an affirmation of social possibility. The poem concludes: "And I won't tell you where it is, so why do I tell you/anything? Because you still listen, because in times like these/to have you listen at all, it's necessary/to talk about trees."

Rich's manner of telling without telling can be read as a commentary on the temporality of a singular America: The poem sidesteps direct presentation, because the time of hope is always already and not-yet, consigned to what might have been and delivered over to what might come. In this context, the pastoral ("trees") is more than nostalgia; it is an interruption of the ongoingness of the present. These trees are like the wilderness that invades the urban ruins of a postapocalyptic landscape—they testify to history's irreducibility to "times like these." Put differently, Rich grapples with the biopolitics of the United States not as if it were a unified continuum—the progressive subsumption of life by power—but as if it were an asymmetrical war between the revolutionary power *of* life and sovereign power *over* life.[61] In times like these, one writes of trees, because trees carry the memory of what might have been, of what still could be.

The temporality of a desire called America bifurcates into the time of the exception ("times like these") and the time of singularity ("the old revolutionary road breaks off into shadows"). Exceptionalism renders the present instant into an index of power; it insists on America's self-presence, the circular fulfillment of its destiny, such that even forward motion is only a realization of national essence. The problem with exceptionalism is that it is not exceptional enough, that it allows for the exception only on the condition that it shores up sovereign order. "Make America Great Again," indeed. In contrast, the time of singularity is eventual; it salvages the surplus potentiality in the present, interrupting the course of things in the name of what might have been or what still could be. Deleuze writes that singularities are "turning points and points of inflection; bottlenecks, knots, foyers, and centers; points of fusion and condensation; points of tears and joy, sickness and health, hope and anxiety, 'sensitive' points."[62] Singularities are zones of transition; they are (non-)places in which extremes touch. They belong to the virtual, which is not the opposite of the actual but its immanent antecedent. The virtual surrounds actual objects as "clouds," that is, as an indeterminate multiplicity of paths of becoming. Singularities are switch-points in the virtual, eventual sites that trigger qualitative transformation (changes of kind, rather than degree).[63] At their most radical, singularities are knots of duration through which one passes from one world to another, or from one timeline to another. If the time of exception is a time of restoration, collapsing the future into a fantasy of history without significant change, the time of singularity is open and indeterminate, evental and dizzying—it is a time of overturning, in which memory breeds creativity and the past spawns futures of monstrous difference. A singular America is the secret time of exceptionalism; it is the old revolutionary road inviting one to dream what could have been, what might still be.

The literary history of a singular America stages itself as a series of revolutionary hauntings that trouble American claims to global hegemony. One of the fundamental premises of this history is the tenuousness of U.S. hegemony. "Times like these" are times of transition, times when the light of protest and the shadows of oppression mingle in a twilight atmosphere. (As I write this paragraph, mass protests loom in recent memory, as well as on the horizon; talk of impeaching the president runs rampant; immigrant families have been divided and imprisoned; income inequality continues to rise in the United States and everywhere else; courageous protesters tear down Confederate statues; and white supremacists celebrate the murder of antiracist activists.) A singular America emerges from the cracks in U.S. hegemony, its utopian possibilities equally legible as phantoms crawling from exceptionalism's abyss. The material condition of possibility of a singular America is thus the instability of American claims to global hegemony. This instability is, however, both cause and effect of a singular America: A singular America is the efflux of hegemony's unraveling, but it is also the militant spirit destroying hegemony from the inside. The literature of a singular America is therefore a literature of extremes, a strange dialectic in which the breakdown of America becomes the occasion for its reimagination.

Giovanni Arrighi, David Harvey, and Immanuel Wallerstein, among others, have diagnosed the contemporary condition of the United States as one of decline: It is not that the United States no longer exercises force on a global scale but rather that this exercise of force no longer coincides with a position of leadership. American hegemony gives way to a tenuous dominance through means of constant warfare—especially global policing operations conducted in the name of exterminating terrorism—and financialization—profit-making practices involving speculation. From this perspective, the post-9/11 wars in Afghanistan and Iraq are less signs of an imperial power in good health than quixotic attempts to prove the continuing relevance of a nation in decline. There is, after all, no compelling reason to believe that only the United States can function as global leader, given that China, the BRICS coalition, the European Union, and OPEC nations are increasingly powerful forces in the capitalist world system. Arrighi traces the roots of this current predicament to what he terms the "signal crisis" of the 1970s, arguing that the combination of a decline in manufacturing profits, military defeat (in the Vietnam War), social revolts, increasing socioeconomic inequalities, and the monetarist counterrevolution (the shift away from Keynesian policies toward currency manipulation) drain U.S. global hegemony of its socioeconomic substance. This signal crisis paves the way for a "terminal crisis" in which the emergence of viable alternatives in respect to hegemony reveals the precariousness of American dominance.[64] The United States may still act as a global power, but it no longer occupies a central position, because, in times like these, there is no center. The present is an interregnum, a time between one global order and another.

Times like these are complicated times, however. It would be a mistake to frame the literary history of a singular America in terms of a simple decline, not least because the time of a singular America is one of futures past. It is a time of breaks with the ongoingness of the present, of leaps into other dimensions of possibility. It refuses linear chronology, because it is written in the name of what might have been. William Burroughs offers the term *retroactive utopia* to describe how the present remains haunted by the incomplete revolutions of the past. The term indexes the unfulfilled potentiality of social movements and political projects, and it implies that this potentiality is not merely counterfactual but a real force disrupting the irreversibility of historical time. Retroactive utopianism revisits the past as a way of inventing other presents. It salvages the jouissance of history, reactualizing it as experiments in living otherwise. Put differently, the retroactive utopianism of a singular America entails the reactualization of America as a revolutionary project, the mining of exceptionalism for that futurity that exceeds its limits. With Slavoj Žižek, one can speak of the repetition of revolution as a creative activity, distinguishing between, on the one hand, the nostalgic desire to return to the past ("Make America Great Again") and, on the other, the recuperation of the "utopian spark" of the event of revolution, that is, the reopening of a "field of possibilities" and the renewal of "missed opportunities."[65] A singular America repeats the revolutionary project of America not for the sake of what has been but in the name of that which in America is more than America: the impossible America whose utopian potential leaves its traces in the desire for another world.

The literature of a singular America is the figuration of this impossible America through the disfiguration of exceptionalism. It is that other vitality interrupting the normal health of American hegemony, turning decline into the production of new bodies and populations. It is a world-systems literature, mapping the dynamic play between capital and culture, political subject and geographical territory, but its internal rhythm exceeds the mimetic relationship between historical condition and textual artifact.[66] The literature of a singular America tropes on the history of U.S. hegemony, but its forms are deformations of exceptionalism and inventions of other kinds of political subjectivity. It is in the zone of the excluded middle, in which complicity and opposition blur, that the literature of a singular America does its work. It is in this libidinal underground that the impossibility of America becomes a positive force.

The literature of a singular America and the new American studies share a devotion to this impossible America. They each attempt to push exceptionalism beyond exceptionalism; they each transform the void at the heart of American exceptionalism into the potential for new forms of life. The New Americanists exemplify the retroactive utopianism of a singular America in their critique of the literary historical category of the American Renaissance. Critics such as Lauren Berlant, Amy Kaplan, and Donald Pease have dismantled the Cold War framework of the "American Renaissance," showing how the fantasy of a superlative instance of American cultural genius (the mid-nineteenth-century moment that includes such authors as Walt Whitman, Henry David Thoreau, and Herman Melville) not only obscures the historical conditions of cultural production but also feeds into the Cold War ideology that promotes the United States as global guarantor of freedom. The New Americanist critique of the American Renaissance is not purely negative, however, for it also recuperates the social energies "beneath" the American Renaissance. Indeed, in *Beneath the American Renaissance*, David Reynolds is careful not to dismiss canonical works of literature by the likes of Whitman and Melville for fear that such dismissal would simply reproduce the dichotomy between major and minor writers on other terms. Instead, he articulates a cultural commons in which "the typical literary text of the American Renaissance is far from being a 'self-sufficient text,' sealed off from its environment. It is indeed what one might call an 'open text,' since it provides an especially democratic meeting place for numerous idioms and voices from other kinds of contemporary texts."[67] The mid-nineteenth-century experiments of literary narrative and poetry are predicated on an unruly mixture of social, political, and cultural elements, so that the American Renaissance has less to do with inventing a properly national culture than with realizing new worlds of possibility through already extant social, political, and cultural potentials. The new American studies begins, one might say, with a critique of F. O. Matthiessen's optative mood, or a critique of the exceptionalist insistence on the subjunctive power of American literature. However, it does not so much abandon the optative mood as convert it into a form of political militance.

What is at stake in the critique of the American Renaissance as an aesthetic category is the expansion of the U.S. political imaginary beyond the terms set by Cold War liberalism. The biopolitical turn in American studies should thus be understood as a culmination, as well as an innovation: The turn to life itself realizes that which is "beneath" the American Renaissance—the social potentiality of America beyond the constraints of exceptionalism. This turn is also an act of self-criticism, an instance in which American studies pushes beyond its own limits, specifically, its failure to reckon with the ontological dimensions of American culture and to develop the jouissance of that desire called America in an affirmative manner. Paraphrasing William Spanos, one might say that the biopolitical turn in American studies conjures up what the New Americanists tended to overlook, even as they unconsciously flirted with it: the errant surplus potentiality of America taking the form of a counter-national community to come.[68]

The literature of a singular America formalizes this speculative effort to make good on that desire called America. It institutionalizes the biopolitical project of liberation as a literary commons—a counter-national canon whose temporal provenance tunnels through centuries like a wormhole, linking the futures past of the American Renaissance to the possibilities opened up by the decline of American hegemony. The unraveling of hegemony enables not only the dismantling of the national canon, as epitomized by the aesthetic category of the American Renaissance, but also the retrieval of the surplus potentiality—the jouissance—for which the American Renaissance stands as both placeholder and tomb. The object of this book, then, is not simply the contemporary period understood as a moment of decline and possibility but also the American Renaissance understood as the immanent anteriority of our present—the exceptionalist presupposition carrying and concealing a singular America. Times like these are complicated times, times when futures past dwell in the present like ghosts demanding their share of justice. It is with this demand for justice in mind, this plea for what might have been, that my analyses consider Whitman alongside Pynchon, Dickinson alongside Burroughs. It is not a question of establishing the linear genesis of the present from the past but of activating the retroactive utopian potential of American literature and culture. What is at stake is nothing less than which utopian figures will rule over our political imaginary.

The chapters that follow eschew chronological order in favor of a systematic thinking through of the concept of a singular America. Beginning with William S. Burroughs's fiction written in the 1980s, I then step backward into the nineteenth century, moving from Walt Whitman's *Leaves of Grass* (1855) to Emily Dickinson's poetry; finally, I return to the contemporary period with Thomas Pynchon's *Against the Day* (2006). Even this description simplifies the temporal and historical trajectories of this study. Burroughs's late trilogy from the eighties is set during the eighteenth and nineteenth centuries, but it also includes elements of science fiction belonging to a distant future. Whitman's poetry occupies a threshold between the pre–Civil War present and a future imagined as the realization of America's revolutionary potentiality, whereas Dickinson steps to the side of the present, into a zone in which time has become wonky in respect to narratives of national progress. Finally, Pynchon's *Against the Day* is a nineteenth-century novel not only in the sense that it mostly takes place during that century but also because it draws on that century's genres—Melville's encyclopedic novel, the American romance, dime-store novels, and border literature—extracting the utopian elements secreted in them. This book thus considers the contemporary period insofar as it is structured by the unfinished business of the eighteenth and nineteenth centuries, especially their unactualized revolutionary potentials, and it considers the literature of the American Renaissance insofar as it unsettles the present's claims to social, historical, and political progress, insofar as it introduces the possibilities of futures past. The temporality that guides this study is less the empirical time of chronology than the no-less-material time of utopian desire.

This book's methodology involves a kind of time travel: not the attempt to visit the past, nor even the attempt to revive it, but rather the recuperation of futures past as forces at work in the present. This isn't presentism, for, in this methodology, the present is exposed to the alterities of a past that has not passed away and a future that disrupts the present. As such, there is no better starting point than William S. Burroughs's late trilogy—*Cities of the Red Night* (1981), *The Place of Dead Roads* (1983), and *The Western Lands* (1987)—which begins with a lament regarding the missed opportunity of the eighteenth-century revolutions: "The chance was there. The chance was missed."[69] Although the 1980s conventionally signifies a time of despair for emancipatory politics, Burroughs's late trilogy deploys the concept of retroactive utopia in order to recuperate the missed opportunities of the American Revolution. In Chapter 1, I argue that Burroughs not only calls attention to the haunting of America by its unfinished revolutionary business but also channels these ghosts into a concrete utopia. His utopian praxis fleshes out the concept of the commons as a political project—the project of escaping from the nation-state and capitalism. In doing so, Burroughs anticipates recent theories of the multitude, as well as the antisystemic revolts that fuel them. At the same time, he complicates the teleological tendencies of these theories by drawing attention to the organizational labor involved in retraining desires for the sake of producing another world. Focusing especially on *The Place of Dead Roads*—a strange hybrid of science fiction and the Western—I show how Burroughs thinks biopolitical utopianism as inextricable from cultural and political revolution.

Chapter 2 demonstrates how the first edition of *Leaves of Grass* constitutes an attempt to reimagine American democracy in nonliberal terms. Whereas Burroughs conceives of the commons in opposition to the hegemonic model of American culture and politics, Whitman conceives of it as the "realization" of America, or the reactualization of the Revolution proper. Whitman proposes a majoritarian utopianism in which the nation need only realize its innermost potential in order to arrive at a better world. The chapter alternates between molecular and molar levels of Whitman's poetry, or between the preindividual common (the shared potentiality of the nation) and the reconstitution of the people as revolutionary force. I argue that there is a constitutive tension between a vitalist democracy and an eventuary democracy in Whitman's poetry. On the one hand, Whitman suggests that poetry might grow utopia from the biological potential of the people in the same way one would grow plants in a garden. On the other hand, his poetry repeatedly considers the need for political division, for a polemical demarcation between the people (as status quo) and the people (as subject of the Revolution). Although Whitman doesn't think through the organizational dynamics of concrete utopianism in as concerted a manner as Burroughs, he does thicken our sense of the ontological basis of a politics of the commons, its rootedness in the vital materiality of bodies.

In the third chapter, I show how Dickinson imagines utopia as an exodus from the nation-state on the part of the women of the republic. Focusing in particular on her poems concerning marriage, I show how she articulates an immanent utopianism on the basis of subtraction from heteronormativity, patriarchy, nationalism, and capitalism. This subtraction operates in tandem with a queer pleasure of preference—a mode of elective affinity in which coupling no longer functions in compulsory terms but depends on a tactile embrace of singular others. Dickinson's marriage poems offer a remarkable entry point for thinking of her poetry in utopian and biopolitical terms, for they not only interrogate the affective economies of marriage (social relations involving emotion, sentiment, and feeling that contribute to the reproduction of capitalism) but also reimagine marriage in queer terms. This chapter brings together queer theory's meditations on alternative socialities with feminist interrogations of socially reproductive labor in order to show how Dickinson's poetry dismantles the bourgeois economy of the household. Dickinson complicates that desire called America, by dissociating the production of new forms of social life from the national body politic and by insisting on the centrality of gender for any thinking of utopian futurity.

Chapter 4 asks whether we might reclaim two traditions of radical praxis from the nineteenth century: idleness as a refusal of capitalist command and the commune as a site for experimenting with alternative socialities. I examine Thomas Pynchon's 2006 *Against the Day*, focusing on its excavation of labor movements and anarchist revolts in the late nineteenth century. More pointedly, I elaborate an aesthetics and politics of idleness that challenges present-day politics of austerity. *Against the Day* articulates an antagonism between capitalist and anticapitalist versions of sloth, or between the mindless pleasures of consumption (to use Pynchon's phrasing) and the refusal of work. This refusal of work should be understood in positive terms, for it not only involves a negation of capitalist discipline but also the construction of a commons. The chapter draws on the work of the Autonomist Marxists, the political activists and intellectuals central to the Italian uprisings of the 1970s, especially their investigations into sabotage, slowdowns, and strikes. It argues that Pynchon and the Autonomists identify the refusal of work with the emergence of a postcapitalist society. This chapter drives home my point that the reactualization of America as a revolutionary project entails a utopianism attuned to the lived experiences of bodies, in this case, the lived experience of capitalism as a rhythm of precarity and of work refusal as an ecstatic dilation of futurity in the present. This overlap of histories—of the nineteenth century with the present—is inextricable from political struggles over how we imagine the future.

Each of these chapters offers a thinking of that desire called America in terms simultaneously philosophical and political. Each examines America as a libidinal attachment to that which in the nation exceeds the nation—a singular America. These attachments do not belong to the United States, even as they concern it, because they trouble what constitutes the nation in the first place. The book's coda bears witness to the counter-national irruption of a singular America by turning, ever so briefly, to contemporary social movements. In doing so, I'm not trying to confirm the concept of a singular America by way of empirical reality but to consider the zone of indistinction between literature and social movement. In this threshold, the concept of a singular America not only finds itself in protest and revolt, but these social and political struggles find in themselves that which exceeds injustice and restitution—the reinvention of America from the place of its impossibility.

CHAPTER 1

A Revolutionary Haunt: Utopian Frontiers in William S. Burroughs's Late Trilogy

During his 1980 presidential campaign, Ronald Reagan delivered a Labor Day speech at Liberty State Park in New Jersey. Reagan promised to replace Jimmy Carter's pessimistic view of stagflation with a hopeful vision of full employment, lower taxes, and general prosperity. This vision would be achieved not only by finding "a way to bring labor and management together for America" but also by "return[ing] to spiritual and moral values." Reagan never specifies what these values are, except to say that they constitute the bedrock of American freedom and that they have "inspired" dissidents in the Soviet Union to escape the stifling regime of communism. Reagan concludes his speech with a call to preserve and protect the American Dream—"that this dream, this last best of hope of man on earth, this nation under God, shall not perish from the earth": "Let us pledge to each other, with this Great Lady looking on [the Statue of Liberty looms in the distance], that we can, and so help us God, we will make America great again."[1] With these words, Reagan casts the emergent political logic of neoliberalism as a national project of renewal—a redemption of American exceptionalism.

Although the slogan "Make America Great Again" (MAGA) has come to be associated with the presidential campaign and administration of Donald Trump, it is Reagan who first popularized it, deploying it as the utopian lure for a full-scale commitment to neoliberalism. It would turn out that the Reagan administration's way of bringing workers and management together meant breaking the power of unions—exemplified by its response to the Air Traffic Controllers' Strike of 1981—and that the restoration of American values involved eliminating public services. Under Reagan, the federal state sacrificed much of its commitment to the social welfare of the nation in favor of deregulating financial markets, destroying unions, spreading "the free market" to the Second World, and cultivating a "morality" that combined homophobia, racism, and misogyny with the worship of entrepreneurship. Even acknowledging their differences, it's difficult not to see Reagan and Trump as variations on the same neoliberal project. They both subordinate the political power of the people to the market, while promising to return America to a golden age. Although their administrations included moderate attempts to ameliorate racism, homophobia, and misogyny, Clinton and Obama did not so much break with this project as dress it in progressive costume—neoliberalism with a soft glove, as it were—suggesting that neoliberalism is less a matter of partisan affiliation than a general transformation of politics. Indeed, as any number of critics have argued, neoliberalism is a global counterrevolution—a transnational project to roll back the social changes associated with the New Deal and the sixties.[2] This project cannot succeed without securing the consent of national peoples, which in the United States has meant not only coercive actions by the state but also the reeducation of the masses to conflate the freedom of the market with freedom in general.

William S. Burroughs's late trilogy, consisting of the novels *Cities of the Red Night* (1981), *The Place of Dead Roads* (1983), and *The Western Lands* (1987), responds to the rise of neoliberalism by salvaging the revolutionary potentials of the past. The trilogy is a revolutionary haunt, conjuring up the social struggles of previous centuries in the name of freedoms to come. Each of the novels introduces what Burroughs terms a "retroactive utopia"—a practice of bearing witness to the possibility that another world "could have happened," or, as Burroughs summarizes, "The chance was there. The chance was missed."[3] The trilogy focuses on moments when history might have changed course, when capitalism and the nation-state might have given way to a more just and egalitarian society. More specifically, it formulates the concept of retroactive utopia in relation to the revolutions of the eighteenth century, not only the American Revolution but also those of Latin America and the Caribbean. The novels do not simply memorialize what might have been, however. They engage in a revolutionary mourning process in which the missed opportunities of history become occasions for reimagining the social possibilities of the present.[4]

Burroughs's late trilogy contests the neoliberal monopoly over the political imagination by demanding that the present make good on the radical hopes of the past. Each novel invents fantastic figures—unruly pirate communes, queer outlaw cowboys, ancient Egyptian proletarians—that embody social alternatives to the possessive individualism of the capitalist market and the hierarchies of the nation-state. These figures are doubly historical. Not only do they respond in a critical manner to the neoliberal axiom that there is no such thing as society, only individuals, but they also constitute attempts to reactivate the lingering specters of past revolutions. "The task of Burroughs's fiction through the late seventies and eighties," Timothy Murphy writes, "is to find some way to fill in the holes, to reconstitute the revolutionary allies, the fantastically active and actively fantasizing *audience*, that he lost at the end of the sixties."[5] Burroughs's fictions from the 1959 *Naked Lunch* to the 1973 *Port of Saints* can be described as actively contributing to the new social movements of the twentieth century; they offer a countercultural vocabulary through which to articulate a dissident politics. In contrast, Burroughs's late fiction grapples with the contraction of political possibility, as neoliberalism not only eliminates radical social movements but also incorporates their aspirations into the capitalist firm—autonomy, creativity, authenticity, and freedom all become attributes of the "flexible" social subject, who is supposedly more than just a worker, because he or she is also an entrepreneur in charge of his or her own human capital.[6] As Jeffrey Nealon usefully summarizes, "If in the United States 'the 60s' functions as a kind of shorthand for resistance and revolution of all kinds, 'the 80s' most immediately signifies the increasing power and ubiquity of markets and privatized corporatization in everyday life."[7] Burroughs's late trilogy challenges the neoliberal co-optation of twentieth-century social movements by salvaging those movements' anti-statist and anticapitalist commitments to the collective social good. Burroughs not only mourns the revolutions of the eighteenth century but also the social movements of the sixties. He reconstitutes his revolutionary allies by recovering the social potential of history's missed opportunities.

Retroactive utopianism is an effort to renew the political imagination by expanding our sense of what a body situated in a particular time and place can do. Of the authors discussed in this book, it is Burroughs who most explicitly frames his work in biopolitical terms. Beginning in his earliest works of fiction, he obsesses over the politics of embodied life—for instance, representing drug addiction less as a personal pathology than as a political problem revolving around how bodies cope with the limits of their social conditions.[8] Throughout his career, Burroughs describes his writing practice as an attempt to transform the human species, and he imagines social revolution as a mutation of the species. As he puts it in *The Western Lands*, "This is a biological revolution, fought with new species and new ways of thinking and feeling."[9] Writing reprograms the human species for new kinds of freedom. It aims to "achieve complete freedom from past conditioning," which is to say that it envisions a life free from the control systems subjugating the human species.[10] From this perspective, utopia is less a place than a reconstitution of what it means to be human. When in an interview conducted shortly after the publication of *Cities of the Red Night*, Burroughs flatly asserts, "I don't think there exists an ideal utopia," he's not rejecting utopia as such but rather abstract utopianism—the idealistic belief in an ultimate resolution to social conflict. Burroughs readily allows for, and even encourages, the social struggles through which people attempt to "create the world they want."[11]

Although Burroughs spent much of his life abroad, his fiction often revolves around the social, political, and cultural dynamics of the United States. On the one hand, Burroughs represents America as an empire, or a global system of control. He refers to it as the "non-dream" and the "anti-dream plan," for it squashes the desire for freedom and the imagination of other ways of living.[12] America is the advanced edge of neoliberalism—the logical conclusion of the latter's conversion of social life into so many market opportunities. On the other hand, in *The Place of Dead Roads*, Burroughs writes of a "Potential America," which is less a place than a political dream—the dream of a world in which history took a different course. Potential America is a specific form of retroactive utopianism, or what I've termed a singular America. It names an interruption of the dialectic between American exceptionalism (the "anti-dream") and its critique (oppositional politics). Burroughs neither abandons that desire called America, nor does he redeem it. Instead, he salvages that which in America is more than America—the dream of a new kind of human species, the imagination of a world in which control has no place.

In what follows, I argue that Burroughs moves beyond the dominant political imaginary of the 1980s by attempting to make good on history's missed opportunities. The late trilogy expresses a fidelity to the history of revolution—less a nostalgia for past moments of struggle than an ongoing commitment to imagining noncapitalist and non-statist forms of social life. This chapter focuses on the second novel of the trilogy, *The Place of Dead Roads*, because, with its strange genre mash-up of science fiction and the western, it reconstitutes the American frontier as a site of biopolitical futurity. The frontier becomes a space in which the forces of neoliberalism ("the Shits") clash with revolutionary dreamers ("the Johnson family"). *The Place of Dead Roads* does more than represent a fantastic struggle against neoliberalism, however. It also educates its readers in the pleasures of the commons, cultivating a desire for forms of social belonging and political action in which cooperation and the common good replace entrepreneurship. In this respect, Burroughs anticipates another utopian project, namely, the politics of the multitude epitomized by the antiglobalization protests of the 1990s and closely associated with the theoretical writings of Michael Hardt and Antonio Negri. As I argue, Burroughs's fiction suggests the inextricability of the politics of the multitude from utopian desire, and, in doing so, it revises the concept of the commons so that it is less a fact of social life than an object of political aspiration. Utopia becomes the political struggle for a life in common, or, as Burroughs writes, "*Paradise actually exists*. . . . This is no vague eternal heaven for the righteous. This is *an actual place* at the end of a very dangerous road."[13]

Retroactive Utopianism

Burroughs begins his late trilogy by launching the reader into a future whose port of entry closed long ago. *Cities of the Red Night* tells the story of an eighteenth-century federation of pirates who live according to "the Articles," a shared code of conduct whose principles include direct democracy, sexual freedom, shared property relations, and general social equality. *Cities* opens with a section titled "Fore!" that combines the direct address of an author's note with the philosophical rumination of an eighteenth-century political treatise. This address offers insights not only into Burroughs's literary-political practice but also into the manner in which the pirates embody the lost possibilities of revolutions past. These pirates settle coastal regions and islands around the globe, spreading their utopian desire to create a new paradise on earth. The section "Fore!" focuses specifically on Captain Mission and his establishment of a settler colony, "Libertatia," off the coast of Madagascar. However, this colony doesn't last long, as it suffers a "surprise attack from the natives." Burroughs generalizes the fate of Captain Mission and his crew, if not the details of their case, describing their overall failure in terms of a missed opportunity to change the course of global history. Had the pirates been able to overcome the assaults by both imperial nations and indigenous peoples, "the history of the world could have been altered. Imagine a number of such fortified positions all through South America and the West Indies, stretching from Africa to Madagascar and Malaya and the East Indies, all offering refuge to fugitives from slavery and oppression: 'Come to us and live under the Articles'" (xiii).

Burroughs doesn't content himself with demonstrating the historical contingency of revolutionary endeavors. He insists on the enduring power of these missed opportunities. His fiction makes a case for a mode of retroactive agency in which it is not the present that rewrites the past but the lost possibilities of the past that remake the present. Burroughs terms this agency "retroactive Utopia," "since it actually could have happened in terms of the techniques and human resources available at the time" (xiv). The missed opportunities of the past unsettle the historical closure of the present by calling up an excess of social potential—the specter of revolution—inhabiting contemporary material conditions. Burroughs's retroactive utopianism condemns the revolutions of the eighteenth century for not going far enough, or for squandering their energies on the construction of the liberal nation-state and industrial capitalism. It reframes present historical conditions as the result of historical processes that could have gone otherwise. This dynamic sense of history doesn't represent a desire to transcend historical determination, because Burroughs makes clear that the forking paths of historical possibility belong to specific material conditions. Burroughs's fiction might even be understood as a kind of historical materialism—a way of surveying and cultivating the social and political potentialities belonging to specific historical moments.

Burroughs's historical materialism becomes clearer when one considers the way he combines and condenses the historical moments of the eighteenth-century revolutions and the Vietnam War. Burroughs draws an analogy between the struggles of the Articulated and those of the Viet Cong on the basis of a shared commitment to anticapitalist, anticolonial struggle and a shared repertoire of guerrilla strategies: "If the whole American army couldn't beat the Viet Cong at a time when fortified positions were rendered obsolete by artillery and air strikes, certainly the armies of Europe, operating in unfamiliar territory and susceptible to all the disabling diseases of tropical countries, could not have beaten guerrilla tactics *plus* fortified positions" (xiii). This sentence's conditional mood speaks to the way that Burroughs's literary-political practice involves realizing an alternative future—a future that is more than an extrapolation of the present—by rerouting the present through the social potentials of the past. More specifically, writing in the early 1980s, Burroughs locates a materialist practice of hope in the U.S. defeat in the Vietnam War and in the lasting sense of loss (Vietnam Syndrome) that followed. *Cities of the Red Night* translates the crisis of global American hegemony into a political opportunity. The failure of American empire thus serves as the condition of possibility for renewing and reimagining that desire called America.[14]

This phoenix-like reversal of defeat into possibility repeats itself in the second book of Burroughs's late trilogy, *The Place of Dead Roads* (1983). At first glance, the novel seems little more than a belated western—an almost reactionary indulgence in a genre whose political content has seldom been subtle.[15] Set in the years between 1899 and 1920, the text positions itself at the close of the frontier, that is, in the wake of Frederick Turner's well-known declaration of the exhaustion of American continental expansion. Of course, U.S. imperial expansion has continued with little, if any, interruption. One need only consider the U.S. adventures in Cuba and the Philippines to get a sense of how the energies invested in continental conquest were redirected into other imperial pursuits.[16] In other words, the frontier does not so much disappear as become displaced. *The Place of Dead Roads* wants to reclaim the futurity of the frontier, transforming the genre of the western into a vehicle for imagining radical political action. As in *Cities of the Red Night*, the second novel in the trilogy formulates this sense of possibility not as a return to the past but as a turn toward a future that might have been: "We will fight any extension of federal authority. . . . We will endeavor to halt the Industrial Revolution before it is too late" (98). This rerouting of nostalgia toward futurity achieves formal consistency in the novel's complex generic fusion of the western and science fiction: Space travel mixes with "Wild West" gunplay, and the novel's narrative machinery constantly invokes the possibilities of futures past—historical roads not taken—against the closure of the present.

Burroughs's late trilogy sustains its commitment to radical politics throughout its three novels. At the same time, this politics is inextricable from the history of settler colonialism, so much so that Burroughs's fictional account of social revolution might just as well be described as a story about the conquest and dispossession of indigenous peoples. After all, Burroughs describes Captain Mission's failure in terms of defeat at the hands of "the natives"—a turn of events suggesting that the recuperation of the Articles might very well entail a (retroactive) victory over indigenous peoples. Burroughs's fiction falls into the same trap that Mark Rifkin finds in American Renaissance literature and Jodi Byrd diagnoses in contemporary critical theory, namely, that the articulation of a nonindigenous political program contesting the status quo ends up depending on the material and discursive disappearance of indigenous peoples.[17] Burroughs's retroactive utopianism operates on behalf of settler colonialism; the futures it opens up—the missed opportunities it revisits—imply the genocide and displacement of indigenous peoples. Moreover, it's difficult not to detect in Burroughs's investment in noncapitalist forms of social cooperation an unacknowledged appropriation of indigenous ways of life. Burroughs's complicity with settler colonialism cannot, and should not, be ignored. At the same time, it would be a mistake to collapse Burroughs's utopianism into settler colonialism, as if it were no more than a colonial ruse. Burroughs occupies the messy terrain between American exceptionalism and its critique, meaning that his fiction is irreducible to a binary opposition between political virtue and vice. He reproduces settler colonialism, but he also circulates a desire to move beyond the nation-state, capitalism, and settler colonialism. This desire—this revolutionary salvage operation—remains a powerful antidote to the U.S. left's ongoing sense of failure and defeat. It expands our political imaginary to include possibilities beyond reform, recognition, and repair. It clears a conceptual, libidinal, and imaginative space for the construction of another world. There is no redeeming America, but, at the same time, there's also no ignoring the utopian aspirations that fall under its name.

"Arrested Evolution": The Politics of Potentiality

Reagan's call to make America great again involves its own kind of retroactive utopianism. Whereas Burroughs wants to replace the nation-state and capitalism with an emancipatory social alternative, Reagan envisions a return to traditional values—the restoration of a golden age of peace and prosperity that never really existed (at least not for everyone). At the same time, this return is utterly modern, or postmodern, insofar as it advances the neoliberal project of expanding the domain of the so-called free market to include every dimension of social life. As Wendy Brown argues, this political tendency—continuously in operation since the late 1970s—involves the hegemony of neoliberal reason in the United States and elsewhere, so that "both persons and states are construed on the model of the contemporary firm, both persons and states are expected to comport themselves in ways that maximize their capital value in the present and enhance their future value, and both persons and states do so through practices of entrepreneurialism, self-investment, and/or attracting investors."[18] From schooling and childcare to pension funds and health care, neoliberalism converts those social services that, under the Keynesian welfare state, had been deemed public responsibilities into private services subject to competition on the market. Moreover, this marketization of social services has penetrated into the domain of subjectivity, refashioning the self as an inherently entrepreneurial creature—a bundle of potentialities (or human capital) measured against its ability to turn risk into private profits. Neoliberalism thus revises the Lockean model of the possessive individual, replacing its emphasis on labor and private property with a no less individualistic, no less possessive emphasis on risk management. With this in mind, Reagan's promise to renew the American dream stands exposed as a way of incorporating the entrepreneurial, speculative, and risk-oriented drives of neoliberalism into the imagined community of the nation.

If neoliberalism can be understood, at least in part, as a counterrevolution with the aim of reformatting social potentials to fit the market, then Burroughs's *The Place of Dead Roads* can be read as an effort not only to expand our social potentials but to reconstitute them in emancipatory terms. Burroughs contrasts "Potential America" to what he terms the "Arrested Evolution" of the human species. The species remains stunted, he contends, because it's too busy rehearsing the rituals of the status quo to evolve beyond its earthbound conditions. Burroughs draws on the conventions of science fiction to imagine social revolution as a literal escape into space—a flight into the unknown. Indeed, one might describe Burroughs as reintroducing the unknown into the social potential of neoliberal subjects, or as expanding the political imaginary so that it exceeds the rules of the market. In short, Burroughs's politics of potentiality replaces the neoliberal evaluation of social life with the demand that the human species live up to its utopian horizons.

The utopian horizons in *The Place of Dead Roads* are inextricable from the American frontier. Not only is the novel set in a fantastic version of the frontier—a semicivilized zone of constant conflict and upheaval—but it also draws on the trappings of the western, including cowboys, cattle rustling, and saloons. Burroughs does not so much reject the western as convert it into a radical social project. He imagines a counter-nation in which the desire for social order and the will to expansion—Manifest Destiny—fulfill themselves in a revolutionary synthesis of solidarity, subversion, and social invention. Kim Carsons, the novel's protagonist, embodies this political reversal, playing the role of cowboy only to undermine its imperial overtones. Kim's quest is not to bestow order on the wilderness but to recover the wildness of social life.[19] The novel describes him as "everything a normal American boy is taught to detest. He is evil and slimy and *insidious*. Perhaps his vices could be forgiven him, but he was also given to the subversive practice of *thinking*" (16). In this context, thinking implies a critique of sanctioned forms of knowledge. It is a "subversive practice," because it refuses to take things at face value, associating knowledge not with authority but with the embrace of the strange, the new, the alien. Liberalism and neoliberalism alike may valorize knowledge, but they do so only insofar as it contributes to "progress," meaning the accumulation of capital, the reinforcement of state power, and the discipline of the market. "Now, American boys are told they should think. But just wait until your thinking is basically different from the thinking of a boss or a teacher. . . . You will find out that you *aren't* supposed to think" (ibid.). Through the character of Kim Carsons, Burroughs articulates a model of critical reason in which negativity—the rejection of "normality"—and positivity—a passion for social difference—come together.

In *The Place of Dead Roads*, critical thought comes to be closely linked to writing fiction. Kim is not only a cowboy but also a writer, with a particular fondness for composing tales packed with outlandish adventures and salacious content. Kim's fictions—extracts of which are included in the novel—mostly belong to the genre of science fiction. This genre choice builds on the characterization of Kim as deviant, connecting his abnormality to a longing for the otherworldly: "Wouldn't mind being reborn as a Mexican, he thought, wistfully, knowing he really can't be reborn anywhere on this planet. He just doesn't *fit* somehow" (304). Burroughs casts science fiction as a misfit genre—a genre of social outcasts devoted to imagining strange worlds and alien forms of life. Kim writes of "the Baron" "rid[ing] his swift Arn": "The Arn is like a stream-lined turtle with a shell of light flexible metal that serves as a means of locomotion and also as a weapon" (29). Elsewhere, he imagines alien sexual difference as an alternative sociality: "On the satellite Fenec, the penis is not confined to a sexual function but serves as a general means of social communication" (30). Kim's role as a science fiction writer suggests that Burroughs's politics of potentiality has less to do with self-realization—in the limited sense of realizing one's inner potentiality—and more to do with the imagination of social alternatives that are so different from the status quo that they cannot help but take the form of other worlds.

Although this isn't the place for an extended discussion of science fiction, it is worth describing how two of the genre's dynamics lend themselves to Burroughs's emphasis on critical thinking and social potentiality. Darko Suvin identifies the genre's critical value with its capacity for estrangement. Revising Bertolt Brecht's concept of *Verfremdungseffekt*, Suvin articulates science fictional estrangement as the effect of an interaction between a zero-degree empirical world and a speculative element: "SF is, then, a literary genre whose necessary and sufficient conditions are the presence and interaction of estrangement and cognition, and whose main formal device is an imaginative framework alternative to the author's empirical environment."[20] Suvin emphasizes science fiction's cognitive rigor, its methodical approach to expanding our perception of the present. SF doesn't simply posit the existence of another world, it draws out the immanent possibility that another world might arise from this one.

Fredric Jameson shares Suvin's assessment of science fiction as a practice of estrangement, but he changes the valence of it, putting the accent on the failure of imagination:

> [Science fiction's] deepest vocation is over and over again to demonstrate our incapacity to imagine the future, to body forth, through apparently full representations which prove on closer inspection to be structurally and constitutively impoverished, the atrophy in our time of what Marcuse has called the *utopian imagination*, the imagination of otherness and radical difference; to succeed by failure, and to serve as unwitting and even unwilling vehicles for a meditation, which, setting forth for the unknown, finds itself irrevocably mired in the all-too-familiar, and thereby becomes unexpectedly transformed into a contemplation of our own absolute limits.[21]

Although Jameson has suggested a more positive role for science fiction as a means of "disrupting" the status quo, he continues to emphasize the genre's critical negativity.[22] Science fiction doesn't deliver the future; instead, it forces us to face the material limits of the present—to acknowledge not only the intractability of our social conditions but also their revocability. Or, as Jameson explains, it is "the answer to the universal ideological conviction that no alternative is possible, that there is no alternative to the system. But it asserts this by forcing us to think the break itself, and not by offering a more traditional picture of what things would be like after the break."[23]

Suvin's and Jameson's descriptions of science fiction are certainly not the only ones available, but they offer a sense of why Burroughs finds himself drawn to the genre. The attraction has less to do with futuristic technology or extraterrestrial beings than with systemic difference—the sense that another social system is possible. *The Place of Dead Roads* identifies its political desires with science fiction's investment in radical difference, or "the break." Kim's stories estrange America; they reveal not only the historical contingency of national formations but also their ability to radically change. In other words, Kim's fiction does more than demystify. It also experiments with new ways of being in the world.

> Kim considers these imaginary space trips to other worlds as practice for the real thing, like target shooting. As a prisoner serving a life sentence can think only of escape, so Kim takes for granted that the only purpose of his life is space travel. He knows that this will involve not just a change of locale, but basic *biologic* alterations, like the switch from water to land. There has to be the air-breathing potential *first*. And what is the medium corresponding to air that we must learn to breathe in? The answer came to Kim in a silver flash. . . . *Silence*. (40)

The metaphor of a prisoner "think[ing] only of escape" suggests that, for Kim, writing is an emancipatory practice. It is an escape from the ordinariness of daily life, from the existential prison of the capitalist lifeworld, but it is also more than "imaginary." Writing, "like target shooting," is "practice for the real thing." It anticipates escape from present-day constraints. In this context, anticipation is neither abstract, nor unreal, but "potential."[24] To "practice" is to suspend the distinction between the actual and the potential in a doing that doubles as the potential to do otherwise. In other words, writing is a practice that actively tarries with the specters of what could have been, that delights in the plurality of possibilities haunting material reality. For other worlds to be imaginable, Burroughs suggests, one must first learn to appreciate the potential for difference and novelty that belongs to this world.

Burroughs elaborates the collective dimension of the politics of potentiality through the language of evolution. Kim's writing draws attention to the "Arrested Evolution" of the human species—a state of historical suspension in which human social potential "stagnates."

> Kim knew he was in a state of Arrested Evolution: A.E. He was no more destined to stagnate in this three-dimensional animal form than a tadpole is designed to remain a tadpole. . . .
>
> Kim knows that the first step toward space exploration is to examine the human artifact with *biologic* alterations in mind that will render our H.A. [Human Artifact] more suitable for space conditions and space travel. . . . We are like water creatures looking up at the land and air and wondering how we can survive in that alien medium. The water we live in is Time. That alien medium we glimpse beyond time is Space. And that is where we are going. (40–41)

Burroughs imagines the possibility of radical otherness, or systemic change, as an evolution that leads the human species from dwelling on earth to voyaging through space. Although Burroughs's language evokes a science fictional imaginary of biotechnology, space travel, and aliens, he nevertheless refuses to offer a definitive image of this otherworldly future. Instead, he emphasizes the encounter with the unimaginable—the moment when our senses can no longer assimilate what appears before us: "We are like water creatures looking up at the land and air and wondering how we can survive in that alien medium." The affective state appropriate to this encounter is, Burroughs suggests, "wonder"—the feeling that arises when the familiarity of the present recedes, but our knowledge of the future remains startling and incomplete. Wonder distinguishes itself from exoticism, because rather than reinforcing the dichotomy between self and other, it opens the door to a transformation of the species. Kim is interested in the exploration of space only insofar as it involves "basic *biologic* alterations": "Kim reads all the science fiction he can find, and he is stunned to discover in all these writings the underlying assumption that there will be no basic changes involved in space travel" (ibid.). Here, "basic" signifies deep or intensive, rather than simple; it suggests a fundamental change in the structure of the human species, as it adapts to the final frontier, "Space." If we're to move beyond our state of "Arrested Evolution," then we must prepare ourselves not only for an "alien medium" but also for our becoming alien to ourselves. This becoming-alien is the essence of Kim's science fiction, which might be understood as a form of utopian praxis whose object is not the invention of new spaces but a radical change of life itself.

Kim's investment in science fiction needs to be understood in relation to neoliberalism and its will to assimilate social life to the so-called free market. Burroughs's focus on the evolutionary potential of the human species stands in stark contrast to the discourses of self-actualization and self-help that were so popular in the 1980s. These discourses frame social problems as personal difficulties to be solved through changes in individual conduct. They foreclose the possibility of social transformation in favor of self-improvement, often in the form of improving one's chances on the market. In other words, self-help discourses channel social potentiality away from politics and toward self-perfection. This drive toward self-improvement is not apolitical, however. As Nikolas Rose argues, such therapeutic practices can be understood in Foucauldian terms as "technologies for the government of the soul," which "operate not through the crushing of subjectivity in the interests of control and profit, but by seeking to align political, social, and institutional goals with individual pleasures and desires, and with the happiness and fulfillment of the self."[25] It would be a mistake to reduce neoliberalism to this subtle form of power, given that neoliberalism so often involves violent expropriation (what David Harvey refers to as "accumulation by dispossession") in the process of creating new markets.[26] However, it would also be a mistake to ignore the way neoliberalism legitimates itself by transforming social potentiality into fodder for self-actualization. Despite Margaret Thatcher's claim to the contrary, neoliberalism does not dissolve all social bonds so much as it subordinates them to individual performance on the market. *The Place of Dead Roads* responds to the neoliberal counterrevolution by insisting that potentiality belongs not to the individual but to the species. For Burroughs, there is no such thing as individual freedom, only collective freedom, and, as Kim Carsons might say, the only worthwhile speculations are those that draw on our freedom to become alien to ourselves.

The Word Virus, or Language as a System of Control

Kim Carsons's commitment to writing as a way of speculating on the future of the human species speaks to Burroughs's more general concern for writing's power over life. For Burroughs, writing is at one and the same time a practice of emancipation and a system of control. In his novels, essays, and interviews, Burroughs elaborates a theory of language as a virus, which replicates itself through the act of communication and, in doing so, alters the human species. Burroughs insists on the literalness of this theory: "I have frequently spoken of word and image as viruses or as acting as viruses, and this is not an allegorical comparison."[27] Burroughs's insistence on the biological dimension of language—on language's capacity to rewrite life itself—suggests that what's at stake in his theory is the nexus of power, embodied subjectivity, population, and language. Not unlike Foucault's genealogical inquiries, Burroughs traces the composition of bodies by specific discursive apparatuses, relations of power, and disciplines of knowledge. He is especially interested in how technologies of mass communication and audiovisual storage—for example, television and the tape recorder—contribute to the formation of a global control system. In elaborating this theory, Burroughs positions his own writing practice as a cure for control—a practice of liberation that not only breaks through the mimetic logic of the word virus but also transforms the human species into a subject of freedom.

One of the ways Burroughs articulates his theory of language is through fictions of the Word's genesis, or accounts of the emergence of language and its infection of the human species. This genesis isn't an isolated event but rather a structural premise of systems of control. "In the beginning was the Word," Burroughs writes, "and the Word was God—and the word was flesh . . . human flesh . . . in the beginning of *writing*."[28] It is language, in its inaugural manifestation as Word or logos, which gives birth to God and Man as twin effects of the same absent cause ("the beginning"). Writing stands at the origin of the Word, or, as Burroughs explains, "I suggest that the spoken word as we know it came after the written word."[29] The Word always already inscribes itself; it is always already articulated as a combination of sign and flesh. The Word remains exposed to the plurality of its usage, which is to say that it opens itself up to a dissemination whose effects are unpredictable. Between the copula linking Word and God ("and the Word was God . . ."), writing intercedes, displacing the myth that attempts to anchor linguistic practice in a transcendent or unified source of enunciation.[30] Burroughs's ellipses—punctuation marks that proliferate throughout his writings—are not gaps in speech but the positive interruption of writing's basic trait: Each point gestures toward the minimal threshold of writing and, in doing so, testifies to the excess of writing over the Word's control.

Burroughs treats the theological vision of the Word's control over expressive action as a myth in need not only of critique but also of a counterhistory. The virus is the vehicle of this counterhistory: "My basic theory is that the written word was actually a virus that made the spoken word possible. The word has not been recognized as a virus because it has achieved a state of stable symbiosis with the host, though this symbiotic relationship is now breaking down" (*Job*, 12). Burroughs presents a short biological history of the human species, marked by three pivotal moments: an evolutionary mutation that makes the initial human-virus symbiosis a genetic mainstay; the manipulation of this symbiosis by governments in the name of "national security"; and an "electronic revolution" that exposes this evolutionary-historical legacy to transformation by anyone in possession of a tape recorder. Burroughs narrates these events with reference to scientific authorities and contemporary events (most notably, the Watergate scandal). As interesting as the twists and turns of this historical account may be, the mode of historicity implied by the narration arguably carries more significance.[31] In this narrative, the human species is an artifact, though not one designed by an individual or collective will. The evolution of the species revolves around transformations in the symbiotic relationship between the "word virus" and human subjects. These transformations may involve communication technologies such as mass print, but they may just as well involve the advent of new political and social formations, such as capitalism and liberalism. In any case, this history is nonteleological and nonlinear. Mutations in the form of the species are neither the realization of some preexisting essence, nor the product of providence, but rather an entirely contingent assemblage of material traits and processes.

The history of the human species, in other words, belies the reproduction of origin or essence. After all, in Burroughs's account, the human capacity for speech emerges from a virus—an entity defined by its capacities for replication and mutation. Burroughs's "electronic revolution" doesn't suggest a simple deviation from the Word's primacy. Instead, it names a fundamental transformation of the relationship between the human species and language, as well as a transformation of the processes that constitute sociality and subject-formation.[32] For Burroughs, the tape recorder exemplifies this revolution because of its ability not only to record but also to mix and splice together diverse materials. Tape recorders invent by combining materials; they produce the new by remixing the old.[33] In addition, the medium of magnetic tape puts into question the ontological distinction between authenticity and imitation.[34] The original is a copy not only because of its mimetic or iconic relation to a referent but also because of its status as immediately reproducible. The original is no more primary than any of the number of tapes that spawn from it and which, in turn, may spawn their own progeny. This indifference regarding originality does not eradicate difference but, to the contrary, allows difference to proliferate, since identity no longer reduces differentiation to the replication of self-identical forms. Rather than difference being an effect of an entity's distance from origin/identity, difference usurps the origin—it becomes difference in itself.[35]

For Burroughs, the electronic revolution is only one of many practices and processes that challenge the dominance of the Word. Burroughs also cites hieroglyphics and the cut-up method of writing (invented by Brion Gysin and him) as practices that trouble the logos. These practices are characterized by kinds of differentiation irreducible to identity or to the exclusivity of the either-or. They are, for Burroughs, contributions to a common project, namely, the "build[ing of] a language" that is a "biological weapon" for waging war against the Word:

> The aim of this project is to build a language in which certain falsifications inherent in all existing Western languages will be made incapable of formulation. The following falsifications to be deleted from the proposed language:

The IS of identity. You are an animal. You are a body. Now whatever you may be you are not an "animal", you are not a "body", because these are verbal labels. The IS of identity always carries the implication of that and nothing else, and it also carries the assignment of permanent condition. To stay that way. All naming calling presupposes the IS of identity. . . .

The definite article THE. THE contains the implication of one and only: THE God, THE universe, THE way, THE right, THE wrong. If there is another, then THAT universe, THAT way is no longer THE universe, THE way. The definite article THE will be deleted and the indefinite article A will take its place.

The whole concept of EITHER/OR. Right or wrong, physical or mental, true or false, the whole concept of OR will be deleted from the language and replaced by juxtaposition, by *and*.[36]

This passage can be read as a commentary on Burroughs's own writing practice, cataloging not only its stylistic traits but also its philosophical and political stakes. For Burroughs, writing isn't about representation—even the kinds of positive representation that make the marginalized more visible—instead it's a means of directly altering the relationship between the human species and language. Burroughs writes of "deleting" and "replacing" linguistic structures, suggesting not only that language has a material history but also that this history can be manipulated through writing. Significantly, the use of the future tense and the passive voice ("will be deleted"; "will take its place"; "to be deleted"; "to build") implies that writing doesn't so much originate in a subject (the author) as pass through it—the writer is less creator than channel of a species to come. These changes—the eradication of the copula; the replacement of definite articles by indefinite articles; the exchange of exclusive disjunctions for inclusive ones—lend themselves to dismantling the primacy of identity and representation. Instead of a tool that the subject uses to manipulate the objects of the world, language constitutes a milieu for the production, reproduction, and transformation of the species, or a laboratory in which the idea of the individual subject might be replaced by more collective models of agency.

The writing practice that Burroughs outlines is performative, which is to say that instead of representing material situations, it invents or intervenes into them.[37] Christopher Breu articulates this point in Lacanian terms, arguing that Burroughs is "interested in accessing the real via the symbolic. In order to do this, though, the symbolic must be used against itself in order to expose that which it attempts but fails to account for and which exists in contradiction to it: the real."[38] Burroughs's critique of the Word doesn't simply substitute one language for another, however. Identity does not get replaced by difference, nor representation by performative language. Such strict reversals would duplicate the sorts of binary truth claims Burroughs criticizes under the heading of the either-or ("Right or wrong, physical or mental, true or false, the whole concept of OR will be deleted"). Instead, Burroughs's linguistic project should be understood as an immanent critique of identity and representation. It does not suggest that identity and representation are false or illusory but rather that they are limiting, that they allude to difference only insofar as they reduce its multiplicity. In concrete terms, it's difficult to deny the power of identity claims in the context of political struggle. Claiming a collective social identity serves as a way of demanding recognition from the liberal state—it's the first step in demanding reparations for historical wrongs or inclusion in public services. At the same time, such demands risk reifying, or fetishizing, the identities that they claim to represent. As Burroughs notes, the "IS of identity" "carries the assignment of permanent condition. To stay that way." Burroughs worries not only about how representation elides the multiplicity of social difference—for instance, the class division that often stratifies ethnic or racial minorities—but also that representation might prohibit radical social change because of the way it links political action to the conservation of identity. To summarize, the object of Burroughs's critique is less representation as such than representation's disavowal of multiplicity, or its conversion of difference into little more than sameness multiplied.

Burroughs's critique of representation dovetails with his more general critique of systems of control. For Burroughs, control describes social processes that deprive subjects of autonomy, foreclose the possibility of radical transformation, and reproduce identity to the exclusion of difference. In "The Limits of Control," Burroughs describes a situation in which governments directly control the mind through "behavior-modification techniques." Even in this situation, language remains essential to the operations of power:

> But words are still the principal instruments of control. Suggestions are words. Persuasions are words. Orders are words. No control machine so far devised can operate without words, and any control machine which attempts to do so relying entirely on external force or entirely on physical control of the mind will soon encounter the limits of control.[39]

Burroughs generalizes the domain of control beyond specifically political institutions. Control is biopolitical in the sense that it concerns the diverse relations among bodies, species/populations, discourses, knowledge, and power. Burroughs begins his essay with a discussion of the state, but he soon expands the scope of his critique to include mass media, intimate relationships, and a variety of social institutions. Any relation or action involving language becomes a potential site of control. Control is qualitatively different from, even if it does not rule out, coercion or "external force." Coercion is the limit of control, or the point at which control admits its parasitic nature, for control, Burroughs clarifies, is not "use": "I *control* a slave, a dog, a worker; but if I establish *complete* control somehow, as by implanting electrodes in the brain, then my subject is little more than a tape recorder, a camera, a robot. You don't *control* a tape recorder—you *use* it."[40] Burroughs relies on a relatively simplistic opposition between living organisms and machinery—a distinction much of his fiction betrays—but the implications of this opposition are nonetheless significant for his theory of control: Vitality supposes at least the potential for resistance, or, conversely, in contrast to pure instrumentalization, which renders social actors into mere means for reproducing the status quo, control requires active participation—it "needs opposition or acquiescence; otherwise it ceases to be control."[41] Control doesn't transform social beings into robots; it conditions them so that they desire their own servitude. Burroughs's novels, I suggest, are extended demonstrations of this thesis. They trace the influence of control in religion, mass media, sexual relations, drug use, and many other areas of social life.[42]

No aspect of human life is left untouched by control. Burroughs goes so far as to claim that "syllabic language" itself facilitates control.

> If I hold up a sign with the word "ROSE" written on it, and you read that sign, you will be forced to repeat the word "ROSE" to yourself. If I show you a picture of a rose you do not have to repeat the word. You can register the image in silence. A syllabic language forces you to verbalize in auditory patterns. A hieroglyphic language does not. . . . It is precisely these automatic reactions to words themselves that enable those who manipulate words to control thought on a mass scale.[43]

Although the binary opposition Burroughs elaborates between hieroglyphic language and syllabic language is more than a little reductive, this passage manages to draw together a number of threads in his theory of language and politics: the relationship between representation and automatization (or the reproduction of sameness); the centrality of self-relation for modes of control ("you will be forced to repeat the word 'ROSE' *to yourself*" [emphasis mine]); and the mutual imbrication of mass sociality (or population) and individual bodies. Although Burroughs employs words such as "manipulate" and "force," it is still "you"—the subjected subject—that acts in the process of control. Control doesn't suspend or eliminate action; it scripts it, so that one functions *as if* one could not do otherwise. Put differently, control takes hold of the relationship between social possibilities in general and the specific practices through which these possibilities come to be actualized. Control governs social potentiality.

Burroughs seldom, if ever, gets cited in the critical discourse of biopolitics, but he has nonetheless influenced it, if only through Gilles Deleuze's writings on control societies. Critics often draw on Deleuze's theorization of control societies as a means of thinking through postmodern or late-capitalist versions of biopolitics, but what gets lost in the process is the debt owed to Burroughs's political imagination. Deleuze explicitly acknowledges this debt in the course of distinguishing disciplinary societies from control societies: "We're moving towards control societies that no longer operate by confining people [as disciplinary societies tend to do] but through continuous control and instant communication. Burroughs was the first to address this."[44] And: "*Control societies* are taking over from disciplinary societies. 'Control' is the name proposed by Burroughs to characterize the new monster, and Foucault sees it fast approaching."[45] Deleuze derives a sense of power's subtlety from Burroughs. It is not simply that Burroughs conceives of control as almost universal in its operations. It's also that he describes how control functions through the complicity of the subjects on which it operates. Control is everywhere, even (or especially) inside of you. It neither eliminates, nor reduces subjectivity; it reconfigures it for the sake of neoliberal forms of governance and the global accumulation of capital. Moreover, Burroughs's emphasis on the inextricability of communication and control anticipates contemporary accounts of communicative or cognitive capitalism—a system of exploitation in which communicative activities generate value that gets extracted by corporations.[46]

At the same time, Deleuze moves beyond Burroughs's theory of control, replacing Burroughs's terminology of command, manipulation, and automation with an analysis of modulation, passwords, and dividuals. Whereas the disciplinary societies described by Foucault "mold" individuals into more or less docile members of national populations, control societies operate in terms of "*modulation*, like a self-transmuting molding continually changing from one moment to the next, or like a sieve whose mesh varies from one point to another."[47] The rigid procedures of normalization belonging to disciplinary societies give way to the infinitely supple modulation of activity—a way of channeling effort so that desire aligns with the demands of corporations and states. In the medical industry, for example, the cure comes to be subordinated to ongoing practices of wellness customized for specific individuals and populations, as if the only way to ensure the reproduction of the status quo were to insist on the relative autonomy of the patient. There is more one could say about what distinguishes control societies, but, at its core, it is a matter of making autonomy, creativity, and communication work on behalf of "the arrogant breed who are our masters" (in particular, the narrow class of individuals whose earnings derive from shares in corporate profits, rather than from wages).[48]

There is another way of describing Deleuze's debt to Burroughs, however. Rather than reading Deleuze as superseding Burroughs—a teleological argument that neither of them would appreciate—we might think of Deleuze as revising the theory of control articulated in Burroughs's prose so that it accounts for his fiction. In other words, Deleuze learns as much, or more, from Burroughs's novels as he does from his essays (which is also to say that Burroughs's fiction outstrips his prose, when it comes to thinking politically). This education is evident in Deleuze's references to Burroughs's fiction in his dialogues with Claire Parnet, as well as in his citations of *Speed* and *Naked Lunch* in *A Thousand Plateaus*.[49] The rhizomatic patterns of writing theorized and practiced in Deleuze's collaborations with Félix Guattari bear more than a passing resemblance to Burroughs's narrative method of stitching together semi-autonomous vignettes into nonlinear plot structures. It's also difficult to imagine that Burroughs's fascination with wandering organs (the infamous talking asshole from *Naked Lunch*, for instance) and his nomadic characters constantly experimenting with new forms of life didn't shape Deleuze and Guattari's philosophy to some degree. If Deleuze moves beyond Burroughs's theory of control, he does so by borrowing elements of Burroughs's fiction. Most important, though, Deleuze inherits a fundamental problem of thought from Burroughs—a question at the heart of any theory of biopolitics: How does one think emancipation in a context of control? How do we imagine and practice freedom in a situation in which our desires and potentialities have been captured and reconstituted by capital and the state? What does it mean to long for freedom, even as one enjoys one's own servitude?

The War against Control

Burroughs wages war against societies of control by imagining language as a "biological weapon." Language is more than a channel for communication.

It is a medium through which the human species can be reconstituted, and it is a set of practices capable of enslaving life to systems of control or of liberating it from them. From one perspective, Burroughs's political theory of language is an extension of the consciousness-raising exercises associated with the sixties—a remnant of the rituals through which activists, hippies, and revolutionaries prepared themselves for a better world. Burroughs's fiction in the 1980s can be understood as an attempt to take language back for radical social movements, to reappropriate culture as a weapon for the left. It is a response not only to neoliberalism's perversion of the social desires of the sixties but also to the culture wars emergent in the 1980s. In particular, Burroughs's fiction constitutes a critique of the moralism that has been a crucial component in neoliberalism's rise to hegemony. Although it's been discussed by many scholars and activists, it is worth recalling that this conservative morality emphasizes personal responsibility, especially in respect to economic support, even as it demonizes racial and sexual minorities as threats to social order.[50] It is a way of neutralizing political antagonism or foreclosing alternatives to neoliberalism. Of course, this moralism is political, despite its protestations to the contrary. Not only does it lend ideological support to coercive efforts such as attacks on organized labor and homophobic legislation, it also lends ethical and spiritual justification to the privatization of public services. In the language of this moralism, the destruction of the welfare state, or the social safety net, translates to the moral activity of helping poor folks "get back on their own feet" by ending their reliance on "entitlements." This moral program—this concerted effort to surrender society to the so-called free market—is a central target of Burroughs's critique.

The Place of Dead Roads is a weapon in Burroughs's struggle against neoliberalism. I've already suggested that one of the ways the novel wages this war is by recovering a kind of social potentiality irreducible to the values of the market. Burroughs builds on this recovery by connecting it to an antagonism between the forces of liberation and the forces of conservative moralism. Indeed, Burroughs substitutes generalized political conflict, or civil war, for the psychological impulse of conventional novels. Not only does the putative protagonist of the novel, Kim Carsons, fail to develop as a character during the course of the narrative, but all of the characters in the novel are little more than functions of collective dynamics. In other words, Burroughs presents characters less as individuals than as indices of social potentials and placeholders for political projects. The novel reinforces this system of characters as social variables in a number of ways, for example, in the revelation that there isn't only one Kim Carsons but many, because he is "one of ten clones derived from Kim Carsons the Founder. Since he was in contact with approximate replicas of himself and with the other clone families . . . , he was under no pressure to maintain the perimeters of a defensive ego and this left him free to *think*" (113). If, for Burroughs, critical thought entails a subversion of identity (or ego) and if emancipation implies the recovery of social potentiality from the limits of possessive individualism, then it makes perfect sense that the protagonist of *The Place of Dead Roads* is not one but many—a figure of multiplicity whose thoughts and actions cannot be construed as anything but collective. This tendency to make characters into social types is arguably one of the defining features of Burroughs's entire corpus, with the exception perhaps of his early semiautobiographical novels. *The Place of Dead Roads* distinguishes itself in gathering these social types into an overarching conflict between two political subjects: the Johnson Family and the Shits. Whereas the Shits are the conservative, moralistic, and politically dominant social element—Burroughs describes them as churchgoing folks with a compulsive need to correct what they see as the flaws in other people—the Johnson Family is a group of outlaws dedicated to emancipating America from systems of control. *The Place of Dead Roads* frames its attempt to imagine an alternative to neoliberalism as the struggle of the Johnson Family against the Shits.

The Johnson Family is representative of what Burroughs terms "Potential America," or "P.A."—a utopian counter-nation situated within American exceptionalism in much the same way that guerrilla forces lurk in the shadow of their enemy. The Johnsons are dedicated to the complete destruction of the Shits: "We seek a Total Solution to the Shit Problem: Slaughter the shits of the world like cows with the aftosa [foot-and-mouth disease]" (155). The novel's biological rhetoric categorizes the Shits as less than human, as diseased cattle waiting for the "slaughter." In other words, Burroughs narrates emancipation in terms of national health, suggesting that liberation from control is analogous to curing a disease. This analogy would seem to suggest that Burroughs's biological weapon—his linguistic project to abolish the "Arrested Evolution" of the human species—has national purification as its aim. The Shits' name is all too appropriate, for Burroughs would like nothing more than to flush them down the toilet. Nor does the novel shy away from literalizing the "Total Solution." One finds several vignettes in which Kim engages in biological warfare against the Shits, for example, infecting an entire churchgoing town with the smallpox (74). The Johnson Family constitutes a revolutionary subject in the sense that it embodies a reactive negation of the social order; the Johnsons are driven by resentment as much as the desire for another world.

The biopolitics of *The Place of Dead Roads* is disturbing. It conjures up the specter of totalitarian regimes, not least of all the Third Reich's quest for a "Final Solution" to the "Jewish Problem." In the context of U.S. history, Kim's deployment of smallpox as a weapon harks back to the genocide of indigenous peoples in North America and to the general history of American empire. At the same time, it is worth distinguishing the revolutionary element in this biopolitics, the way in which Burroughs represents it as an anticapitalist political project. In short, this is class war. Burroughs seems to repeat and reinforce the racial logic of Soviet biopolitics, as described by Michel Foucault: The antagonism between the working class (the Johnson Family) and the bourgeoisie (the Shits) amounts to a race war in which the death of one class contributes to the health of the other.[51] The horizon of revolution is a healthy national social body, and this health can be achieved only through the elimination of the disease, namely, capitalism as embodied by the bourgeoisie.

Burroughs's description of the Johnson Family's revolutionary efforts breaks with the logic of race war, however. The novel deconstructs the opposition between the Johnson Family and the Shits by articulating the problem of class in viral terms. Class is biological not in the sense of being a natural fact or an effect of evolution but in the sense that it is a question of how bodies are organized, or the ways in which populations are composed by specific material conditions. In other words, class is not essential, it is historically contingent.

> You are a Shit Spotter. It's satisfying work. Somebody throws your change on a morphine script back at you and his name goes down on a list. We have observed that most of the trouble in the world is caused by ten or twenty percent of folks who can't mind their own business because they *have* no business of their own to mind any more than a smallpox virus. Now your virus is an obligate cellular parasite, and my contention is that what we call evil is quite literally a virus parasite occupying a certain brain area which we may term the RIGHT center. The mark of a basic shit is that he has to be *right*. And right here we must make a diagnostic distinction between a hard-core virus-occupied shit and a plain ordinary mean no-good son of a bitch. Some of these sons of bitches don't cause any trouble at all, just want to be left alone. Others cause minor trouble, like barroom fights and bank robberies. To put it country simple—former narcotics commissioner Harry J. Anslinger *diseased* was an obligate shit. Jesse James, Billy the Kid, Dillinger, were just sons of bitches. (154–55)

The smallpox virus figures the historical contingency of class as a kind of parasitism. "The mark of a basic shit" has little to do with consciousness or intention. One does not choose to be a shit, instead shittiness—for lack of a better way of putting it—occupies the subject, taking over their cognitive faculties in an act of psychic colonialism. With this in mind, Burroughs's "Total Solution" is less an act of genocide than a kind of cultural revolution or decolonial struggle. Instead of pursuing the elimination of a people, it aims at curing the disease of moral rectitude ("The mark of a basic shit is that he has to be *right*"). It is an almost Nietzschean exercise in dismantling the moral system through which those in power disguise their operations of control as divinely ordained expressions of the good. There is a tension in Burroughs's articulation of the Shit problem, however. On the one hand, Burroughs insists on a "diagnostic distinction between a hard-core virus-occupied shit and a plain ordinary mean no-good son of a bitch," implying that the political dynamics of this virus conform to discrete subject positions. One is or is not a Shit, just as one is on one side of the law or the other. On the other hand, viruses cross the boundaries between subjects—they replicate and circulate across the membranes distinguishing one organism from another. One isn't born a law enforcement agent, like Harry J. Anslinger; one becomes one, and the same presumably holds for sons of bitches. There seems to be a contradiction in Burroughs's political imaginary between class division and biological fluidity, or between the binary structure of political antagonism and the multiplicity and mobility of viral infection. "To put it country simple," the Johnson Family appears caught between wanting to tear down the entire social order and needing to be in the right.

This tension between the logics of antagonism and infection might be rephrased as a question: How does one engage in political struggle without reproducing the ideological structures of the status quo? How does one acknowledge the changeability of political subjectivity without dissolving antagonism? Burroughs's response, I suggest, is embedded in the rhetorical dimensions of the text, specifically, in the way that the above passage not only operates as description and diagnosis but also as revolutionary call to arms. This critique of the Shits reads like a recruitment effort, the text's "we" opening itself up to others through the indeterminacy of the second-person, "you": "You are a Shit Spotter." Even as Burroughs marks the division between the Johnson Family and the Shits, he invites the reader into the Family, as if to suggest that the very act of reading *The Place of Dead Roads* were an act of political conversion—a process of becoming revolutionary through the biological weapon of language. This interpellative process gestures toward an understanding of political antagonism that reconciles class division and viral multiplicity, without necessarily dissolving the tension between them. The binary structure of antagonism does not cancel the mobility and multiplicity of the virus. Instead, it organizes viral itineraries into provisional unities, or contingent political assemblies. One might say that Burroughs's model of antagonism is performative, because it produces the political subjects that it purports to describe. Yes, one is or is not a Shit, but this diagnosis is itself the result of social processes that underlie and cut across this dualism. Indeed, the very act of diagnosing a Shit transforms one into a member of the Johnson Family, suggesting that Burroughs's interest in drawing a line of social and political division is synonymous with his desire to recruit agents for his "Potential America." Antagonism is therefore relational—it is the strategic reorganization of lines of social force into real but contingent political assemblies.

If Burroughs is so interested in reframing America as an antagonism between the Johnson Family and the Shits, it is because he sees the United States as a vanguard of global control that needs to be opposed. Citing the post–World War II expansion of U.S. influence abroad (via the Marshall Plan, Cold War containment policy, and institutions such as NATO), as well as the country's role as an innovator of control technologies (television news broadcasting, the atomic bomb, etc.), Burroughs argues that the United States is the cutting edge of the "Western control machine."[52] America is a global hegemon, or "superpower." As such, it is also an incubation chamber for the future of global politics—a vast apparatus making some political possibilities likely (neoliberal market culture, for example), while shutting other ones down (not least of all socialism and communism). Asked by an interviewer to expand on his description of "America as a nightmare," Burroughs responds that the United States is more precisely a "non-dream": "The American non-dream is precisely to wipe the dream out of existence. The dream is a spontaneous happening and therefore dangerous to a control system set up by the non-dreamers."[53] Burroughs draws an opposition between an anti-utopian containment of social potentiality and the "spontaneous happening" of utopian alternatives. America is a control machine inasmuch as it is suppresses utopian dreams, which is to say that control is parasitical, relying on the social potentiality it wishes to eradicate: "All control systems try to make control as tight as possible, but at the same time, if they succeeded completely, there would be nothing left to control."[54] There is an ontological asymmetry, then, between control and utopia, for against the positivity of the dreamers, there stands not another positive entity but a diffuse system of negativity. *The Place of Dead*

Roads hints at this asymmetry in its praise of the Johnson Family's creativity: "That his [Kim's] dream of a takeover by the Johnson Family, by those who actually do the work, the creative thinkers and artists and technicians, was not just science fiction" (104). Much like Marx's analysis of capitalist exploitation, Burroughs's critique of the Shits of the world implies that political control depends on the theft of social potentiality. It is more than a coincidence, then, when Burroughs, in the third book of the late trilogy, *The Western Lands*, arrives at the same figure as Marx to represent exploitation: the vampire—an undead creature who only has as much life as it drains from others.[55]

Burroughs articulates America as a constitutive antagonism between systems of control and dreams of other worlds. He harbors no illusions about the destructive nature of American empire, but he also recognizes "that a cultural revolution of unprecedented dimensions has taken place in America during the last thirty years, and since America is now the model for the rest of the Western world, this revolution is worldwide."[56] This cultural revolution is immanent in the American system of control—it is at one and the same time a determinate negation of American exceptionalism and the imagination of alternatives to it. The Johnson Family and its Potential America are figures of this cultural revolution, ways of linking the subversive social energies of the 1960s to a long history of resistance and revolution, as well as to the political urgency of the neoliberal present. Burroughs's retroactive utopianism is not only a perspective on history but also a political strategy for waging war against all the Shits of the world.

The Happiness of the Commons

The Place of Dead Roads is utopian because it dreams up alternatives to neoliberalism and its systems of control. Burroughs does not simply insist that another America is possible. He also develops concrete figures of this possibility—forms of life that contribute to a pedagogy of utopian desire. Burroughs straddles the line between refusing to represent utopia and imagining utopia as an object of political aspiration. In doing so, he responds to a fundamental dilemma in the politics of utopianism: Making an image of utopia risks dissolving utopia's appeal as a form of radical alterity, but leaving utopia a complete unknown risks reducing it to the most abstract of horizons—little more than a shooting star glimpsed in the night sky. Burroughs cuts through this dilemma by presenting not utopia as such but forms of social potentiality that mediate between the material limits of the present and the real possibility of alternative futures. He is less interested in picturing the geography of utopia than in imagining the kinds of social life that would inhabit it. To hazard an analogy, Burroughs doesn't offer a recipe for utopia, but he does suggest some of its ingredients. These ingredients include egalitarian forms of communal belonging, participatory democracy, and nonhierarchical modes of social cooperation. They belong to a pedagogy of utopian desire not because they provide a solution to political impasses but because they teach one to appreciate the pleasures of radically other forms of life.

Burroughs's retroactive utopianism is biopolitical in the sense that it hopes for the revolutionary transformation of the human species, more than the invention of the good place. It anticipates the antiglobalization protests of the late 1990s (exemplified by the 1999 Seattle WTO protests), as well as the cycle of antisystemic struggles running from the early 2000s to the present (e.g., the Occupy Movement, the Indignados, Idle No More, #BlackLivesMatter). It's not simply that Burroughs criticizes the same neoliberalism and social conservatism targeted by these movements but also that he cultivates a form of political subjectivity that operates beyond the dichotomies of public and private, socialist and liberal, universalist and pluralist, collective and individual. Burroughs's fiction and prose contribute to the invention of a new political grammar—the grammar of the multitude, as it's sometimes called—in which collective liberation occurs for, rather than at the expense of, individuals and in which universal emancipation from capitalism occurs through, not despite of, a plurality of struggles over matters of race, gender, and sexuality. Although seldom acknowledged as such, this politics of the multitude is fundamentally utopian because of its commitment to radically transforming human subjectivity and its belief that another world is possible.[57]

Burroughs doesn't simply anticipate the politics of the multitude, however. His retroactive utopianism troubles the theorization of the multitude by interrupting its paradigm of immanence. In brief, theoretical accounts of the multitude tend to emphasize how its politics is the realization of already existing social potentialities. This emphasis implies a certain realism and materialism, opposed not just to idealism but to any kind of political normativity. The historical movement of the multitude is teleological, but this teleology is resolutely materialist—its goal is not an abstract ideal but rather the complete expression of human potentiality. This insistence that the multitude's aspirations are entirely immanent, that what the multitude wants is nothing more than to realize itself, stems in large part from the history of the new left and its wish to unbridle itself from the restrictions of both union and party politics.[58] It is an attempt to articulate a form of direct democracy in which struggles against patriarchy, racism, heteronormativity, and capitalism do not need to be subordinated to official representatives in order to be effective. This refusal of hierarchy and delegation is one of the crucial strengths of the multitude. Theoretical accounts of the multitude suffer, however, from their unwillingness to think through a fundamental tension—the tension between the multitude's self-realization and its radical transformation. If the multitude desires another world, if it's committed to systemic change, then how can its politics possibly be reduced to an extrapolation of already existing social potentiality? Burroughs's retroactive utopianism draws attention to this tension, suggesting that rather than an impasse, it is actually the motor of the multitude—its utopian heart. The politics of the multitude, one might say, plays across the gap between self-realization and becoming-alien, or between this world and another. As Kim Carsons might say, radical politics is science fiction, but science fiction is very real.

The politics of the multitude finds its most concerted theoretical expression in the collaborations of Michael Hardt and Antonio Negri. Hardt and Negri's work theorizes the multitude as a revolutionary subject existing within, yet opposed to, a global empire of control (what they term "empire"). In *Multitude: War and Democracy in the Age of Empire* (2004), they define the multitude as a decentralized, horizontally articulated network of singularities in which commonality is not a presupposed essence but rather the presupposition and the result of cooperative relations productive of subjectivity. In other words, the multitude is not a collection of discrete individuals but an assemblage in which social relations compose the individuals that they also link together. Hardt and Negri specify the cooperative fabric weaving together the multitude as "the common," which is to the multitude what private property is to capitalism. It is a set of social relations and institutions enabling a nonappropriative mode of sharing the world. The common doesn't stand above individuals, in the manner in which the liberal public sphere stands above the private life of citizens. Instead, it weaves itself out of the diverse interactions of singularities, through their labors and political actions but also through the most quotidian moments of their existence. According to Hardt and Negri, the common is revolutionary, because it challenges top-down models of government through collaborative and egalitarian decision making and because it liberates social production from private property. The common is the material basis of the multitude, its condition of possibility and its vital motor.[59] It names a utopian horizon insofar as it gestures beyond the global social totality that is capitalism. It is a multivalent concept whose strength is its capacity to gather together anti- and noncapitalist practices without collapsing them into a homogenous mass.

Hardt and Negri actually distinguish two multitudes, or two subjects of the common. On the one hand, there is the "ontological multitude," the multitude as potential for resistance and freedom inherent in the human species. This version of the multitude—derived in large part from Baruch Spinoza—is "always-already," which is to say that although its actual forms may change from one historical period to another, the capacities it embodies persist as the basis of political struggle. On the other hand, there is the "historical multitude," which is also the political multitude: "Really, the not-yet multitude. This multitude has never yet existed."[60] The historical multitude is a project in the sense that it postulates a subject whose concrete form blurs the line between present and future. Hardt and Negri argue that these two multitudes inhere in one another as necessary complements: "These two multitudes, however, although conceptually distinct, are not really separable. If the multitude were not already latent and implicit in our social being, we could not even imagine it as a political project; and, similarly, we can only hope to realize it today because it already exists as a real potential" (222). Although the capacity for resistance is insufficient in itself to challenge global empire, the political project that would transform the multitude from mere possibility into a revolutionary movement is immanent in the ontological multitude. In contrast to both party politics and vanguardism, the politics of the multitude is a decentralized and plural welling-up of resistance—an emancipatory movement in which everyone governs, without hierarchy or delegation.

Hardt and Negri's distinction between the ontological multitude and the historical multitude raises a question: How does the first multitude actualize itself in the second, or, conversely, how does the second multitude become adequate to the first? In this regard, it's telling that Hardt and Negri rely on the phrase "not-yet" to describe the temporality of the political multitude—the same phrase Ernst Bloch uses to describe concrete utopianism in *The Principle of Hope*. Although Hardt and Negri insist that the multitude is anything but utopian, that it is the very image of a "revolutionary realism," it is not against utopia as such that they polemicize but rather (much like Burroughs) against abstract utopianism (356). The political project of the multitude is utopian insofar as it relies on a gap between the present and the future, or potentiality and actuality, which in turn serves as the space of figuration for another world. As the last lines of *Multitude* read: "We can already recognize that today time is split between a present that is already dead and a future that is already living—and the yawning abyss between them is becoming enormous" (358). This "yawning abyss" is the necessary condition for imagining an alternative to capitalism and global empire. Hardt and Negri's commitment to building another society is a form of concrete utopianism, because it excavates the possibility of another world from neoliberalism's doctrine of TINA ("There Is No Alternative"). In this view, the common is a mediating figure, which heralds a society to come, while remaining rooted in the material conditions of the present.

In more recent work, Hardt and Negri revise their political theory in an attempt to flesh out the multitude's organizational dynamics and respond to the historical fortunes of social movements. In *Commonwealth* (2009), they elaborate a theory of revolutionary parallelism, that is, a program for building institutions of the multitude that would progressively take over the functions of governance without reproducing the hierarchies of formal government.[61] In *Assembly* (2017), they pose the question of leadership—the question of how to make sure the institutions of revolution are coherent enough to endure. "Our hypothesis," they write, "is that decision-making and assembly do not require centralized rule but instead can be accomplished together by the multitude, democratically."[62] They do not dismiss the need for leadership but suggest instead that it needs to remain tactical, or "limited to short-term action and tied to specific occasions."[63] Despite Hardt and Negri's efforts to fill in the gap between the two multitudes, it remains a constitutive element of their political imaginary. It returns as the space between the revolutionary institutions of the multitude and the residual institutions of capitalism and the state, or as the discrepancy between tactical leadership and strategic assemblies. In any case, this gap is indispensable to the politics of the multitude, which cannot truly be revolutionary, unless it leaps across the chasm separating the world we have from the world we want. "Revolution is not for the faint of heart," Hardt and Negri write. "It is for monsters. You have to lose who you are to discover what you can become."[64]

Despite his general reluctance to embrace utopianism, Negri offers a useful term to encompass the constitutive tension between the immanence of the multitude's politics and its utopianism—"disutopia." Far removed from the negative connotations of "dystopia," disutopia designates "the sense of an overflowing constitutive activity, as intense as a utopia but without its illusion, and fully material."[65] Whereas the conventional understanding of utopia implies that it is a transcendent elsewhere that resolves the social contradictions of the present, Negri's "disutopia" implies a production of subjectivity that is primarily temporal—a historical movement that dissolves the fixed spaces of formal government, unleashing a democratic "strength" (*potenza*) fully immersed in material social relations. This strength isn't pure positivity but "continual dislocation," or the mixing of "absence, void, and desire." "The expansiveness of strength and its productivity are grounded in the void of limitations, in the absence of positive determinations, in this fullness of absence."[66] The "dis" in "disutopia" alludes to this confluence of positivity and negativity, surplus and void. In sum, disutopia does more than realize the multitude. It constitutes an immanent utopianism characterized by antagonism and invention—a tense struggle to respond to the desires of the multitude by experimenting with new forms of political life.

Burroughs's *The Place of Dead Roads* is disutopian in the sense that it figures utopia not as an elsewhere or a distant future but as ongoing political struggle. The novel's political imaginary inhabits the gap between the ontological and historical multitudes, putting into focus the process of mediation through which the social desires of the present satisfy themselves in the alterity of the future. In doing so, it highlights what a number of critics contend Hardt and Negri neglect, namely, the practicalities of political organization.[67] Nowhere in *The Place of Dead Roads* does Burroughs fill in the constitutive alterity of utopia with a rigid program, but he does make utopia concrete by transforming the potentiality of Kim Carsons's fiction writing—the potentiality for humans to move beyond a state of "Arrested Evolution"—into an alternative social entity: the Johnson Family. The novel oscillates between narrating Kim's adventures as if he were the text's sole protagonist and displacing Kim to the role of mere exemplar of the Johnson Family—"Kim is just another Johnson" (132). In the gap between Kim and the Johnson Family, the novel elaborates its own version of the commons, understood as the concrete figuration of another world.

In an author's note Burroughs introduces the Johnson Family before the novel even begins. The note suggests that the Johnson Family is less a distinct group of characters than a generic potential for certain kinds of social practice:

> The original title of this book was *The Johnson Family*. "The Johnson Family" was a turn-of-the-century expression to designate good bums and thieves. A Johnson honors his obligations. His word is good and he is a good man to do business with. He is not a snoopy, self-righteous, trouble-making person. A Johnson will give help when help is needed. He will not stand by while someone is drowning or trapped under a burning car. (Author's Note)

This note frames the novel as mourning the loss of a specific form of social life. If Burroughs doesn't explicitly write of the Johnson Family as an object of mourning, he nonetheless implies the activity of mourning in the act of losing the novel's original title, as if to say, "This novel is written in the name of the Johnson Family, in the place of their loss." In the manner of retroactive utopianism, the novel does not wistfully remember the Johnson Family but recalls it with an eye toward rescuing and reinventing it. It describes the Johnsons not in terms of what they did but in terms of what they do or will do. Instead of a discrete set of individuals, then, the Johnsons constitute a genre of subjectivity that one becomes through praxis, as indicated by the passage designating not *the* Johnson Family but rather "a Johnson." The indefinite article opens the Johnson Family to the future, dispensing with a narrow mode of historicism that would merely catalog past historical formations. The indefinite article also alludes to the multiplicity of the Johnson Family's existence: If the Johnsons are characterized by a specific ethos, they nevertheless actualize that ethos in numerous ways. Retroactive utopianism thus implies not the past's restoration but rather its recuperation as social potentiality that remains open to the future.

The author's note goes on to define the Johnson Family in terms of a virtuous cycle between individuality and cooperation, as well as singularity and commonality.

> The only thing that could unite the planet is a united space program. . . . The earth becomes a space station and war is simply *out*, irrelevant, flatly insane in a context of research centers, spaceports, and the exhilaration of working with people you like and respect toward an agreed-upon objective, an objective from which all workers will gain. *Happiness is a byproduct of function*. The planetary space station will give all participants an opportunity to function. (Ibid.)

In contrast to the Shits' obsessive rectitude, members of the Johnson Family mind their own business—they live and let live. At the same time, they also help when help is needed. These traits might appear to correspond in a simple manner: A Johnson is an individual going his own way, until an instance arises when someone needs assistance, at which point he lends a hand. In this view, premised on a negative conception of liberty (liberty as freedom *from*), a Johnson is first an individual and then a cooperative being. However, the second paragraph of the passage, with its vision of space-bound exodus, contradicts this view. Individuality isn't prior to collectivity but an effect of it: "*Happiness is a byproduct of function.* The planetary space station will give all participants an opportunity to function." The passage suggests that what defines the individual—his or her "function"—emerges through a common project. Nor is this commonality imposed, for it is an "agreed-upon objective" organizing a specific kind of collectivity. The text marks the immanence of this political project to the collectivity engendering it by revising utopianism so that it is a process through which "earth becomes a space station": One doesn't leave for utopia; one *becomes* utopian with others. Burroughs presents his utopian praxis as a cooperative exodus of people from the forms of bondage entailed by capital and the state.[68]

The novel describes this process of becoming utopian as the functionalization of social life, as if to suggest that the longing for another world can only be fulfilled if all find their proper role in society. "The planetary space station will give all participants an opportunity to function." This notion of function, repeatedly invoked throughout the novel, has little to do with a reductive version of functionalist sociology, however. In place of functionalism's assumption that the reproduction of society requires each subject to inhabit his or her proper place, Burroughs's notion of functionality is entirely immanent; the passage describes abandoning preconceived goals in favor of the joy of working together: "The exhilaration of working with people you like and respect toward an agreed-upon objective, an objective from which all workers will gain." This negation of the kind of teleological command in which the end dictates the means is what Burroughs means when he writes, "*Happiness is a byproduct of function.*" Function is not determined by a given conception of happiness, but rather happiness—the goal—is determined by the functioning of the social. Satisfaction becomes a positive affect inhering in praxis, but, as the "agreed-upon objective" implies, the emotional tonality of this political project doesn't consist in the individualistic pleasures of liberalism or neoliberalism. Instead, the text's language suggests that the "exhilaration" of this collectivity depends on constant negotiation between the singular ("all participants [will have] an opportunity to function") and the common (a "united space program"), as well as between the here and now (present needs and desires) and the then and there (the "happiness" that will be the "byproduct" of achieved "function"). The Johnson Family is, to borrow Negri's term, disutopic, existing in a process of "continual dislocation"—a flight through space that is also a flight into the future.

In *The Place of Dead Roads*, the Johnson Family is a figure for the happiness of the commons. It traces the contours of a political organization in which the potentiality of the commons becomes partially actualized, if not fully realized. In this context, the commons is utopian, because it projects the possibility of a radically other world within and against the pervasive individualism and entrepreneurial drive of contemporary social life. The figurative, or literary, quality of the commons in Burroughs's novel suggests that the political form of the commons is not given in advance by its social potentiality but instead requires the political imagination of futurity. Implied, here, is a distinction between *the* common as social potentiality and the common*s* as political organization, or, as Cesare Casarino explains, "the common as potentiality as such" is political not in itself but insofar as it involves "the forms of the common, including and especially our bodies."[69] In sum, the politics of the multitude are utopian insofar as they ask us to imagine a world in which our common social potentialities—our needs, desires, and capacities—would be realized in concrete political forms.

The Place of Dead Roads scatters descriptions of the Johnson Family's organization across its pages. Indeed, the actions of the plot are less means of narrative development than ways of modeling the social dynamic of the Johnson Family. It is as if Burroughs couldn't decide whether he wanted to write a work of fiction or an instruction manual for fighting neoliberalism. The novel's explanatory bent echoes the formal dynamics of the literary genre of utopia, which, Phillip Wegner notes, "occupies a middle ground between the phenomenological concreteness of the literary aesthetic and the abstract systematicity of the theoretical."[70] At the same time, the narrative dimension of utopian fiction is not incidental; it's what makes such texts an education in political desire. It is the narrative momentum of fiction, or the process of attempting to work out the resolution of a specific social conflict, that transforms the presentation of utopia from a static model or abstract ideal into a concrete object of political aspiration. In Jameson's words: "We might think of the new onset of the Utopian process as a kind of desiring to desire, a learning to desire, the invention of the desire called Utopia in the first place, along with new rules for the fantasizing or daydreaming of such a thing."[71]

The Place of Dead Roads teaches its readers not only to recognize the injustices of neoliberalism but also to enjoy the commons, to see the commons as a material possibility and to desire it as a way of life. Take the following passage, for example.

> Porters stagger under their luggage. Kim gives them each a bright new dime. They snarl after him.
> For the roles rotate. You can be *fils de famille* today and busboy tomorrow—*son cosas de la vida*. Besides it's more interesting that way.

> Kim loves to play the acne-scarred blackmailing chauffeur or the insolent bell-hop tipped back in a chair, his face flushed from drinking the bottle of champagne he has delivered.
>
> . . .
>
> This system of rotating parts operates on the basis of a complex lottery. . . . Some people achieved a lottery-exempt status for a time but for most it was maybe a month, often less, before they got the dread call. Turn in your tycoon suit and report to casting.
>
> The Johnson Family is a cooperative structure. There isn't any boss man. People know what they are supposed to do and they do it. We're all actors and we change roles. Today's millionaire may be tomorrow's busboy. There's none of that ruling-class old school tie. . . .
>
> We are showing that an organization and a very effective organization can run without boss-man dog-eat-dog fear. (114–15)

Two qualities of this social arrangement stand out: the autonomy of the system in respect to its parts (or the loose relationship between individuals and the social roles they occupy) and the "rotation" of individuals between parts (or the frequent change in individuals' respective social positions). This coupling of the contingency and the variation of social roles suggests a specific form of equality—what we might call the equality of acting, for everyone plays one position and then another: "We're all actors and we change roles." Temporality is crucial, here, for it is not the individual social roles that contest the social order but the manner in which they change over time. The social organization is never complete or whole, because the rotation of the roles as dictated by a "complex lottery" ensures that the gap between player and role remains open. The evident randomness of the lottery means that there's no mistaking the differences among the roles as the effect of natural hierarchy or innate disposition. "Today's millionaire," Burroughs writes, "may be tomorrow's busboy." No matter what a Johnson is doing, there's an element of counter-actualization involved, which is to say that the Johnson Family never exhausts its social potentiality but always brings it into play with a trace of negation, so that in performing a role, one simultaneously is and is not that role—one could always be/act otherwise. Being a Johnson thus implies a constitutive exposure to alterity, a willingness to become alien to oneself.

In narrative terms, the constitutive alterity of the Johnson Family takes the form of a discrepancy between general descriptions of the Johnson Family as a social system and the exemplification of the Family's functioning in character-driven vignettes. The vignettes Burroughs employs to illustrate the Johnson Family's operations do not simply explain or clarify;

they also disrupt the smooth reproduction of the system and, in doing so, highlight a utopian surplus of potentiality. In the witty banter between two Johnsons, one witnesses the novel's experimentation with social performance, its openness to social difference.

> Kim loves to play the acne-scarred blackmailing chauffeur or the insolent bell-hop tipped back in a chair, his face flushed from drinking the bottle of champagne he has delivered.
> "What is the meaning of this?" Tom snaps. . . . The boy rubs his crotch and insolently squirts Tom in the crotch with a soda siphon.
> "Oh sir, you've had an accident." He bustles around, loosening Tom's belt and trying to shove his pants down.
> "What the bloody hell are you doing?"
> "Just changing your didies, sir."
> Or maybe Tom is coming on and Kim the bellboy is playing it cool.
> "Oh, sir, I *couldn't* sit down at the table with you. I know me place, sir, if you'll pardon the expression, sir." (114–15)

The affect at work in this passage is "insolence"—a sauciness that brooks no hierarchy and is linked to a lack of moderation. As an adverb ("insolently squirts"), it suggests a practice that challenges the social order, or, in linguistic terms, a disruptive traversal of communication by an excess of (non)sense. It's tempting to read this dialogic back-and-forth as a reflexive allegorization of meaning's relation to the language system. The question, "What is the meaning of this?" is a response to the aleatory swerve of signification, the "accident" of language produced when Kim aborts the busboy script to squirt out an event that overturns convention. Indeed, the homoerotic gestures—the undoing of pants, the ejaculatory squirting—suggests the polysemic dimensions of conversation, the way in which a trope queers the straight course of communication with splashes of linguistic excess.

This bodily and linguistic excess speaks to an irreducibility of exemplification to strict determination. The above passage plays with various possibilities (Kim as chauffeur, Kim as bellboy), which, in turn, contain other potential variations. It epitomizes Burroughs's call for a linguistic practice that dismantles the rigidity of identity, the determination of the definite article, and the exclusive disjunction of the either-or in favor of variable becomings, the multiplicity of the indefinite article ("Kim is just another Johnson"), and the inclusive disjunctions involved in shifting from one role to another ("Or maybe Tom is coming on and Kim the bellboy is playing it cool"). The text multiplies possible paths, layering one atop another in a virtual map of possible worlds and stories. Rather than developing a linear plot, the narrative obsessively repeats a moment, experimenting with the deviating trajectories that might emerge from any instant. The Johnson Family operates not through the reproduction of sameness but through repetition with a difference—repetition as the multiplication of performances that modify the very system they instantiate. Repetition is therefore a creative act, involving the swerve of (non)sense in a gestural, affective, and tropological break with dominant social scripts.

The Johnson Family models a political alternative not only to neoconservatism and neoliberalism but also to the left-wing nostalgia for the earlier days of New Deal liberalism. Burroughs traces the outlines of a social formation in which collectivity or communal belonging is no longer mediated by the state and in which the variation of social roles—a substitute for the promise of upward social mobility—goes hand in hand with egalitarianism. Moreover, the Johnson Family is a postcapitalist project, replacing the irrationality of capitalist markets with institutions designed to promote the common good. In this respect, Burroughs is a political theorist of the multitude, though one who acknowledges that the hope for another world can become concrete only through a process of cultural revolution. At the same time, it's worth recalling the limits of this utopian project, which include the homosociality of the Johnson Family (it largely consists of men) and the settler colonialism underlying its counter-national ambitions. Burroughs's political imagination is inextricable from the violences associated with American exceptionalism. Indeed, Burroughs can write for the sake of a "Potential America" only insofar as he draws on the libidinal energies of exceptionalism, repeating the latter's dream of reinventing the human species in the name of the New World. This complicity does not cancel out Burroughs's utopianism, nor, I would argue, does it reduce it to a reactionary project. Instead, it inscribes his utopianism in the excluded middle between American exceptionalism and its critique; it roots his utopianism in the material history of the United States—in the injustices constitutive of the nation—without for all that being reducible to this history. Burroughs's retroactive utopianism owns up to the "non-dream" that is America, but it does so for the sake of that which in America is more than America—"Potential America."

To conclude, the utopianism of the Johnson Family is threefold. First, it offers an alternative social structure as a model, or mimetic site of identification, for the desires of readers. Although a work of fiction may not be able to demonstrate the feasibility of a social program, it can make such social possibilities thinkable and desirable in the first place. Put differently, Burroughs—like Kim Carsons—risks thinking differently about the world; he hazards a vision of social life that runs against the grain of the neoliberal counterrevolution. He expands the political imaginary beyond the parameters of the nation-state and capitalism, introducing social relations in which individuality and collectivity support, rather than contradict, each other. Second, the Johnson Family serves as a utopian figure because of its form as much as its content, specifically, because of its ability to simulate historical change. One sees this in the way that Kim leaps from one occupation to another, working as a busboy one moment, a science fiction writer in another, a bank-robbing bandit in yet another. However, this sense of flux exceeds the roles of characters, belonging more generally to the narrative style of the novel. This text positions its readers on a hinge between one world and another, between what has so far been the case and what may yet become the case. Of course, one could say that this temporal pivot characterizes the genre of the novel as such, but what distinguishes Burroughs's fiction—and indicates its affinity with the genre of utopian fiction—is that the subject of change is never an individual character but always a collective entity. The Johnson Family is utopian not only because it embodies a collective ethos that refuses the status quo but also because it insists on the mutability of social form and the contingency of political practices. Finally, the Johnson Family serves as a kind of time machine through which readers revisit the revolutionary possibilities of the past. The new social movements of the sixties and the revolutions of the eighteenth century return not as inert relics but as material specters enabling transformations of political subjectivity. In this light, Burroughs's fidelity to the Johnson Family—his inscription of the novel in the place of their loss—is a commitment to make good on the unfinished business of past revolutions. History becomes science fiction, as Burroughs transforms past and present into shimmering portals opening onto alien worlds.

Futures Past

When Reagan and Trump propose that we "Make America Great Again," they are practicing their own version of retroactive utopianism. They are fantasizing about a moment of peace, prosperity, and family values—an era when American dominance was supposedly unquestionable. This golden age never really existed, except perhaps in economic terms as a short historical period following World War II, during which capital and labor reached a compromise and the Fordist family wage allowed households to rely on a sole male breadwinner. The family wage was largely confined to white families in which adults conformed to the regulations of heteronormativity and patriarchy. It excluded nonwhite Americans, as well as nonnormative family structures (e.g., single mothers, gay and lesbian couples). Moreover, this period of peace and prosperity had less to do with innately American values than with a concerted effort to dissuade U.S. citizens from embracing the "evils" of communism. In other words, this fantasy of a golden age is the expression of a desire to eliminate political challenges to the universality of capitalism and to the social ideal of the white, heteronormative family. From this perspective, the Reagan and Trump administrations can be viewed as segments in a long cycle of right-wing political regression. They may differ in a number of respects, but they both represent combinations of neoliberalism and social conservatism. That is, both administrations deploy neoliberal policy measures to destroy public services and universalize entrepreneurship, while at the same time promoting "family values" (discrimination against nonnormative social structures), "law and order" (criminalization of nonwhite and foreign-born residents), and the general expansion of state power. As Wendy Brown and Melinda Cooper have argued, if this blend of neoliberalism and social conservatism appears contradictory, it is a necessary contradiction insofar as the social despair and political chaos unleashed by neoliberalism prepare the ground for the authoritarian tendencies of social conservatism.[72]

Burroughs's late trilogy mobilizes retroactive utopianism as a way of responding to the neoliberal counterrevolution. This utopianism is not purely reactive, however. It also a way of salvaging the revolutionary energies of history, of trying to make good on the promises of past social struggles. Burroughs doesn't want to make America great again. He wants to reinvent America as a counter-nation—a post-state, postcapitalist social formation in which the common good, individual liberty, and equality support one another in a virtuous circle. Although Burroughs sometimes articulates this vision of the future in programmatic terms, it is still the formal dynamics of his fiction that make novels such as *The Place of Dead Roads* an education in utopian desire. In other words, Burroughs's utopianism has less to do with the picture he draws of the future (the Johnson Family's flight into space) than the way he narrates the struggle for that future (short vignettes linked in a nonlinear fashion, combining the elements of two genres—the western and science fiction). This formal experimentation constitutes a radical pedagogy of desire, because it not only estranges readers from neoliberal common sense (the belief, however unconscious, that no alternative is possible) but also teaches them to see their relations with others as a pleasure and a strength, rather than an obstacle to individual liberty. *The Place of Dead Roads* asks that we struggle for Potential America against the American non-dream, that we fight for a future free of the Shits and their systems of control.

Burroughs's utopian pedagogy depends on the ability of his fiction to unsettle linear forms of history, or to trouble normative models of chronology. *The Place of Dead Roads* is in many respects a nineteenth-century novel written in the 1980s with the aim of transforming several centuries worth of revolutionary struggle into the seeds of a radically other future. Put differently, the novel locates the frontier simultaneously in the past (the eighteenth and nineteenth centuries, as well as the 1960s), in the present (the 1980s, or the neoliberal era more generally), and in the future (concrete figurations of social alternatives). If I begin this book with Burroughs, breaking with the chronology of publication history, it is in the hopes of making retroactive utopianism into a literary critical methodology. This methodology asks what it would mean to consider American literary history not only as a series of discrete periods but also as an unfulfilled revolutionary project that continues to haunt us. It asks what it would mean to read not only oppositionally, in the name of critique, but also affirmatively, in the name of utopia.

In the next section of the book, I turn to nineteenth-century U.S. literature not in an effort to trace the empirical sources of the Johnson Family but to think through the continuities between the American Renaissance and our current period of socioeconomic decline. Imagine it as an adventure in time travel, the object of which is not to bear witness to what's already passed but to change the past and, in doing so, release an alternative timeline. This alternative timeline constitutes a counter-national trajectory—a turning of exceptionalism against itself. Walt Whitman is an especially useful starting point for this adventure, for not only does he imagine America as a project to be realized. He also grapples with the difficulties of thinking through concrete political struggles without abandoning utopian hope. Indeed, both Whitman and Emily Dickinson offer distinct practices of dismantling American exceptionalism, while recuperating its utopian potential. Each writer enacts the flight of a singular America beyond exceptionalism, imagining not a redeemed nation but a people to come. Each introduces a future past not as source of regret but as the possibility of realizing that in America which is more than America.

CHAPTER 2

The People and the People: Democracy and Vitalism in Walt Whitman's 1855 *Leaves of Grass*

On February 15, 1856, a review of the first edition of *Leaves of Grass* appeared in the *Washington Daily National Intelligencer*. The review acknowledges the originality of the work, but it also accuses Walt Whitman of a dangerous speculative bent: "It is in every way a singular volume: singular in its form, singular in its arrangement, singular in its style, and most singular of all in its rhapsodical fancies."[1] The reviewer isolates a particularly troubling trait in Whitman's poetry: pantheism.

> The reader who has proceeded only thus far begins already to discover that Walter Whitman is a pantheist. Without, perhaps, ever having read Spinoza, he is a Spinozist. Without, perhaps, much deep insight into Plato the divine, he is a Platonist "in the rough," and believes profoundly in the "immanence of all in each," without ever once mouthing that grand phrase of the Greek philosopher. Without knowing how to chop the formal logic of the schools, he is a necessitarian and fatalist, with whom "whatever is is right." The world as he finds it, and man as he is, good or bad, high or low, ignorant or learned, holy or vicious, are all alike good enough for Walter Whitman, who is in himself a

"kosmos," and whose emotional nature is at once the sensorium of humanity and the sounding board which catches up and intones each note of joy or sorrow in the "gamut of human feeling."

It's difficult to tell from this passage whether Whitman's gravest sin is his pantheistic tendencies or the way he flirts with philosophy. Whitman's belief in the pure immanence of God/Being in nature/existence overturns the ontological order of things. It transgresses against a Christian, anthropocentric, neo-Platonic worldview, according to which the value of a being is measured against a scale descending from divine perfection to the stupidity of inanimate matter, with humans falling somewhere in between the grace of angels and the cunning of cats. In contrast to this divinely ordained hierarchy, Whitman "believes profoundly in 'the immanence of all in each,'" which is to say that he constructs existence as a plane of material consistency without vertical hierarchy. There are differences among beings, of course, differences of degrees and even of kind, but there's no difference of substance, no inherent distinctions that place humans or God in a transcendent relation to anteaters, volcanoes, or blades of grass. Pantheism implies monism, or the idea that there is only one substance—call it God or Nature, it's all the same—composing the universe. This is what makes Whitman a Spinozist, even if he hasn't read Spinoza. That the review's objection to Spinozism is political becomes clear in the author's complaint regarding Whitman's conflation of "high or low": "good or bad, high or low, ignorant or learned, holy or vicious, are all alike good enough for Walter Whitman." Pantheism may not be a political program, but it contradicts the ontological foundations on which the liberal social order rests. Whitman's "rhapsodical fancies" would seem to have as much to do with political subversion as doctrinal heresy.

That the *Washington Daily National Intelligencer* review is critical, at times even scathing, doesn't stop it from being an astute reading of Whitman. Few accounts so vividly articulate the connections among ontology, politics, and aesthetics in the 1855 edition of *Leaves of Grass*. The review establishes that the ambivalent reaction to the first edition of *Leaves* results as much from its philosophical and political orientation as from its experimental literary style. In fact, it would be better to say that these matters are bound up with one another, that literary form and political-philosophical content are mutually imbricated. It's precisely this transdisciplinary embrace that the *Daily*'s reviewer finds so bewildering and troubling. It would be easier to reject the arguments of one who "know[s] how to chop the formal logic of the schools" than to contend with a writing that refuses to acknowledge the difference between poetry and philosophical speculation or the sensuous domain of aesthetics and the rational realm of the concept. One could say that this blurring of boundaries between poetry and philosophy is Whitman's perverse manner of demonstrating the truth of his pantheism.

Although Whitman likes to describe his poetry in terms of candor, transparency, and ease, the political thinking it performs is far from simple. In this chapter, I argue that Whitman's poetry elaborates two concepts of democracy—a vital democracy and an eventual democracy—each of which involves its own set of literary and philosophical operations. These concepts aren't mutually exclusive, but they are contradictory, the one imagining democracy as the expression of material life force and the other imagining it as the realization of a revolutionary event. On the one hand, Whitman articulates democracy in vitalist terms as the organic realization of political futurity. He draws on the medical, physiological, and natural historical discourses of his time to articulate democracy less as a historically contingent practice of governance than as an ecosystem (or meta-organism) through which the creatures of America realize their destiny.[2] This Whitman is a not-so-new materialist. He introduces a poetics of individuation in which the life of matter is not only collective, relational, plural, and nonanthropocentric but also irreducible to the distinction between the organic and inorganic. Not unlike Jane Bennett, Mel Y. Chen, and Rosi Braidotti, Whitman expands the register of animacy—the sense of what counts as living—so that it cuts across the boundary separating carbon-based life forms from other kinds of vibrant intensity.[3] For Whitman the pantheist, democracy entails a kind of promiscuity: the cultivation of a vitality that respects social, cultural, and biological differences only insofar as they participate in an egalitarian community of matter.

Even though this vision of a vitalist democracy would seem to imply a kind of political universalism, Whitman nevertheless invests America with a special intensity of life. America names the realization of democracy; it is both the origin and the telos of political futurity, as if the primal truth of democracy were only disclosed when it reached the shores of the New World. Whitman's exceptionalism betrays his vitalism, but it is equally accurate to say that it is only through this exceptionalism—through the act of taking exception to the status quo by raising America to the status of an exceptional nation—that Whitman's poetry articulates democracy as social struggle or political contestation. Whitman's investment in America as an exceptional site of geopolitics and culture transforms democracy from an ontological condition into a political project. Democracy becomes the project of realizing the American Revolution through the invention of another people; it is no longer the becoming-actual of a potential life force but rather the interruption of everyday life by an exceptional historical event. Whereas for the vitalist Whitman the test of poetry is its ability to express life in all of its intensity and breadth, for the revolutionary Whitman the test is poetry's capacity to enact a break with life, to realize another life in and against the daily business of the people.

Whitman's poetry can thus be said to contain a constitutive tension between a universal vitalism and an exceptionalism of the event, or between an ontology of life and a revolutionary praxis. It's this tension that saves Whitman from blind nationalism. Although his patriotic fervor is undeniable, Whitman's faith in America is double: It is faith in the people, in the goodwill, hardiness, and resources of the nation; and it is faith in a people to come, in the arrival of a counter-nation in which America finally makes good on its exceptional promise. It is from this doubleness—this tango between the people (as they actually exist) and the people (to come)— that a singular America emerges in Whitman's poetry, as if it were only by pushing exceptionalism to its extreme conclusion that some other America could appear. In this respect, Whitman is simultaneously the comrade in arms of William S. Burroughs and his opposite. Whitman's faith in America—what F. O. Matthiessen described as his optative mood—is a far cry from Burroughs's emphasis on revolutionary antagonism.[4] Whitman spends more time singing the nation's praises than imagining its radical transformation. At the same time, Whitman shares Burroughs's sense of a "potential America," his commitment to that which in America is more than America. Whitman anticipates Burroughs's concept of retroactive utopianism when he frames the truth of American democracy as a future that will have arrived from out of the history of the Revolution. The two writers differentiate themselves from each other not by whether or not they bear witness to a singular America but by how they do so: Whereas Burroughs saves America from itself through an act of revolutionary purification, Whitman wavers between nurturing the latent potential in the American people and reinventing the people. It's the difference between imagining a singular America as the determinate negation of the United States and imagining it as the nation's fruit.

Although there are six U.S. editions of *Leaves of Grass*, this chapter focuses solely on the first edition. It does so not because the 1855 version of *Leaves* possesses some special authenticity, as if the origin of the work were pure in its democratic convictions, but rather because of the edition's roughness. The 1855 edition is a hodge-podge of prose and poetry, messy and contradictory in its politics, aesthetics, and philosophy. This messiness can be seen in its relative anonymity, signaled by the absence of Whitman's name on the cover, as well as by the lack of individual poem titles; it can also be seen in the refusal of the conventional constraints of lyric poetry, or in the absence of regular meter and line lengths, as well as the heterogeneity of voice and pronoun usage. Moreover, the 1855 edition's prose preface, which reads like a manifesto for poetry and politics (or for poetry *as* politics), announces *Leaves of Grass* as a project whose aim is nothing less than the reconstitution of American life. It frames the volume as both revolutionary praxis and song of life, which is to say that it introduces the doubleness of Whitman's democracy as an optics through which to read the poems that follow. In sum, the speculative ambition of Whitman's poetry is never clearer, never more bombastic, than in its 1855 incarnation. Although this ambition doesn't disappear from subsequent editions, it does, as many scholars note, become tempered, especially after the Civil War. From the third edition on, the messiness of Whitman's poetry gets organized around discrete sections, usually labeled in thematic terms; the poems receive titles, attaching their significance to specific dates, places, and philosophical problems; and, in all but one edition, the poem "Walt Whitman" inscribes the power of the poetry under the proper name of the author. None of which is to suggest that these editions lack complexity. The complexities are simply of a different kind. What distinguishes the 1855 edition, I suggest, is that its prefatory framing, anonymity, and compactness (in comparison to the length of the other editions) all contribute to heightening the tension between Whitman's ontology of life and his revolutionary praxis.

Whitman's pantheism is a double voicing of democracy, a lyric practice through which the truth of politics is both always already and to come. In other words, there's the people and then there's the people. On the one hand, Whitman elaborates a vitalist ontology. He sidesteps a liberal philosophy of individualism in favor of a song for all that is common. The people are an egalitarian assemblage in which the self emerges from a shared materiality, or shared life force, without ever leaving the common behind. I discuss this vitalism as a poetics of individuation in the next section, arguing that what might seem egoism—the song of the self—is really a manner of thinking collectivity as generosity and reciprocity, rather than as sacrifice and suffering. In Whitman, this sense of collectivity explicates itself as a queer erotics—a cruising of capitalist political economy in which propriety and property gives way to a passion for excess, abandonment, and change. On the other hand, the evental Whitman is an apostle of the Revolution. It's not simply that he keeps faith with the revolutionary desire at America's origins but that he longs for a people that would live up to the belief in America as exception. This is the properly utopian Whitman, the one who believes in a singular America. It is the Whitman that emerges through the interruption of the ontology of life, through a material-symbolic death and resurrection of the people. Whitman realizes not the people but that which in the people is more than them—a people to come, or a counter-nation. This is also the Whitman for whom the peculiar institution of slavery, the problem of gender inequality, and the struggle for the autonomy of workers are not merely obstacles to vitalism but rather tests of the speculative value of America. They are the crucible through which America proves itself something more than just another nation. As the reviewer for the *Daily* knew all too well, Whitman's heresy has less to do with how he sees America than with his rhapsodical fancies about what America might realize.

Whitman's Ontology of Life

Whitman's first vision of democracy is identical with an ontology of life. It's nothing more and nothing less than the outflow and intensification of all that is lively in the material world. Democracy becomes synonymous with the self-production of life on egalitarian terms. That this concept of democracy can also go by the name of pantheism already suggests the strange continuity between multiplicity and unity, change and endurance, that Whitman's poetry strives to enact: The plurality of social life in Whitman's poetry depends on the oneness of the universe; it's only through the abolition of division, through the overcoming of not only social but also ontological separations between entities, that democracy becomes a material fact. Although this emphasis on ontology might sound austere, abstract, and even pedantic, Whitman's pantheism presents the being of the universe as a wonderful, strange, and queer matter. The philosophical promiscuity through which Whitman confuses high and low, transcendence and immanence, spirit and matter, discovers its most vital expression in a queer form of tactility, in an eroticism that causes the self-presence and self-sufficiency of the modern, Cartesian subject to give way to the mutability, permeability, and ecstasy of embodied life. Queerness is the phenomenality of Whitman's material commonwealth, which is another way of saying that it's the queer pleasure in material sensation, the perverse gratification of the spirit in the flesh, that differentiates Whitman's vitalist democracy from the representational apparatus of liberal democracy. For

Whitman, democracy is not the representation of the people; it is instead the way in which the people share a life in common. In other words, democracy isn't the delegation of power but the material experience of it. It's a queer mode of governance.

Whitman's pantheism initially expresses itself in the dismantling of a series of binary oppositions constitutive of liberal democracy and the capitalist social order. The materialist commonality that Whitman fabricates through his poetry not only overturns divisions between mind (or soul) and body but also between public and private, representative democracy and participatory democracy, formal equality and real equality. It is, however, by dismantling the first opposition (soul and body) that Whitman is able to dismantle the others. In the 1855 *Leaves of Grass*, Whitman reinvents democracy by plunging it into the complexities of bodily life. Democracy is not a set of principles or a formal constitution standing above the political subjects that make up the nation but rather a process conducted *through* bodies. This concept of democracy distinguishes itself from liberal democracy's articulation of political subjectivity in terms of individualism, private property, and rational deliberation. Liberalism depends on what C. B. Macpherson called the "possessive individual": a "conception of the individual as essentially the proprietor of his own person or capacities, owing nothing to society."[5] In contrast, Whitman's poetry relies on fundamentally different understandings of property and of the relationship between subjectivity and corporeality. It proceeds from the premise of a material world shared in common.

Whitman's recuperation of corporeality and commonality sets the stage for an alternative basis for democracy. This vision of democracy predicates itself on a social fabric in which individuality proceeds from commonality. Rather than beginning with individuals, Whitman traces the contours of a process of individuation in which beings emerge from the sharing of collective knowledges, desires, affects, fantasies, bodies.[6] The "merge" toward which Whitman beckons the reader ("Who need be afraid of the merge?") is not a call for readers to establish a political sphere separate from everyday life, as in the liberal social contract, but rather a call for them to "realize" the powers that are the basis of their subjectivity.[7] The constant metamorphosis of subjectivity in *Leaves*—the way in which Whitman becomes one person and then another in an incessant process of change—depends on a commonality not simply anterior to the life of individuals but *immanent* in it: "I do not ask the wounded person how he feels . . . . I myself become the wounded/person,/My hurt turns livid upon me as I lean on a cane and observe" (39). The boundaries between individuals blur in these lines, the verb "become" undercutting the discrete positions implied by "observe." Sympathy gives way to transmutation, as the wound becomes a singular point enfolding both persons, bleeding into and out of them to form a new unity of life. The implication of this mutual becoming is that individuality doesn't consist in self-sufficiency, identity, or tautology (X = X, or "I am that I am"). Instead, individuality is the surface effect of a comprehensive plane of commonality. In this ontology, individuals "enclose" a primordial material commonality; they produce themselves out of the common, by taking a share in it, one which they, in turn, share with others so as to create new social formations: "I am an acme of things accomplished, and I an encloser of things to be" (50). What results is a new kind of public sphere, not a public mind standing above private bodies, but a collective and cooperative cultural intelligence of bodies—a publicness without the private as its opposite. This new mode of political being is the corollary of Whitman's pantheism, for, in asserting the immanence of universal substance, Whitman deprives political theory of the metaphysical grounds for dividing political subjectivity (citizenship) from the body, or the public from the private. There is only the common, and politics can only be a political contestation over the forms of social life belonging to the common.

Whitman's poetry situates itself in terms of the common by generating an image of selfhood that overturns the modern, Cartesian subject. This form of subjectivity—what, following Heidegger, one can parse as the *sub-jectum*—entails a movement by which the subject subtracts itself from the world (places itself under—*sub*—the world) in order to grasp the world through the activity of representation.[8] The modernity of the subject not only implies mastery of the world, or the conquest of Nature, but also the fundamental separation of subject and world. In contrast, Whitman's poetry asserts a fundamental continuity between the subject and the world. As Mark Noble argues, one can understand this continuity as an example of atomism (in the philosophical and scientific sense): "For Whitman this means not only reimagining the kinds of experience subjects qua matter might discover and the kinds of adhesive connections they might form to one another, but also relocating the spiritual power of subjectivity immanently within the material."[9] The opening lines of the poem that would come to be named "Song of Myself" offer a concise performance of atomism:

> I celebrate myself,
> And what I assume you shall assume,
> For every atom belonging to me as good belongs to you. (13)

These lines oscillate between a comprehending embrace of others and a fluid dissemination of the self. On the one hand, self-valorization involves a mirror relationship in which the identities of others echo the identity of the "I." The "you" becomes a function of the "I" insofar as one understands the verb "assume" in terms of engendering identity. One assumes not merely properties but that which makes one *one*. What matters is not only that the "you" follows the "I," that what the "you" "assumes" follows from what the "I" assumes, but also that the "I" returns to itself in the use of the reflexive pronoun. The "I" capitalizes on the "you," expanding itself through investments in others. This entrepreneurial spirit is a refrain in "Song of Myself," signaled by the use of economic language and by the continual return to the "I" as the identifying marker of an ever-expanding reservoir of linguistic capital: "What is commonest and cheapest and nearest and easiest is Me, /Me going in for my chances, spending for vast returns, /Adorning myself to bestow myself on the first that will take me, /Not asking the sky to come down to my goodwill, /Scattering it freely forever" (21). The capitalist economy of the self falters, or goes default, as every embrace, every return on the investment of the self in others, gets radically redistributed. There is a kind of conceptual rhyming that occurs between the concluding lines of these passages: "For every atom belonging to me as good belongs to you" and "Scattering it freely forever." Between these lines unfolds the idea that there's no fixed individual legislating the sharing of bodily life. Productivity—life's expansiveness—depends on multiplication and commonality, not on private accumulation.

This commonality expresses itself through the dissemination of matter. The closure of the self comes undone as the atoms composing the self resolve themselves into a preindividual commonwealth of matter—a nonexclusive, nonindividualistic merge of properties. Conversely, the self and the other emerge from a common substance that, rather than being permanently enclosed by individuals, plays between subjects in the process of poetic enunciation and syntactical connection. In sum, self and other disseminate into a common substance from which they also emerge. However, this dissemination entails a more radical implication than the inseparability of self and other, for commonality is not a consequence of the joining together of separate entities but rather of an ontologically prior process of individuation. If we read the "for" of the third line as a causal statement ("For every atom belonging to me as good belongs to you"), then the self-reflexive identification of the first line and the interpenetration of self and other in the second line presuppose the mutual "belonging" (or sharing out) of a common process. It's not simply that subjectivity deconstructs itself but also that the production of subjectivity implies a preindividual medium—not a fixed and solid substrate but a dynamic and fluid milieu.[10] The ontological priority of this process implies a shift to a molecular perspective that resists the fixed boundaries of identity. Before the existence of individuals, yet inhering in individuals as a material surplus of potentiality, there is the preindividual zone of the common—a life in common.

In this view, Whitman belongs less to those mystical traditions emphasizing the spiritual unity of the cosmos than to a subterranean lineage of materialist thought passing from Spinoza through Marx to contemporary thinkers such as Louis Althusser, Jean-Luc Nancy, and Antonio Negri.[11] The fundamental premise shared by these thinkers is that being is neither a closed set of self-sufficient entities nor an inert substrate, but rather a process of individuation in which the singular emerges from the common and the common from the singular in an infinite play of sharing. Singularity, in this instance, means not unique self-identity but a difference that emerges in and through relation—a difference *of* relation. From this perspective, the term *subject* reifies a prior process of sharing; it freezes the preindividual potential and transindividual connections of being into a rigid mold. Jean-Luc Nancy puts it as follows: "Singular beings" "are themselves constituted by sharing, they are distributed and placed, or rather *spaced*, by the sharing that makes them *others*: other for one another, and other, infinitely other for the Subject of their fusion, which is engulfed in the sharing, in the ecstasy of sharing: 'communicating' by not 'communing.'"[12] This ontological axiom of commonality avoids not only liberal social contract theory (with its delegation of power to a sovereign body) but also the communal fallacy, which imagines community as an organism whose members belong to it like so many limbs. What Nancy calls the "ecstasy of sharing" is a production of personhood in which individuality and collectivity are reciprocal and in which politics is entirely immanent in life.

Whitman's materialist articulation of a life in common depends on an idea of the body as bearer of an excess of potentiality. The mutability, mutuality, and expansiveness that Whitman attributes to life implies an irreducibility of the flesh to the given, or of the body to identity. In the poem that would come to be called "I Sing the Body Electric," Whitman suggests that poetry is the demonstration of this surplus of vitality through language.

> The expression of the body of man or woman balks account,
> The male is perfect and that of the female is perfect.

> The expression of a wellmade man appears not only in his face,
> It is in his limbs and joints also . . . . it is curiously in the joints of his hips and wrists,
> It is in his walk . . the carriage of his neck . . the flex of his waist and knees . . . . dress does not hide him,
>
> The strong sweet supple quality he has strikes through the cotton and flannel;
> To see him pass conveys as much as the best poem . . perhaps more,
> You linger to see his back and the back of his neck and shoulderside.
>   (77–78)

This passage demonstrates Whitman's patient attention to the body not merely as an object to be dissected but as a spectacle exceeding the subject-object relationship. These lines notably lack an "I" that would unify the images into the sensory wealth of a detached ego. Instead, the passive construction of "It is in . . ." constructs the body itself as speaking being. It is the body that articulates itself into an "expression," and it's the body that the poem attempts to follow, record, voice, and embody. That the body's movements are a form of writing is evident not only in the reference to "the *expression* of the body" but also in the focus on clothing. If the clothing of the "wellmade man" "does not hide him," if the body "strikes through the cotton and flannel," it's because the relationship between clothing and flesh is akin to that between signifier and signified: The one does not obscure the other but gives expression to it through a chain of metonymic displacements in which the signifier/clothing at one moment expresses the signified/bodily appearance and then in another gives way ("strikes through") to the body, which, in turn, becomes signifier. This metonymic process takes place in the fall from one line to another as an unfolding of the body across the space of the poem. Line becomes limb, and poetry becomes prosthetic technicity—a strange fusion of the mechanical and the vital, of machine and organism. But what is striking is not simply that the body takes center stage but that the poem indicates that the body is already a poem. The "wellmade man" is a poem so complex, so fine, that the poem can only hope to live up to it: "To see him pass conveys as much as the best poem . . perhaps more." Whitman opens up a zone of indistinguishability between body and language, with poetry possessing the mission to live up to the expressive movements of the body, and the body in turn excited by the play of language. Poetry thus belongs to both language and body; it names less a genre of writing than a particular intensity of life—an excess of expression over form, of potentiality ("perhaps more") over "limbs and joints."

But what of the excess of the body over the poem, the "perhaps more" of bodily expression? This surplus is nothing other than life itself. "I am less the reminder of property or qualities," Whitman writes, "and more the reminder of life" (28). Whitman doesn't eschew the specificity of poetic labor, but he assigns it the task of increasing the power of life. More specifically, he gives language over to the democratic project of liberating humans in order to maximize their vital intensities. Referring to religions, museums, governments, and corporations, among other institutions, Whitman sums up the vitalist principle of his poetry: "It is not they who give the life . . . . it is you who give the life" (60). Life, in this instance, is distinct from a notion of bare biological life. It's not a set of basic instincts or drives. Nor can it be reduced to an undifferentiated force. Instead, life names the immanent surplus of the common insofar as it embodies itself in concrete forms. It's a process of differentiating the common, an actualization of potentiality that does not exhaust itself in this or that form. Whitman's poetry is a return of life to itself ("it is you who give the life"), with poetry being understood as an activity that not only gives expression to life but that also belongs to it. Poetry's immanence in life may be an ontological matter, but that doesn't mean it's neutral in political terms. Poetry constitutes a technology for amplifying life, for cultivating the excess of bodily potential over the given order of things, and, as such, its spirit is unruly, subversive, and even anarchic.

It's worth pausing for a moment over the radical implications of Whitman's linguistic practice. Whitman surrenders language to life; he makes language a prosthetic extension of the vital processes through which subjects come into being. Language thus abolishes itself in the realization of life. At the same time, however, Whitman locates in expressive capacity a surplus of potentiality through which bodies become "perhaps more" than the "best poem." It is only by signifying that bodies realize the life in them. Paradoxically, then, Whitman's poetic mode implies both the abolition of language for the sake of life and the proliferation of language for the sake of life. This conclusion is born out in the educational program that Whitman espouses to his readers in the 1855 Preface. Following the injunction, "This is what you shall do," Whitman lists a series of practices that include appreciating nature, hating tyrants, and mingling with people regardless of social class. He concludes this list by asking his reader to "read these leaves in the open air every season of every year of your life, reexamine all you have been told at school or church or in any book, dismiss whatever insults your own soul, and your very flesh shall be a great poem and have the richest fluency not only in its words but in the silent lines of its lips and face and between the lashes of your eyes and in every motion and joint of your body" (vi). In this circular logic, the immanence of life and language finds its guarantee in the activity of reading *Leaves of Grass*. The book does not so much redeem the flesh through the word as discover the continuity (or "fluency") between linguistic expression and bodily expression. Language abolishes itself in embodied life ("your very flesh shall be a great poem") only insofar as life expresses itself in a language of "silent lines."[13]

Whitman's ontology of life and language is the condition of possibility of a polity in which there's no gap between the people's lives and the domain of governance. Whitman's pantheism leads to a nation that would be without division, that would gather up fleshy presence, without becoming an inert mass. Whitman gives this alternative national form at least two names: "America" and "democracy." I discuss what it means that Whitman treats these words as synonyms in the next section, for, in this slippage, Whitman's concept of history appears as a teleological course at the end of which democracy culminates in "America." For now, I want to focus on the idea of democracy as ontology, which is to say the idea of the people (*demos*) as the organic extension of being. Betsy Erkkila describes Whitman's political ontology as a "politics of Nature." The aptness of this phrase consists in the way it ties politics to a logic of organic development: Politics cultivates the people as a union of being, as the circular return of life to itself. Erkkila breaks down the stakes of this logic in the following: "Through the invention of an organic self who is like the Union, many in one, Whitman seeks to manage and resolve poetically the conflicting and paradoxical energies of the Union."[14] This reading moves in two directions. On the one hand, it locates Whitman in a historically situated struggle over the state of the Union. Whitman's poetry becomes an attempt to resolve the historical contradictions between free states and slaveholding states, Federalism and Anti-Federalism, constitutionalism and constituent power, as they expressed themselves in the 1840s and '50s.

On the other hand, one can also read Whitman's "politics of Nature" in a literal fashion. Union is not merely the end goal of politics. It is its presupposition. The "organic self" that Whitman invents isn't "like the Union"; it *is* the Union. Macroscopic and microscopic levels of politics replicate one another in a fractal geometry, a repetition of organic patterns at different scales. In Whitman's words, "An individual is as superb as a nation when he has the qualities which make a superb nation" (xii). This commensurability between nation and individual goes hand in hand with Whitman's assertion that the "United States themselves are essentially the greatest poem" (iii). The merging of poetry and flesh enables the organic continuity between individual and nation, for poetry names nothing less than the process of individuating the common. That is, poetry is the expression of singularity through (and not despite of) commonality, and the totality of this expression is the nation. As Jason Frank remarks, "For Whitman it was not enough that democratic egalitarianism be conceptualized as a formal principle; it must be further inscribed in flesh. Affection, eros, amativeness, attachment were essential components of this embodiment, of the manner through which the democratic people could become 'a great passionate body.'"[15]

In this reciprocity between singularity and commonality, Whitman finds himself again in the company of Spinoza, specifically the Spinoza of the *Ethics*. "The highest good of those who follow virtue is common to all, and all can enjoy it equally."[16] Spinoza suggests that freedom is an effect of commonality. Freedom doesn't come at the expense of collective bonds, as if individual liberty were synonymous with breaking away from association. Instead, freedom involves the mutual composition of interests, powers, and affinities, such that the actualization of the self is also the realization of the common, and vice versa. Crucially, this process of composing the common not only produces the common good as a result, it also transforms the participants that compose the common. There are a number of ways of reading Spinoza's theorization of commonality, some more optimistic than others, but what can't be denied is that, for Spinoza, political power is entirely immanent in Nature (or God—the two are the same for him).[17] There's no exit from the state of nature into politics, no transcendence of the political over the social. Instead, politics names the process of constructing and reconstructing the relations that make up nature, and nature is nothing but this relational dynamic.

Whitman's monism, his Spinozan bent, unfolds as a rethinking of nationality on immanent and egalitarian terms. The division between citizen and bare life gives way to "the merge," or to the individuation of a life in common. The boundary line separating citizen from noncitizen dissolves; the stranger no longer serves as the constitutively excluded element of the polity but as its fundamental basis—the strangeness of singularity, of difference in itself, becomes the very force of relation. Anonymity is thus the essence of national belonging; it is the necessary namelessness of universal participation in governance. Put differently, democracy is only worth its name if anyone and everyone participates. What typically gets labeled "the public sphere" doesn't vanish in this context, but it does generalize itself to the point where the liberal version of privacy no longer exists: Domestic life coincides immediately with public life. A public of strangers, or a strange public; a common demos, or the becoming-demos of the common—however one phrases it, the translation of being into polis implies the mutual constitution of individual and collective in an endless process of organic growth. As Gilles Deleuze—another Spinozist—writes:

> "Camaraderie" is the great word Whitman uses to designate the highest human relation, not by virtue of the totality of a situation but as a function of particular traits, emotional circumstances, and the "interiority" of the relevant fragments. . . . In this way is woven a web of variable relations, which are not merged into a whole, but produce the only whole that man is capable of conquering in a given situation. Camaraderie is the variability that implies an encounter with the Outside, a march of souls in the open air, on the "Open Road."[18]

The merge knows no outside, because it doesn't found itself on constitutive abjection or foreignness. At the same time, the essence of the merge is "the Outside" in the sense of an intimate strangeness: The outside opens up the inside not through destruction but through the never-ending renegotiation of the common with the singularities that compose it. This is why Deleuze can conceptualize wholeness in Whitman as nontotalizing, as a "web of variable relations": In this instance, organic unity—what Whitman sometimes calls the "organic compact"—is neither self-same, nor permanent, but mutable, heterogeneous, and, above all, egalitarian.

The most concerted manner through which Whitman translates being into democracy is eroticism. Whitman elaborates a politics in which nationality coincides immediately with a free-flowing sexual energy. In Peter Coviello's words, Whitman's America consists of "specifically affective attachments"; it involves a "utopian vision of America given coherence not by the state but by the passionate ties that join together its far-flung citizens."[19] In contrast to the regime of "sexuality" that emerges in the eighteenth and nineteenth centuries—the system of discipline and control Foucault describes in *The History of Sexuality*—Whitman's erotic art consists of fluid relations in which bodies are made and unmade in a perpetual flux of the common.[20] Sexual acts transform bodies in and through their relations with others. Discrete acts are not, however, the primary expression of sexuality in Whitman's 1855 *Leaves*. Sexuality is irreducible not only to identity but also to act. The fluidity of sexuality is not an contingent feature of the merge but a constitutive dimension, which is to say that life in common *is* erotic, that the democratic nation *is* sexual relation. When Whitman writes, "Ever love .... ever the sobbing liquid of life," he names the solution to the problem of how belonging can correspond with fluidity: "Love," which blurs the line between physical eroticism and passion in general, allows "life" to maintain a consistency—a "liquid" coherence—even as it mutates (47).

Whitman's sexual mode of being conforms neither to the regime of sexuality as Foucault articulates it, nor to the queer liberal counterdiscourses that have emerged to contest it. Whitman writes in the midst of sexuality's emergence as one of the most significant regimes of identity production in modernity. As a number of critics have explained, Whitman's expression of sexuality cannot help but articulate itself by way of contemporary discourses of sexuality, including those found in moral hygiene movements, temperance movements, phrenology, and medicine.[21] That Whitman's response to these discourses is critical and nonnormative has been well established, but the debate remains open regarding the degree to which it manages to break from the regime of sexuality. For instance, it's difficult not to identify a liberal demand for the tolerance of diverse sexual identities in the following lines: "Through me forbidden voices,/ Voices of sexes and lusts .... voices veiled, and I remove the veil,/ Voices indecent by me clarified and transfigured" (29). Whitman seems to anticipate the collective coming out of the Stonewall generation, announcing the promise of a world in which the once forbidden would be redeemed ("transfigured") and the once closeted would become spectacular ("clarified"). The logic is one of deconcealment and incorporation, which is to say of revaluation through inclusion. It corresponds to what Foucault calls a counterdiscourse, or a reshuffling of power relations that cannot help but reinforce the more general apparatus of sexuality.

Although there are moments in which the counterdiscourse of queer identity prevails in the 1855 edition of *Leaves*, more commonplace is a liquid version of sexuality, or an erotics of energy, that defies identitarian and proprietary forms of sexuality. Whitman confounds the regime of sexuality on ontological grounds, not so much contesting it as avoiding it altogether. This position differs from later editions of *Leaves* in which a dialectics of secrecy and confession articulates queer sexuality as a marginal or dissident form of life. In the 1855 edition, the logic of sexuality proceeds from Whitman's claim that: "Not one is dissatisfied ... not one is demented with the mania of owning things" (34). These lines are the sexual corollary to Whitman's atomism, his refutation of possessive individualism through the sheer dissemination of matter. Sexuality is common, not private or proprietary; it consists in a relationality that undermines identity, which is not to say that it does not involve difference. In contrast to an identitarian regime of sexuality, Whitman's sexual economy is characterized by variable relations among affects, desires, and conducts and by the constant production of new forms of life through connections between bodies. Whitman's sexuality might be called performative, because subjectivity as identity gives way to subjectivity as an effect of discourse and practice, but this description would need to be qualified not only by the specific continuity Whitman establishes between language and flesh but also by Whitman's valorization of nonnormative difference only insofar as it participates in the common.[22] These emphases come across in a pointed manner in the following lines: "Is this then a touch? .... quivering me to a new identity, / Flames and ether making a rush for my veins, / Treacherous tip of me reaching and crowding to help them, / My flesh and blood playing out lightning, to strike what is hardly different from myself" (32). Identity is always tentative, exposed to the possibility of a "quivering" through which one arrangement of flesh gives way to another, but this tentativeness has less to do with the instability of subjectivity in a deconstructive sense than with the preindividual commonality in which Whitman roots subjectivity. If the chain reaction through which a "touch" becomes fire and lightning results in a "strik[ing of] what is hardly different from myself," it is because autoeroticism and sexual contact with another become indistinguishable in the common. Sexual relation is the common touching itself.

The most repeated sexual encounter in the 1855 *Leaves* is that which occurs between the "I" of the lyric person and the poem's second-person addressee. Here's a telling example:

> Divine am I inside and out, and I make holy whatever I touch or am touched from;
> The scent of these arm-pits is aroma finer than prayer,
> This head is more than churches or bibles or creeds.
> If I worship any particular thing it shall be some of the spread of my body;
> Translucent mould of me it shall be you, ...
> Whatever goes to the tilth of me it shall be you,
> You my rich blood, your milky stream pale strippings of my life;
> Breast that presses against other breasts it shall be you,
> My brain it shall be your occult convolutions, ...
> Mixed tussled hay of head and beard and brawn it shall be you,
> Trickling sap of maple, fibre of manly wheat, it shall be you;

> Sun so generous it shall be you, . . .
> Winds whose soft-tickling genitals rub against me it shall be you,
> Broad muscular fields, branches of liveoak, loving lounger in my winding paths, it shall be you,
> Hands I have taken, face I have kissed, mortal I have ever touched, it shall be you. (29–30)

The opening line of this passage repeats Whitman's deconstruction of Cartesian dualism. It does so in a way that links the unity of being (its immanence or monism) to the absorption of divinity, rather than to a secular materialism. The body comprehends spirit: The scent of armpits is "finer than the prayer," the "head" greater than religious institutions. The "divine" becomes an immanent effect of corporeal movement and connection. It is only in the touch that joins bodies, in the affective connection between beings, that spirit comes to life: "If I worship any particular thing it shall be some of the spread of my body." The "spread" of Whitman's body encompasses not only the universe of the poem but also the position of the reader ("you"). There is ambiguity, here, as the address could presumably constitute an apostrophe—a speech act not directly aimed at the reader—due to the lability of the pronoun. But this ambiguity only amplifies the queer divinity of Whitman's sexuality: Sexuality, as a kind of corporeal poiesis, blurs the lines between flesh and text, presence and absence, the actual and the virtual, transcendence and immanence. The poem becomes flesh in a process of communication that does not work through separation but through a mingling of material entities that generates a third term without negating or subsuming the preceding terms. This communication of bodies through the merge is the most characteristic element of Whitman's sexuality. Touch brings together that which is "inside and out" in a zone of indistinguishability; it isn't a discrete zone of contact between solid, self-contained objects but a becoming fluid of the solid and a becoming solid of the fluid: The pressing of breasts against breasts pours forth from the milky stream of life; "tussled hay of head and beard and brawn" bifurcate into "trickling sap of maple" and "fibre of manly wheat." The divinity opening this passage thus indicates the irreducibility of the flesh to oneness; it gestures toward the surplus of potentiality that belongs to the common—an excess of life over private property, individuality, and even personhood.

Whitman's queer erotics of the common is perhaps best described as ecstatic. Ecstasy (*ek-stasis*) suggests a being-outside-of-oneself without the abolition of the person. In *Leaves*, life in common individuates itself as a series of ecstatic creatures. The "milky stream" in the above passage figures this ecstasy, its not so subtle reference to ejaculation (or coming outside of oneself) threading a continuity between the first-person and second-person: "*your* milky stream pale strippings of *my* life" (emphasis added). Indeed, ecstasy might serve not only as a description of the common but also as a reference to the tone of the 1855 *Leaves*, with its frequent exhortations and ejaculations, and even to the syntax, with its tendency to favor the weak pauses of commas over the period's decisive stop. Elaborating on this point, one can interpret the "It shall be you" mantra of the passage as mutual ejaculation, a kind of ecstatic commoning: The "I" ejaculates to become the "you," but only insofar as the "you" already belongs to the "I" as condition of its existence. Rather than possessing the other in a sexual encounter, each individual remakes himself or herself through a dispossession of self that's also a joining with another. Individuals do not so much merge as return to the preindividual common that always already constitutes the self.

The 1855 edition of *Leaves* doesn't allow for anything so rigid as heterosexuality. In the context of its queer ontology, heterosexuality can appear as only an encrustation or blockage. It's a parasitic economy in which being finds itself impoverished. In contrast, there is a way in which homoeroticism, if not exactly homosexuality, belongs to the text, not least because of the thinly veiled descriptions of Whitman's penetration by phallic objects throughout the volume—for instance, in the above passage: "Broad muscular fields, branches of liveoak, loving lounger in my winding paths, it shall be you." Although one cannot pin down the language to a specific sexual act, one also cannot rule out anal eroticism: the "branches of liveoak" entering into Whitman by way of his "winding paths." In fact, it's the indeterminateness of these lines that makes Whitman's poetry so queer, the way in which the words gesture toward Whitman's bodily orifices in male-male penetration and, at the same time, disseminate into the "winding paths" of the indiscriminate, generic, and preindividual common of *Leaves*. I hesitate to name this queerness "gay," even if, as Robert Martin so eloquently argues, one shouldn't shirk away from the queer content of Whitman's life and work.[23] Rather, Whitman's poetry performs a more general queering of social life through its refusal of identificatory regimes and its replacement of the poverty of heteronormativity with the plenitude of the common. Michael Moon echoes this point when he associates Whitman not only with the sex radicals of his day but also with Fourier's utopianism: Whitman's seriality ("his coming to see himself as both part of and constituted by virtually endless series or chains of association") "draws on and contributes to a stream of anarchic political and erotic aspirations in which sexual variance in its myriad forms has not been a marginal or tolerated feature, but a central and fundamental value."[24] Moon's analysis rhymes with my own articulation of a life in common, not least in the way it fuses liquidity with multiplicity, seriality with variance. Anarchy, in Moon's argument, isn't chaos but rather "potentially world-making, life-affirming practices."[25] There's a utopian dimension to Whitman's erotics, a way in which it draws forth another world through that which is most near.

To call Whitman queer, then, is not to identify him in a strict sense. Instead, it's a way of allowing the sexual energy of his work to affirm life in all of its multiplicity and commonality. This is perhaps how one should read the absence of Whitman's proper name on the cover of *Leaves*, its inclusion only in the copyright information and in two lines of poetry (once the full name "Walt Whitman" [29] another time "Walt" [31]). Rather than describe this elision as a deconstructive play of presence and absence, one would do better to think of it as the freeing of singularity into a life in common. It's not disappearance, then, but dissemination, provided one acknowledges that such "scattering" always involves "returns." As Michael Warner suggests, one can understand this valorization of anonymity as gay cruising.[26] If entering into Whitman's merge implies a loss of personal recognition, *Leaves* more than compensates for this loss through the tactile and verbal pleasures of its common language.

The politics of Whitman's ontology is exemplified by this queer erotics. Democracy is an orgy. It's the anonymous mingling of flesh in a multiplication of differences. The pantheistic, or Spinozist, avenue down which I've pursued this insight suggests that, for the 1855 *Leaves*, the normative dimension of democracy is identical to the expression of being. Democracy is no more and no less than the articulation of being as a life in common, which is to say that Whitman derives a concept of politics from an ontology. This derivation implies an identity between being and praxis; it means that praxis is synonymous with the unfolding of being in all of its modes. The trickiness of this political ontology is that it seems to leave little room for decisive ruptures: If politics says itself as being, or if politics is but the lively expression of being, then how does one break with the status quo? Where can one discover the possibility of an epochal rupture with the way things are? Whereas William Burroughs positions the commons as an object of political aspiration, Whitman sees it as a natural tendency, as the givenness of life itself. Jane Bennett writes of Whitman's politics and poetics: "Good judgment may require one to periodically inhabit the role of falling sun, for this accepting, nonranking illumination can reveal things as possessing a certain performativity, or what Whitman calls 'the pulsation in all matter, all spirit, throbbing forever, eternal systole and diastole of life in all things.'"[27] Can a politics without judgment, or a praxis without a normative thrust, be anything other than a reiteration of the status quo? If politics is like sunlight falling on a blade of grass, is it anything more than a halo surrounding the given?[28]

The ultimate truth of Whitman's vitalist democracy may lie in his poetry's praise of eternity as a grand equilibrium of being. "The clock indicates the moment . . . but what does eternity indicate?" (49). "It is not chaos or death . . . it is form and union and plan. . . . It is eternal life" (55). "The law of the living cannot be eluded. . . . It is eternal" (68). "The eternal equilibrium of things is great, and the eternal overthrow of things is great" (95). Insofar as life is common, it is eternal, for life belongs not to the finite individual but to the common. The impersonal flow of life is greater than any one epoch, more powerful than any social order. The "union and plan" of being swallow up historical difference, and even political "overthrow" signifies but an eddy in the "eternal equilibrium." Allen Grossman has argued that Whitman shares with Abraham Lincoln a "common conservatism," that Whitman's desire to invest the Union with the grandeur of eternity serves the ideological function of consecrating the United States in providential terms.[29] The identity between being and democracy entails the positive valuation of the given as an expression of an overarching truth. Another way of putting this would be to say that Whitman ends up repeating a political doctrine that dates back at least to Plato's *Republic*, namely, the argument that political virtue derives from the allotment of each to his or her proper place. "Nothing out of its place is good," Whitman writes, "and nothing in its place is bad" (iv). It is difficult to imagine how this vision of democracy might reckon with the injustices of slavery, patriarchy, capitalism, or settler colonialism. However, as I argue in the next section, there's another democracy in Whitman's *Leaves*, a democracy whose essence is not life but struggle, not flow but break.

Whitman's Two Democracies

In the 1855 edition of *Leaves of Grass*, democracy divides into two. Democracy as life in common is not so much replaced as interrupted by another democracy. This second democracy takes place as an exception—an evental rupture—that simultaneously breaks up the continuity of Whitman's political thinking and maintains it. If Whitman articulates democracy as an expression of life in common, he nevertheless introduces a division of the common along temporal, historical, and political lines. In temporal terms, Whitman posits the democratic life in common as both always already and not-yet. In historical terms, he associates this superlative form of political life with the founding of the United States, that is, with the American Revolution understood as the culmination of world history. Whitman, however, views the Revolution as only incompletely realized. As such, he bestows on poetry and politics (on poetry *as* politics) the historical mission of realizing the Revolution in the present. Finally, this sense of an unfulfilled revolution depends on a recognition of social inequalities in the present. In this section, I focus on two structures of inequality, each of which is foundational to the life of the nation: wage labor and slavery. These divisions of the common do not negate Whitman's monism, but they do constitute immanent objections to any assertion of direct continuity between ontology and politics. Politics becomes a project, an event-oriented praxis, through which being throws itself forward, exceeds itself, catches itself off guard. This second version of democracy doesn't grow in an organic manner. Instead, it cuts the world in two; it splits the common into a life of unfulfilled potentiality and a life that would realize the Revolution. It insists that there's the people (as they already exist) and then there's the people (to come).

From this perspective, if democracy means anything, it is only insofar as it betrays ontology. The political gravity of Whitman's poetry emerges in those moments when a gap interrupts the continuity between being and politics (or between life in common and the struggle for equality). This second notion of democracy appears at those moments when Whitman doesn't simply assert democracy as a material fact but declares it an imperative one must live up to. These acts of declaration coincide, in a conceptual and rhetorical sense, with Whitman's self-designation as the exemplary incarnation of democracy. In contrast to the critics who view this rhetorical operation as imperial, I argue that the structure of exemplary self-reference actually opens up a space for political contestation.[30] Rather than suturing the social body closed through a fantasy of universal equality and belonging, Whitman's performances of exemplarity imply a strange conjunction of surplus and void. In modeling democracy, Whitman betrays the insufficiency of the American social body in respect to its own democratic potential. This disjunction between the virtuality of democracy as a generic truth and the singularity of democracy as an event is the utopian motor of the 1855 *Leaves of Grass*. Put differently, Whitman's utopianism consists in calling out the inadequacy of the United States in respect to the promise of America and in transforming this sense of inadequacy into the vision of a counter-nation to come. It's as if Whitman could imagine a singular America—an America beyond nation-state and capitalism—only by doubling down on exceptionalism, by keeping faith to the idea that it's the destiny of the American nation to fulfill the course of world history.

In the poem eventually titled "Song of Myself," the reader comes across a number of moments in which the poem demands democracy, rather than simply asserting its existence. These demands are declarations of equality in which the lyric person of Whitman functions as the guarantee of a time to come. The following is one of the most well known instances:

> Walt Whitman, an American, one of the roughs, a kosmos,
> Disorderly fleshy and sensual . . . . eating drinking and breeding,
> No sentimentalist . . . . no stander above men and women or apart from them . . . no more modest than immodest.
>
> Unscrew the locks from the doors!
> Unscrew the doors themselves from their jambs!
>
> Whoever degrades another degrades me . . . . and whatever is done or said returns at last to me,
> And whatever I do or say I also return.
>
> Through me the afflatus surging and surging . . . . through me the current and index.
>
> I speak the password primeval . . . . I give the sign of democracy;
> By God! I will accept nothing which all cannot have their counterpart of on the same terms.
>
> Through me many long dumb voices,
> Voices of the interminable generations of slaves,
> Voices of prostitutes and of deformed persons,
> Voices of the diseased and despairing, and of thieves and dwarfs,
> Voices of cycles of preparation and accretion,
> And of the threads that connect the stars—and of wombs, and of the fatherstuff,
> And of the rights of them the others are down upon,
> Of the trivial and flat and foolish and despised,
> Of fog in the air and beetles rolling balls of dung.
>
> Through me forbidden voices,
> Voices of sexes and lusts . . . . voices veiled, and I remove the veil,
> Voices indecent by me clarified and transfigured. (29)

It is tempting to read this passage as a spectacular moment of bravado in which Whitman nominates himself the messiah of a democratic salvation. He becomes a messianic figure through which the people will, in the final hour, be "clarified and transfigured." The circular pattern generated by the repetition of "I" and "me," as well as the anaphoric repetition, ensures that the transformation of social multiplicity into political unity occurs through the singular point of Whitman's person. Whitman is thus not only the "current"—that which runs with the stream of the masses—but also the "index"—that which introduces a vertical axis, or typological relation, through which the earthly gestures toward redemption. This reading would seem to be confirmed by the passage's enactment of an equality in line with a Christian doctrine of salvation: The lowest become the highest only insofar as they give themselves over to a faith that supersedes other obligations. The passage implies a Pauline conceptualization of the messiah as that figure capable of engendering a heavenly body (a resurrected body) subtracted from earthly flesh.[31] *Leaves* thus becomes synonymous with an event of resurrection, and democracy comes to mean the transcendence of the people over mere flesh.

At the same time, the opening lines of the passage appear to radically undermine this reading: Whitman is no exceptional individual but only "an American, one of the roughs, a kosmos . . . no stander above men and women or apart from them." These lines suggest a refusal of transcendence. The indefinite article insists on the serial dimension of politics, the ordinariness of a democracy wholly immanent in the life of the people. The figure of the poet is not only of the people in the sense of being formally equal to them (a like being) but also in the sense of being inextricable from them (being *with* them): Whitman is a body among bodies, and even if his body performs the function of the poet, this function is always already in the process of being disseminated, or shared out in the individuation of the common. This refusal of transcendence cements itself in the passage's praise of the flesh as the element of democracy: "Disorderly fleshy and sensual . . . eating drinking and breeding." Democracy comes to name the becoming-horizontal of social life, less an event than the recognition that no one stands above another, that the people (Whitman included) are all "of wombs, and of the fatherstuff." Democracy, in short, is the immanence of a life in common.

The contradiction at the heart of this passage—the split between a messianic democracy and an immanentist one—constitutes the gap through which politics reappears in the 1855 *Leaves*. The equivocation between democracy as event (resurrection) and democracy as life in common (flesh) generates a space in which political struggle takes place. In evental democracy, the common becomes the outcome of a project, rather than an ontological presupposition. Democracy takes place as a materialist teleology in which the end is constantly re-created through praxis. In this logic, the people become adequate to themselves only by becoming more than themselves. The point is not that this evental mode of democracy substitutes for the ontological mode but rather that it interrupts the latter, introducing historicity into the process. The irreducibility of this split can be seen in the ambiguity of the passage's call to "Unscrew the locks from the door!/Unscrew the doors themselves from the jambs!" On the one hand, these lines constitute a demand: a negation of closure or privacy affirming a democracy to come. It is both suspension of domesticity and march into the streets. In entering the streets, the people reconstitute themselves as a new kind of commonality: They become a people whose solidarity is predicated on fidelity to the revolutionary event. On the other hand, opening a door is no more than a disclosure of presence. It's the deconcealment of an already existing commonality. Whitman merely allows the people to reveal themselves in their ordinary glory.

Whitman serves as the mediating figure between two concepts of democracy. He doesn't synthesize them but rather provides a rhetorical-corporeal topos through which their differences can be registered. Whitman is a union of opposites, as he himself suggests when claiming the right to contradiction: "Do I contradict myself?/Very well then .... I contradict myself" (55). Another way of articulating this doubleness would be to say that Whitman *exemplifies* democracy. As Giorgio Agamben writes, the example is "excluded from the normal case not because it does not belong to it but, on the contrary because it exhibits its own belonging to it. The example is truly a *paradigm* in the etymological sense: it is what is 'shown beside,' and a class can contain everything except its own paradigm."[32] Whitman may be "no stander above men and women or apart from them," but in the act of designating himself the embodiment of democracy, he becomes a supernumerary element—a surplus member. He is of but not with; he belongs only insofar as he exceeds. Democratic flesh (*demos*) thus divides itself between the people and the poet, between life in common and the surplus body giving voice to this life. Whitman becomes the gap through which democracy transforms from structure into event, from the given into the to-come, and from social being into political struggle. He's simultaneously what binds the people together and what splits them in two.

My general argument should be clear by now. The 1855 edition of *Leaves of Grass* offers democracy as a life in common, but, at the same time, it takes exception to this vitalist version of democracy in the name of a democracy to come. The figure of Whitman doesn't resolve this contradiction but instead makes it productive. This productivity is the result not of one logic of democracy or the other but of the gap between them. This gap can be parsed, on the one hand, as the impossibility of absolute immanence, or the fundamental nonidentity of being with itself, and, on the other hand, as the space of the event, the minimal difference enabling temporal rupture to take place. One can also articulate this gap in terms of the formal sequence that it supports (a sequence whose temporality is logical, not empirical): Life in common expresses itself as a monistic stream of being (logic of democracy #1); in order for being's expression to have coherence, it requires an act of self-reference or exemplification (the event of Walt Whitman's presence, which is also the poem as event); self-reference engenders a political surplus element that is immanent in yet in excess of life in common (logic of democracy #2). This sequence can also be understood in linguistic terms as the coming together and pulling apart of the syntactic and semantic dimensions of *Leaves*. Life in common would correspond to the syntactic dimension (the serial iteration of the people), while the redemptive version of democracy would correspond to the semantic dimension (the people as reserve of potentiality waiting to be actualized). These linguistic axes converge and diverge through the singular point that is Walt Whitman's presence in the text, through those moments in which the act of enunciation makes an appearance in the text as the trace of voice.

Whitman's doubling of democracy along conceptual and linguistic lines is synonymous with his utopianism. I've already suggested that the erotics of the 1855 *Leaves of Grass* can be read as utopian, because, in loosening the ego's hold over life, it gives birth to a new kind of ecstatic subjectivity. At the same time, this utopianism risks an elision of political struggle because of the seamlessness of the social field that it presupposes. In a dialectical reversal, radical alterity comes to be folded back into the commonality of the merge—after all, an orgy that has become universal cannot differentiate itself from the pleasures of the everyday. This utopianism is nearly identical with the procedural formalism for which Wai Chee Dimock impugns Whitman—a democracy whose proof consists in serial equivalence is perhaps not worth its name.[33] In contrast, the evental concept of democracy implies a more resolute utopian praxis. It introduces the future into the present not as an extrapolation of what already is but as the eruption of the new and different. Jason Frank articulates this utopianism as a "democratic regeneration" of the people through "their constitutive futurity, in their remaining forever a people that is not . . . yet."[34] He elaborates: "The people invoked by Whitman do not aim at the realization of a common essence or at the construction of such an essence, but are only realized through their continual political reinvention out of a collective reservoir of sublime potentiality."[35] More than an attribute or state of being, the commonality of the people is something like an immanent sense of futurity, a constitutive demand to become more than oneself. What Frank doesn't take into account, however, is the incommensurability between the people and the people, between the "not" and the "yet." There's an equivocation in his argument insofar as he tries to reconcile the common and the sublime, or, in my terms, the first version of democracy and the second. What's missing, I suggest, is an encounter with death.

In the 1855 *Leaves*, the people can't realize their potentiality without first dying, because their potentiality exceeds the limits of their contemporary mode of existence. As Whitman puts it in the preface: "The greatest poet forms the consistence of what is to be from what has been and is. He drags the dead out of their coffins and stands them again on their feet. . . . He says to the past, Rise and walk before me that I may *realize* you. He learns the lesson. . . . He places himself where the future becomes present" (vi, emphasis added). Realization constitutes a utopian praxis when it becomes resurrection, when it implies the death of one form of existence and the emergence of another. The operator of resurrection is, of course, Whitman. Whitman becomes the place in which the future not only enters into the present and past but also exceeds them; "consistence" ("the consistence of what is to be from what has been and is") gives way to rupture (the gap between the subject of the coffin and the risen subject). The most resolutely utopian praxis that one finds in the 1855 *Leaves* is rebirth through death, or materialist resurrection.[36]

This formal logic of utopia takes on specific historical content, when one considers that Whitman's materialist resurrection is nothing less than the reactualization of the American Revolution. It's a commonplace to note that, for Whitman, "America" signifies more than a geographical entity or a nation-state. It names the possibility of a new politics. America is a state of nature, an organic unity of life in common. However, in distinction to the philosophies of Locke and Hegel, this state of nature is not the presupposition of politics but rather the space in which politics finally realizes itself in a manner adequate to nature. The event of Revolution, however, interrupts this organic model of politics. It introduces a gap between the continental imaginary of the New World and the no less continental imaginary of the revolutionary nation. The latter doesn't erase the former but temporalizes it: The revolutionary nation resurrects the New World; it actualizes the potentiality of the New World only insofar as it brings about a singular America—an America without precedent. Whitman's poetry, then, constitutes a repetition not of the New World in itself but of the Revolution as that which realizes the potentiality of the New World.[37] It is repetition squared. This imaginary can't help but reinscribe the exceptionalism that it also exceeds, which is to say that the emergence of a singular America in Whitman's poetry doesn't escape the pull of history's thanatopolitical drift, including settler colonialism, the institution of slavery, and capitalist-imperial expansion. In Whitman, the event of Revolution is always double, a narrative not only of liberation but also of conquest.[38]

The American Revolution, I'm arguing, doesn't simply serve as the condition of possibility for the 1855 *Leaves*. It is also the materialist teleology of the text, the historical trajectory of its utopian praxis. This sense of history suggests that (at least in this edition of *Leaves*) Whitman's futurity can't be reduced to what D. H. Lawrence terms "the quivering nimble hour of the present" or what Cody Marrs describes as "but the present remade."[39] The immanent futurity of the 1855 edition exceeds the self-identity of the present because the Revolution cannot be subsumed in the actuality of the United States. America does not yet live up to its promise, which means that the Revolution hangs over it as a demand or even a warning. This structure of demand depends on the recognition of the present as a moment of crisis, as a moment in which a decision must be made because the present is divided from itself. As Betsy Erkkila argues:

> It was, at least in part, out of his desire to revive the dead body of republican America that he turned his main energies in 1854 to completing the poems of *Leaves of Grass*. The poems were not, as is commonly assumed, a product of Whitman's unbounded faith in the democratic dream of America; on the contrary, they were an impassioned response to the signs of the death of republican traditions he saw throughout the land and his growing fear that the ship of American liberty had run aground.[40]

This indictment of America's degeneration begins in Whitman's pre-*Leaves* poetry, notably in "Song for Certain Congressmen," "Blood-Money," and "Resurgemus." In these poems, Whitman denounces political corruption, the increasing dominance of market relations, and compromise with the slave system. He sees these social forms as eclipsing, or at least attenuating, republican virtues of autonomy and cooperation, virtues that he associates not only with the American Revolution but also the French Revolution (as indicated by "Resurgemus" [1850], included in revised form in the 1855 edition as the poem that would eventually be named "Europe: The 72nd and 73rd Years of these States"). David Reynolds frames Whitman's poetic response to this historical crisis in terms of an opposition between union and strife: "Into the vacuum created by the dissolution of the nation's political structure rushed Whitman's gargantuan 'I,' assimilating images from virtually every aspect of antebellum American culture in a poetic document of togetherness offered to a nation that seemed on the verge of unraveling."[41] Reynolds, however, sees in this valorization of togetherness not a revolutionary impulse but a reformist one. He goes so far as to suggest that Whitman flirts with the right-wing nationalism of the nineteenth-century Know Nothings. According to this argument, Whitman's organicist nationalism too easily covers over the social contradictions and conflicts of the period. In contrast, I'm arguing for the revolutionary force of the 1855 *Leaves of Grass* not on the basis of Whitman's personal politics—Reynolds is right in that regard—but because of the philosophical and political dynamics of the text.[42]

The 1855 *Leaves* constitutes a revolutionary document because of its condemnation of the status quo and its demand for a materialist resurrection of America. This desire to resurrect America receives its most explicit formulation in "A Boston Ballad." In this poem, Whitman summons the ghost of the revolution past to condemn present-day corruption: "What troubles you, Yankee Phantoms?" (89). He then imagines King George's return as a living dead incarnation of all that blocks the people of the United States from realizing their singular potentiality: "The crown is come to its own and more than its own" (90). This poem has all the marks of the American jeremiad in its combination of admonishment, warning, consecration, and unification.[43] This condemnation doesn't limit itself to negativity, for it also serves as a symbolic renewal of the Union. However, Whitman's jeremiad doesn't institute consensus, nor does it found the social compact on an experience of shame. Instead, it projects social unity into the future anterior as that state in which satisfaction will have been achieved, in which freedom, equality, and association will have become reciprocal elements in American life. It predicates democracy as life in common on democracy as event, with the space between these two political logics occupied by the decrepitude of a living dead nation.

The drama of reactualizing the Revolution repeats itself in the 1855 edition of *Leaves of Grass* through the trope of unaccountable life: an apostrophe in which Whitman speaks to that which in the people is more than the people—their singular excess of potentiality. I want to conclude this chapter by showing how this trope functions in two poems, those that would come to be named "Song for Occupations" and "I Sing the Body Electric." These poems offer the most condensed and incisive instances of the knot between the two logics of democracy. In both poems, Whitman raises up life in a manner that divides it from itself, that creates a cleavage between a morbid element and a vital element. The historical event of revolution inscribes itself in the gap between these elements, the movement from one side to the other being the kinesis through which the potentiality of American life realizes itself. This potentiality is immeasurable not only because it escapes objective measurement but also because Whitman's drama of resurrection contests capitalist and statist forms of identification. The political subjectivity emerging from Whitman's revolutionary scission exceeds the forms of the worker and the citizen. These two forms of identification require measurement as a form of discipline, a way of restricting and channeling life toward selfish, productive, and nationalistic ends. In contrast, Whitman dedicates his efforts to unblocking revolutionary potential. His poetry insists that the people cannot be tamed by identitarian systems of control. In doing so, Whitman marks his distance from a reactive politics of injury—a struggle for the recognition and restitution of an injured social identity—and pleads the importance of utopian praxis—an affirmative biopolitics whose aim is not life's restoration but its reinvention.[44]

"A Song for Occupations" connects the politics of labor to the Revolution by singing the nonidentity between abstract labor and living labor. The poem performs three actions in respect to labor. First, it catalogs the plurality of activities that make up labor. Second, it asserts the equality among different kinds of labor. This equality is not equivalence but rather the rejection of hierarchy in respect to activity. These first two actions take place through the formal features for which Whitman is most well known, namely, parataxis, syntactical parallelism, and anaphora. These formal structures enact a break not only with classical poetry's concern for elevated subject matter but also with ideologies that establish an essential division between skilled labor and unskilled labor. However, the seriality of these formal features also risks rendering the discrete semantic elements into equivalent units, which is to say that it risks collapsing the diversity of labor into the average measure of capital. There's a risk that the seriality of Whitman's poetry is nothing except a formal analogue to the circulation of labor as commodity. The third and final action, however, prevents this abstract leveling of activity from occurring. It marks the nonidentity of an occupation with itself on the basis of an excess of life (potentiality, or living labor) in respect to market abstractions. This reading has little to do with scholarship that interprets Whitman's poetry through his empirical identity as a lower-middle-class artisan (printer, journalist, poet). Although such interpretations offer compelling accounts of the class conflicts of the antebellum United States, they fail to grasp the ways in which Whitman's poetics of labor exceeds social identity.[45] The political subjectivity of labor that Whitman cultivates is a matter of nonidentity, of irreducibility and excess, in respect to abstract labor. Although his poetry may reproduce a capitalist logic of equivalence in its syntax, on the semantic and rhetorical levels, it undermines this bourgeois class content by insisting on labor's revolutionary potential.

Whitman may not be a Marxist, but he does invent a concept of living labor at almost the same moment as Marx.[46] Living labor defines itself in opposition to abstract or dead labor. It's the embodied potentiality that lends life to the commodity; it's the vital surplus in activity that instills use-value into material substance and enables the extraction of surplus-value (the valorization of capital). As Marx puts it in a discussion regarding the productive consumption of machinery and raw materials:

> Living labour must seize on these things, awaken them from the dead, change them from merely possible into real and effective use-values. Bathed in the fire of labour, appropriated as part of the organism, and infused with vital energy for the performance of the functions appropriate to their concept and to their vocation in the process, they [the machinery/raw materials] are indeed consumed, but to some purpose, as elements in the formation of new use-values, new products, which are capable of entering into individual consumption as means of subsistence or into a new labour process as means of production.[47]

Marx articulates his own drama of resurrection in the form of capital's valorization through the extraction of labor's life force: The dead labor of capital is brought back to life only through constantly renewed encounters with the vitality of workers. Marx crucially distinguishes material substance ("dead," inert, thingly) from the incarnate yet protean "energy" of labor ("fire of labour," "vital energy"). The latter constitutes a surplus not only over matter but also over labor-power. If labor-power is activity that has been purchased and reduced to the measure of the wage, then living labor is that excess of embodied time irreducible to linear measure. Marx also articulates this concept in terms of an opposition between space ("*objectified labor*, i.e. labor which is *present in space*") and time ("labor which is present in time ... present only as the living subject, in which it exists as capacity, as possibility").[48] This formulation suggests that the contradiction between labor-power and living labor is also a conflict between capital's spatialization of labor in the form of the commodity and the surplus of life embodied by workers.

There are, of course, significant differences between Marx and Whitman. Whereas Marx identifies a dialectical tendency of capitalism to self-destruct through the production of its own negation (the proletariat), Whitman's vision is more ambiguous and nationalistic. He envisions an overcoming of the capitalist value-form that may or may not imply the abolition of capitalism, and he does so through a utopian vision of the American people as the proper incarnation of living labor. That being said, Whitman's critique of capital is no less immanent than Marx's; it operates not by separating itself from social existence but by exploding it from within. Take the following lines from "Song for Occupations": "The wife—and she is not one jot less than the husband, / The daughter—and she is just as good as the son, / The mother—and she is every bit as much as the father" (58). On the one hand, given the contemporary social constraints on women, one can read these lines as a progressive political declaration—an insistence on equality whose implicit premise is the recognition of patriarchy's injustice. The sequence of verbs, moving from the negation of inequality ("not one jot less") to the assertion of equality ("is just as good as," "is every bit as much as"), translates the force of critique into the affirmation of subjectivity. These lines enfold women into the political subject of the people; they overcome the constitutive exclusion of women from the people through sheer repetition of the copula. On the other hand, the almost arithmetic-like quality of these lines also suggests their limitation: They do not so much enact a political subjectivization as institute equivalence through a mathematical ontology. Whitman appears to take on the seriality of capital itself, borrowing the critical force of his poetry from capital's ability to act as a solvent with respect to traditional social bonds. In the syntax of his poetry, Whitman repeats the passage from living labor to abstract labor, reformatting social life for the sake of capital. In a poem that repeatedly circles back to the question of labor, the implication would seem to be that egalitarian politics, including feminist struggles against patriarchy, happens through, not despite of, the processes of capital accumulation.

What distinguishes Whitman's poetry from free market ideology, however, is that even as it reproduces the logic of capitalism, it insists on the irreducibility of living labor to abstract labor. Much like Marx's critique of political economy, Whitman's poetry acknowledges the ways in which capital loosens certain kinds of oppressive relations (feudal bonds, for example). At the same time, it doesn't stop there. "Song for Occupations" repeatedly undercuts the articulation of equivalence by introducing a scission into the capitalist value-form: "I bring what you much need, yet always have,/I bring not money or amours or dress or eating . . . . but I bring as good;/And send no agent or medium . . . . and offer no representative of value—but offer/the value itself" (59). The poem distinguishes "value itself" from its representation through money or commodities. One might understand this negation of mediation as conforming to capital: Capital is not the commodity (value's representation) but the relationship organizing value's extraction through exploitation ("value itself"). However, these lines also assert that this value is always already present in the reader. "Value itself" seems to signify the *source* of value, a potentiality irreducible to quantitative measure.

"Song for Occupations" celebrates living labor by articulating the source of value in opposition to objective forms of value. The poem elaborates this source as an indistinct yet singular something, found everywhere and at every moment:

> There is something that comes home to one now and perpetually,
> It is not what is printed or preached or discussed . . . . it eludes discussion and print,
> It is not to be put in a book . . . . it is not in this book,
> It is for you whoever you are . . . . it is no farther from you than your hearing and sight are from you,
> It is hinted by nearest and commonest and readiest . . . . it is not them, though it is endlessly provoked by them . . . . What is there ready and near you now? (Ibid.)

These lines confirm an interpretation of "value itself" as potentiality, for the "something" that value has become defines itself through the manner in which it "eludes" actuality. Potentiality emerges in the gap between the present simple and the past participle as that which gives presence without being reducible to a given form of presence. At first glance, this division appears to conform to an opposition between subject and object: The "something" belongs to "you" without being reducible to common nouns such as "book," "discussion," and "print." However, this subjectivization doesn't imply a Cartesian transcendence of subject (spirit) over object (matter) but rather an immanent subjectivization of matter. The difference belongs to matter itself, as suggested by the strange proximity of being "no farther from you than your hearing and your sight are from you." In this reference to the senses, Whitman locates potentiality in the embodied person as that which exceeds a given arrangement of the flesh without ever leaving the body behind. The division between abstract and living labor is not about substance but relation and movement: Living labor is potentiality that "eludes" capture by abstract labor; it is energy that shapes matter without exhausting itself in the actual.

One could imagine a reading in which this surplus of potentiality merely reinscribes Whitman's vitalist version of democracy. Living labor would coincide with the universal flow of life in common. However, in insisting on the gap between potentiality and actuality, Whitman creates the space for eventual democracy. Into this space, Whitman inserts himself as the vehicle through which the Revolution reactualizes itself in the people:

> Old institutions . . . . these arts libraries legends collections—and the practice handed along in manufactures . . . . will we rate them so high?
> Will we rate our prudence and business so high? . . . . I have no objection,
> I rate them as high as the highest . . . . but a child born of a woman and man I rate beyond all rate.
>
> We thought our Union grand and our Constitution grand;
> I do not say they are not grand and good—for they are,
> I am this day just as much in love with them as you,
> But I am eternally in love with you and with all my fellows upon the earth.
>
> We consider the bibles and religions divine . . . . I do not say they are not divine,
> I say they have all grown out of you and may grow out of you still,
> It is not they who give the life . . . . it is you who give the life;
> Leaves are not more shed from trees or trees from the earth than they are shed out of you. (60)

This passage transforms living labor into constituent power and abstract labor into constituted power. It rearticulates the surplus potentiality of labor as the excess of force that founds a polity. Antonio Negri defines constituent power less as the condition of possibility of governments than as a democratic power (in the Italian, *potenza*: potentiality) characterized by self-governance, futurity, and crisis; it is "a force that bursts apart, breaks, interrupts, unhinges any preexisting equilibrium and any possible continuity. Constituent power is tied to the notion of democracy as absolute power."[49] In the above passage, Whitman repeatedly extracts constituent power from its constituted forms. He does so through a peculiar kind of negation, one that doesn't destroy but instead returns constituted forms to the source of their value. The skeptical deployment of subjective verbs ("thought," "consider"), the interrogative mood, and the syntactic refrain of "not . . . but" suspend the actuality of value as fixed in a given institution. These formal features establish the contingency of institutional forms in respect to the potentiality that gives birth to them. If Whitman judges the objective value of "libraries," "manufactures," "our Union," and "our Constitution" to be "as high as the highest," it's only because quantitative value reveals its relative poverty in the face of what "rate[s] beyond all rate." There is a kind of value that precedes and exceeds measurable value—the source of value as surplus potentiality. Whitman once again locates this surplus potentiality in the American people through his use of second-person address. He marks a division in the people between their identification with institutions of governance—their citizenship—and their power to generate material realities—their social puissance. "It is not they who give the life . . . . it is you who give the life."

"Song for Occupations" reactualizes the Revolution by discovering a surplus potentiality in the daily occupations of the people. On the level of syntax, the people expresses itself in a serial equality ultimately indistinguishable from the circulation of capital. On the semantic level, however, the trope of unaccountable life—Whitman's apostrophe to the life that "rate[s] beyond all rate"—marks the irreducibility of the people to the relations of production. In short, living labor "eludes" determination by bourgeois power. Jason Stacy is right to argue that, in the 1855 *Leaves*, Whitman redefines "the work nexus" to privilege process over product and subject/verb over object.[50] However, this argument remains incomplete without considering how this processual, subject-oriented labor is immanent in abstract labor. "Occupation" names both the identification of the people with their proper social positions and the evental process of putting surplus life (living labor) into play. The people thus divide into two. They are a mass of individuals defined in relation to capitalism but also a collective force of creation whose time is still to come. Whitman mediates between these two peoples, a process which can be traced in the shift of pronouns from "we" (the people as defined by dominant social arrangements) to "I" (Whitman as site of the event, as channel of revolutionary potential) to "you" (the subjectivization of the event: the people as site and source of utopian praxis).

In serving as mediator of the Revolution, Whitman ensures that the people do not become identical to their present conditions, that they remain delivered over to utopian possibilities. In positioning himself this way, however, Whitman determines the constitution of the people to come. This determination includes the democratic content that circulates throughout the 1855 *Leaves* (the insistence on social equality, collective self-governance, and life in common), but it also includes the violences associated with American exceptionalism: settler colonialism, slavery, imperial power. As Donald Pease argues, Whitman's renewal of U.S. democracy is inextricable from colonial violence: "Whitman literally regenerated the US body politics out of the forgetting [of the Battle] of Goliad as an instance of colonial violence and the remembering of it as the site of the celebratory enunciation of his song."[51] The surplus potentiality that circulates in *Leaves* has as its condition of possibility not only the imperial acquisition of territory (Pease's example is the Mexican territory that would become Texas) but also the racialized division of peoples into those worthy of democratic life and those excluded from it. If Whitman's exemplification of America is what enables the political subjectivization of a life in common to occur, it's also the magnet to which threads of historical violence are attracted. This is not to suggest that this violence erases the utopian potential of Whitman's poetry. Instead, it foils exceptionalist visions of a redeemed America. Whitman's utopian praxis doesn't transcend contemporary material conditions so much as open a space of radical alterity within them. A singular America emerges both within and against American exceptionalism. In Whitman's case, this immanence means that he not only remembers colonial violence but also sometimes reinforces it. Even as his poetry introduces new forms of freedom, equality, and solidarity, it also lends itself to the consecration of empire.[52] It's worth recalling that as a figure of the American Renaissance, Whitman belongs not only to a moment of crisis—a moment when the United States longs for the Revolution's renewal—but also to the period during which the United States begins its ascent to global hegemony. Writers such as Whitman do not so much reflect this transitional period as *figure* it: They transform immanent historical tendencies into line of flights; they mine the present for futures that exceed or realize it. In the case of the American Renaissance, these futures include an overlapping array of social movements, ecstatic orgies, insurgencies, intentional communities, fugitive flights, colonial subjugation, bondage, and war.

Whitman's poem "I Sing the Body Electric" brings the dialectical intertwining of liberation and bondage, freedom and empire, to a fever pitch. I've already discussed how it elaborates a vitalism in which the power or life force of the people expresses itself in corporeal terms. The good body is a poetic body, a body that "conveys as much as the best poem . . . perhaps more." However, Whitman's vitalism finds its true test in how it reckons with the social condition of slavery. The well-known auction scenes concluding "I Sing the Body Electric" ask what it might mean to reframe a desire called America in terms of the social death of slavery. The central conceptual and poetic maneuver of these scenes consists in uncoupling constituent power from citizenship by incorporating the slave into the people:

> A slave at auction!
> I help the auctioneer . . . . the sloven does not half know his business.
>
> Gentlemen look on this curious creature,
> Whatever the bids of the bidders they cannot be high enough for him,
> For him the globe lay preparing quintillions of years without one animal or plant,
> For him the revolving cycles truly and steadily rolled.
>
> In that head the allbaffling brain,
> In it and below it the making of the attributes of heroes. (80–81)

In usurping the role of the auctioneer, Whitman sets up a dialectical reversal not unlike the one in "Song for Occupations." Whitman doesn't reduce the slave to the measure of the commodity. Instead, he articulates the immeasurability of the slave, or the irreducibility of the human to exchange. The passage frames this invaluable dimension in terms of a time beyond measure—"the quintillions of years" involved in "preparing" for the presence of this singular slave. The slave thus becomes the telos of democracy insofar as democracy names a life in common (a life without social division). This democratic vision would seem to require an egalitarian politics, for it implies another kind of materialist resurrection—the abolition of what Orlando Patterson terms slavery's social death.[53] The constitutive exclusion involved in citizenship gives way to an identification of politics with the remainder of the nation-state: The horizon of political possibility comes to coincide with slavery and its abolition. Put differently, it's precisely the slave's status as the abject element of liberal democracy, his occupation of the void in the political order, that enables Whitman to transform him into the future of a radically democratic America.

Whitman insists on the constitutive futurity of the slave, which is to say that the figure of the slave becomes nothing less than the symbolic and material horizon of a properly American utopianism. The slave becomes "not only one man . . . . He is the father of those who shall be fathers in their turns, / In him the start of populous states and rich republics, / Of him countless immortal lives with countless embodiments and enjoyments" (81). The immeasurable potentiality of the slave pluralizes itself; it is a matter now not only of the irreducibility of a body to the capitalist value-form but also of Black subjectivity as the condition of possibility for new nations. Constituent power no longer confines itself to the people, at least not to the people as defined by white supremacism. Whitman stumbles onto the para-ontology of blackness, that immense productivity of being excluded from Being—the generative force of singular existences that shadow forth from a zone of nonexistence.[54] Although Whitman doesn't directly participate in the aesthetics of the Black radical tradition, as envisioned by Fred Moten, he nevertheless lights onto one of its fundamental tenets, namely, that the power of Black life (as it emerges from slavery and its aftermath) consists in breaking the hold of ontology, in overturning life's predication on a division between Being (so often articulated in terms of whiteness and purity) and beings.[55] In many respects, the scene gives readers the most radical version of Whitman's democratic politics, for it links the reactualization of the Revolution to the success of abolition—the people only realizes itself by incorporating the constituent power of liberal democracy's remainder. At the same time, as Martin Klammer argues, one can also read this passage in terms of Whitman's personal support (along with Lincoln) for colonization schemes, that is, for the relocation of Black Americans to Africa following emancipation.[56] This interpretation reads the phrase "rich republics" in a literal manner, suggesting that Whitman in fact delineates two historical trajectories—one for whites in America, one for Blacks in Africa. This reading also highlights the eugenic dimension of Whitman's poetry, the way in which it reiterates a racialized hierarchy through a valorization of Black generativity. These ambiguities are irresolvable. It's not only that there are discrepancies between biography and poetry at play, here, but that the poetry itself is caught between marking the alterity of blackness in ontological terms and discovering in blackness the evental force of democracy. This irresolvability should be understood as a contradiction between Whitman's investment in slavery and his desire to abolish it. If Whitman profits from slavery in the sense that his condition as a white writer depends on the labor of enslaved masses, he also makes abolition the telos of democracy—the people realizes itself only through the eruption of blackness as constituent power.

Whitman's evental version of democracy serves as a corrective to his vitalist democracy, but one could just as well argue that it is only by way of Whitman's vitalism that the dream of Revolution maintains its faith in the people. There is no democracy to come without the people's flesh. In other words, Whitman's utopian praxis is rooted in the social. Political subjectivity surpasses the given social order only insofar as it realizes the surplus potentiality that belongs to sociality. In the 1855 *Leaves*, this surplus potentiality is the living labor or constituent power of the people—their power to reinvent themselves by reactualizing the Revolution. This surplus of life is inseparable from death. The utopian birth of a new people, of a people that would finally live up to itself, only comes about through the death of contemporary forms of life. In other words, Whitman's second version of democracy depends on the passage from one life to another—from one people to another—through a valley of death. Whitman's poetry thinks in biopolitical terms, because it neither escapes from life, nor settles into it. It seizes onto that element in life that is both void and surplus, impossibility and alterity, death and resurrection. There's no saintliness in this poetry, no standing above the body. Political subjectivity is one of the roughs—an American, no more and no less.

Whitman as Textual Commons for the Future

In times like these, one wonders what Whitman would have said. One wonders how he would have reckoned with the Trump era, how he would have suffered and struggled through the seeming extinction of America's utopian promise. The years after Obama's presidency would have been a massive letdown, not least because in President Obama's statesmanship Whitman would likely have heard echoes of his beloved President Lincoln. Of course, as Keeanga-Yamahtta Taylor reminds us, there were plenty of promises broken by the Obama administration, too.[57] Indeed, one should probably write the history of that desire called America as a series of broken promises, rather than trying to tally up its successes. But perhaps this approach is all wrong. Instead of asking what Whitman would have said, maybe we should instead consider how Whitman remains a resource not only for the present but for the future. With this in mind, Whitman is less a historical figure than he is a utopian horizon—a literary space in which the potential for a radical democracy finds sanctuary. Ben Lerner has described this sanctuary as a "textual commons for the future," a phrase that he elaborates as follows: "Walt Whitman is himself a *place* for the genuine, an open space or textual commons where American readers of the future can forge and renew their sense of possibility and interconnectedness."[58] To understand Whitman as a place of hope, as an abode sheltering a sense of political possibility and social connection, is to read Whitman for the future, to read him for that which in America is more than America—a singular America. It means avoiding the bitter consolation of imagining Whitman weeping at what the United States has become and instead laboring and fighting for an America in which commonality, equality, and liberty are inseparable from one another.

This chapter has presented the most radical political dimensions of Whitman's poetry. Whitman's two democracies offer a sense of the people as divided by its own utopian potential. There's the people and then there's the people, which is to say that there is life as status quo and a life to come, or nation as consecration of inequality and counter-nation as egalitarian rebirth of political subjectivity. At the same time, there are limits to Whitman's futurity, constitutive historical determinations circumscribing the social and political possibilities opened up by his textual commons. Whitman's utopian praxis depends on the conceptual-libidinal topos of America in a way that cannot help but reproduce American exceptionalism, even or especially when it gives life to a singular America. Whereas Burroughs could imagine two American political subjects—the Johnson Family (revolutionary outlaws) and the Shits (the bourgeoisie)—Whitman can imagine only an all-comprehending multitude. Whitman's utopian praxis would appear to limit, if not to foreclose, political antagonism by constricting the divisive force of political difference to a single subject: the people. I've already addressed some of the limits of Whitman's poetics of the merge, especially in regard to its complicity with empire and slavery, but it's worth recalling another. Whitman's valorization of the generativity of the common as a kind of masculine bravado risks repeating the marginalization of women in the antebellum United States. More specifically, Whitman's insistence on the unity of the people would seem to imply a blindness to the way in which the social reproduction of the United States depends on the subordination of women. The next chapter, on Emily Dickinson's poetry, shows how Dickinson contests this subordination not only by parodying patriarchy and heteronormativity but also by cultivating an alternative vision of America in the form of a queer, utopian separatism. This utopianism could not be more different from Whitman's in its emphasis on retreat, silence, and obscurity. If Whitman imagines utopia as an egalitarian orgy of continental proportions, Dickinson imagines it as two bees buzzing through a field of grass, enjoying unspoken pleasures.

CHAPTER 3

Nobody's Wife: Affective Economies of Marriage in Emily Dickinson

In an 1885 letter to Mabel Loomis Todd, Emily Dickinson ponders the social dimensions of a desire called America, not least of all its gendering.

> "Sweet Land of Liberty" is a superfluous Carol till it concern ourselves—then it outrealms the Birds.
> I saw the American Flag last Night in the shutting West, and I felt for every Exile.
> I trust you are homesick. That is the sweetest courtesy we pay an absent friend. The Honey you went so far to seek, I trust too you obtain.
> Though was not there a "Humbler" Bee?
> "I will sail by thee alone, thou animated Torrid Zone." . . .
> Touch Shakespeare for me.
> The Savior's only signature to the Letter he wrote to all mankind, was, A Stranger and ye took me in.[1]

Todd is summering in Europe when Dickinson writes this letter, a situation that provides Dickinson with the opportunity to meditate on America's libidinal pull. The "American Flag" encapsulates this desire in a symbolic object. In the distance between the old world and the new, Dickinson traces the path of the flag, as if it stood not only for national allegiance but also for a world-historical destiny. Not unlike Hegel's story of a westward-bound historical reason, the flag comes to rest in "the shutting West." It's tempting to read this trajectory with an emphasis on dusk, on the way in which Dickinson spots the flag as it fades into darkness. However, in doing so, one would also have to consider the cyclical rhythm of day and night, the way in which "the shutting West" is less a tomb than a crossroads—a place of repeated passage, a prelude to the coming of the sun. Dickinson assumes Todd is "homesick," she puts her "trust" in it; it's an act of faith, but this faith is backed by the guarantee of the flag's return. Just as the earth's rotation ensures the sun's reappearance, so too will Todd circle back to America, returning from exile to the soil the flag marks as home.

At the same time, even as Dickinson traces this exceptional circle of desire, she also undoes it by marking her exclusion from it. "'Sweet Land of Liberty' is a superfluous Carol till it concern ourselves—then it outrealms the Birds." Dickinson sends a letter across the Atlantic Ocean and, in doing so, she breaks the spell of American exceptionalism. She does so not by praising the deep roots of European culture—"Touch Shakespeare for me" is more ironic aside than sincere request—but by framing that desire called America as a promise that has not yet been kept. The letter makes a couple of Dickinson and Todd; it turns them into a pair abandoned by their nation, even as they are pulled westward by its symbols. This sense of abandonment culminates in the reference to "the Savior," an allusion to a scene in the biblical book of Matthew, in which Jesus is refused shelter, turned away because he is a stranger. "The Savior's only signature to the Letter he wrote to all mankind, was, A Stranger and ye took me in." Dickinson doesn't spurn a desire called America. Instead, she asks that it "concern" Todd and herself, that it live up to its liberatory promise through a kind of radical hospitality. Dickinson wants America to be a place for strangers, a home for those it has abandoned.

In a provocative gesture, Dickinson signs the letter to Todd not "Emily" but "America." In signing as the nation, or in countersigning the nation, Dickinson suggests that the political task at hand is not so much the abolition of a desire called America but its revision. That "concern" exceeds inclusion and recognition comes across in the way Dickinson imagines America taking flight. When America concerns itself with Dickinson and Todd, it "outrealms the Birds." Dickinson doesn't break the circular spell of the flag because she wants to integrate herself into America. She breaks it so as to convert America into something more than itself. In the phrase "outrealms the Birds," one should hear not only a wish to compete with our avian brethren but also an unworking of sovereignty—a decoupling of national desire from state sovereignty. A singular America takes place in Dickinson's letter as a counter-nation in which two women turn toward America only insofar as America makes good on its "Carol" of liberty.

This chapter reads a series of Dickinson's poems—those that might be called her marriage poems—as practices of outrealming liberty. These poems perform the diurnal rhythms of national desire in the household; they show how domestic sentiment reproduces the national body politic in the spatial figure of "Home." They also parody the heteronormative and patriarchal institution of marriage, introducing discontent with the status quo as a means of reimagining society. In many respects, Dickinson's marriage poems can be read as social reproduction theory, which is to say as a theoretical practice grappling with the various ways in which the reproduction of households through so-called domestic labor structures capitalist society. Dickinson's poems reveal how the sexual division of labor in and outside of the household is integral to national sovereignty; how the figure of the housewife functions as a libidinal trap, conscripting people into the position of national and capitalist subjects; and how the daily rhythms of marriage are not simply a mirror of the daily grind but also a failure of social and political imagination. In short, Dickinson's poetry addresses itself to a biopolitics of marriage, a meshwork of power that includes sentiment, chores, religious rituals, demography, state policies, and a slew of other practices integrating romance, eroticism, labor, and nation.

Dickinson's poetry does more than demystify, however. It also composes a queer sort of coupling, an erotic relationality that echoes the rituals of marriage only insofar as it overturns them. This is the positive dimension of outrealming liberty, the utopianism immanent in its critique. Dickinson converts the discontent with marriage into the basis of a queer romance in which the bond between partners no longer takes the form of duty or obligation but preference or inclination. It's a genre of autonomy that makes a virtue of contingency, that substitutes the fleeting pleasures of secrecy for the permanent spectacle of sovereignty. Secrecy, in this context, has less to do with the closet than with the power to withdraw from normative social structures. Dickinson secretes queer passion into her poems, and, in turn, her poems constitute zones of opacity, or what Foucault terms heterotopias—"counter-emplacements, kinds of effectively real utopias in which the real emplacements, all the other real emplacements that one finds in culture's interior are at once represented, contested, and inverted."[2] In poems such as "I'm Nobody! Who are you?" Dickinson transforms the troubling void in the marriage complex into a surplus of potentiality: What cannot be recognized in the reproduction of the nation—truly queer desire—becomes the possibility of a noncapitalist, nonheteronormative sociality.

To read Dickinson this way is to acknowledge that she's as much a materialist as a metaphysician—a queer materialist, perhaps, but a materialist nevertheless. For all of its attention to theological niceties, Dickinson's poetry concerns itself with sensuous textures, not least of all the matters and metabolisms of nonhuman nature. Birds, bees, spiders, grass, and trees populate her poems as thickly as if she were writing a treatise on natural history. Even Dickinson's seemingly sentimental musings on domesticity include architectural details that entrench the bourgeois home in infrastructures of brick and mortar. In short, the speculative orientation in Dickinson's poetry is inextricable from her ongoing investigation into the material economies that make up nineteenth-century social life in the United States. In what follows, I argue that Dickinson's poetry can be understood as a critical labor on the affective economies of marriage, meaning that her poetry shows how what we usually call emotion, sentiment, or feeling is an element in a complex ideological apparatus that produces subjects for the nation-state and capital. Dickinson theorizes the social reproduction of America by decomposing and recomposing the affects, feelings, and sentiments that make love into a labor, and labor into love. This affective approach builds on the materialist insights of manuscript studies and the New Historicism in Dickinson scholarship, but it does so at a slant.[3] Instead of focusing on social and historical context or on the circulation of manuscripts, I'm more interested in the ways Dickinson's poetry constitutes a material practice that not only dissects the affective composition of the bourgeoisie but also crafts queer modes of relationality in which social life reproduces itself in nonnormative terms. Of course, contextual and manuscript matters inform Dickinson's lyric practice, but the temporal and spatial scales on which her poetry operates exceed the constraints not only of the nineteenth-century Amherst in which Dickinson lived but also of the aesthetic domain of the poem. Dickinson's poetry, I argue, has something to say about the social reproduction of capitalism in the contemporary moment, especially about how the so-called feminization of labor in the service sector still relies on the heteronormative and patriarchal affective economies of the nineteenth century.

This chapter analyzes what might be thought of as the two faces of Dickinson's marriage poems: the killjoy and the nobody. The killjoy insists on her right to be unhappy; she parodies domestic bliss, allowing her vicious laughter to echo throughout the cushioned rooms of the bourgeois household. She objects to the marriage between capitalism and patriarchy, and she bemoans the reduction of woman to wife. The killjoy interrupts the affective economy of the household by exposing how it exploits women in the name of national prosperity. She is a voice of refusal, and this refusal takes place not for the sake of a better home and garden but in the hopes of radically transforming the affects, social relations, and political conducts involved in living together. In other words, Dickinson seeks to redefine what it means to couple. She does so by inventing a form of life irreducible to the housewife. This is the nobody: a queer figure who turns the refusal of domestic bliss into another way of sharing a life. The nobody disidentifies from the nation-state and capital; she composes a counter-nation of singular beings who reject gendered exceptionalism, cultivate a generosity in excess of bourgeois thrift, and touch one another with an erotic intensity that knows no secure boundaries. "Till it concerns ourselves—then it outrealms the Birds." Whereas Whitman writes poems that affirm the nation's limitless promise, Dickinson dwells in the betrayal of national promise. She composes a counter-nation, small but intense, secret but tactile. She writes a commons in which women refuse to play wife.

Housewives and Killjoys

Dickinson's marriage poems trace a trajectory from the housewife to the killjoy, which is to say that they articulate a political passage from the social reproduction of the housewife to the malcontent who rejects domestic bliss. Although comparing Dickinson to Marxist feminists such as Selma James, Mariarosa Dalla Costa, and Silvia Federici might seem odd, they not only share an object of critique—the housewife as subject of social reproduction—but also a commitment to popping the balloon of bourgeois romance. Love, these thinkers demonstrate, costs a great deal, especially for the women to whom affection has been assigned as a labor and a duty. Dickinson shares with these feminists the viewpoint of social reproduction, a viewpoint, as Maya Gonzalez explains, that recognizes that

> not only is all labor "unpaid" and yet appears to be paid for the work it actually performs, but that this fetish inherent to the wage-relation and our very understanding of justice requires that all life outside of work appear absolutely "free" of work for capital. However, for those who are given the duty of reproduction in this sphere of life, as their biologically determined role, there are no illusions as to its "worklike" character.[4]

The illusion that the reproduction of the household is not really work, that despite all appearances it is merely an act of love, is a necessary condition of capitalism and a point of political contestation. One could describe this as a conflict over the visibility of social reproduction, but one would have to qualify this assessment by acknowledging that what's at stake has as much to do with affect and desire as epistemology. Dickinson's marriage poems struggle with the invisibility of housework less in epistemological terms than in affective terms. Not only does Dickinson investigate the production of the housewife as a biopolitical figure integral to the reproduction of nation-state and capital. She also offers readers the killjoy—in Sara Ahmed's words, the one who exercises "the freedom to be unhappy," "to live a life that deviates from the paths of happiness," "to cause unhappiness by acts of deviation."[5] Dickinson's poetry doesn't simply represent the bourgeois household and its social pathologies. It outrealms liberty by offering the freedom to be unhappy with domestic bliss.

Dickinson's critique of the housewife begins by inspecting the conflation of woman and wife, or the way in which becoming a proper woman entails conscription into the capitalist system of social reproduction.

> She rose to His Requirement—dropt
> The Playthings of Her Life
> To take the honorable Work
> Of Woman, and of Wife—[6]

These few lines already intimate the outlines of the political economy of marriage in the nineteenth-century United States. It's not simply that womanhood, or normative femininity, depends on the opposition between "honorable Work" and "Playthings," but that the entire teleological course running from girlhood to womanhood orients itself around "His Requirement." Becoming-wife implies giving oneself over to another; it requires a sacrifice of childish pursuits for the sake of earning a place in the system of social reproduction. The "honor" associated with the labor of the housewife has to do with its being unwaged. The absence of the wage, the fact that her work is unpaid, lends it the air of sacred duty. It suggests a realm in excess of the factory or the office, a place of pleasure, comfort, peace, and rest. In "drop[ping]/The Playthings of Her Life," she not only becomes "Wife" but also transforms into the foundation of the household, not just the material complement of the workplace but also a site of libidinal compensation for the daily grind. In sum, the housewife is a crucial biopolitical technology in the nineteenth century, first, because in taking care of the household—in performing daily chores, managing family activities, raising children, and so on—she produces and reproduces the labor power on which capital depends, and, second, because, in addition to managing the material reproduction of the labor force, she also manages its affective and libidinal life, converting the quotidian rhythms of the workday into the sweet hum of providence. The rhyme between "Wife" and "Life" is no coincidence; it is a sign not only of the housewife's role in maintaining the life of the nation but also of her duty to do so with a smile. Marriage, this rhyme suggests, should have all the euphony of a well-constructed poem.

Dickinson's critique of the political economy of marriage doesn't simply demystify the housewife's role as unpaid labor. It also parodies the material and affective exchanges required to reproduce capitalism. Dickinson's poems dealing with marriage are linguistic zones of commerce through which women, money, law, and labor traffic in a complex and contradictory manner. Take the following poem, for instance.

> I gave Myself to Him—
> And took Himself, for Pay—
> The solemn contract of a Life
> Was ratified, this way—
>
> The Wealth might disappoint—
> Myself a poorer prove
> Than this great Purchaser suspect,
> The Daily Own—of Love
>
> Depreciate the Vision—
> But till the Merchant buy—
> Still Fable—in the Isles of spice—
> The subtle Cargoes—lie—
>
> At least—'tis Mutual—Risk—
> Some—found it—Mutual Gain—
> Sweet Debt of Life—Each Night to owe—
> Insolvent—every Noon— (426)

The poem describes marriage as an heteronormative exchange generating "the solemn contract of a Life," meaning that Dickinson's verse doesn't just parody the symbolic act of exchanging vows but also dissects the long-term social and economic implications of entering into the bond of marriage. The parallelism of the first two lines seems to indicate an equal exchange between two autonomous subjects—"myself" for "himself." The economic language of the poem extends this instant of exchange into the ongoing time of financial investment: Ideally, marriage is "Mutual Gain," an endeavor in which one receives a return on one's investment of time and energy. However, marriage, like any other investment, may just as well return a loss. "Risk" is intrinsic to any sort of exchange involving promise, expectation, and the deferral of profits, so that just as a ship involved in the spice trade might wreck at sea, so too might a marriage run aground. The poem can thus be read as an attempt to assess this risk, to calculate the discrepant ways in which husband and wife bear the risks and rewards involved in coupling.

The temporality of the poem is even more complex than this logic of risk and reward suggests, however. This complexity becomes evident in the tense shifts from verse to verse: The poem starts with the simple past tense in the first stanza but then alternates between present and future tenses in the next three stanzas. This transition from punctual instant to recursive loop between presence and expectation makes sense. It's nothing but the verb-form of marriage—a moment of "solemn contract" that gives way to the ongoing labors and expectations involved in living as a couple or a family. However, this ongoing loop becomes complicated by the superimposition of the long-term rhythm of mercantile trade (the voyage to "the Isles of spice" and back) onto the shorter term intervals of days spent performing chores and exchanging signs of affection ("Each Night," "every Noon"). The cycles of transatlantic trade and household reproduction support one another. The former provides the latter with commodities such as sugar, tea, and coffee—all of which are raw materials that the housewife transforms into the elements of domestic satisfaction. At the same time, there's an incommensurability between these scales, a tension between the linear protraction of the ship crossing the Atlantic and the incessant repetition of daily life in the bourgeois home. Adventures at sea don't quite fit into the cramped constraints of brick and mortar. The poem registers this disjunction in its rhyme and meter. The poem's meter is regular (iambic trimeter in the first, second, and fourth lines of each stanza, broken up by iambic tetrameter in the third), suggesting the daily rhythms of marriage, but its rhyme scheme is erratic: The second and fourth lines of the first and third stanza compose perfect rhymes, but the second stanza produces a slant rhyme at best, and the fourth stanza makes no attempt to rhyme at all. The acoustics of the poem cross difference with repetition, or regularity with chance, to form an heterogeneous assemblage of moments, durations, loops, and interruptions. It's as if the poem were trying to make the complex temporalities of capitalism audible, as if it were trying to sound out the exchanges between the household and global capital.

The figure of the housewife is what keeps this tangle of timelines running. It's the housewife that bridges the gap between the different scales of circulation, ensuring the smooth reproduction of labor for capital. In formal terms, one can speak of this virtual housewife as the voice of the poem. It's the voice of the poem that binds the discrepant temporalities, scales, and rhetorical figures into a unified linguistic act. Voice is the absent cause of the poem; it is the material trace of the act of enunciation. Put differently, voice is the necessary fiction of a body having spoken the poem. There's a homology, here, between Marx's understanding of labor power and Roland Barthes's articulation of the grain of the voice. Labor power names both the physical body of the laborer and the capacity to labor; it is the unity of objective materiality and subjective potentiality.[7] Likewise, Barthes elaborates the grain of the voice as "meaning in its potential voluptuousness": "The 'grain' is the body in the voice as it sings, the hand as it writes, the limb as it performs."[8] The grain of the voice has less to do with meaning or communication than with sensuous potentiality; it names all of those qualities that belong to an aesthetic practice without being reducible to the objective dimensions of form or content. It is, one might say, the poem's mode of expression. In the case of Dickinson's poem, this mode of expression implies not only a fragile synthesis of the discrepant scales of global capitalism but also the power to keep things going, or to make them grind to a halt.

"I gave Myself to Him," I'm arguing, is not only a poem *about* labor but also a poem *of* labor. It doesn't simply represent the social reproduction of capitalism. It rehearses the affective and symbolic labors involved in producing the housewife as material foundation of capitalism. The invisibility of the housewife's labor—its being passed off as sacred duty—is an ideological necessity: Capitalism requires what Silvia Federici terms *the patriarchy of the wage*, or the exclusion of women from the wage and their consequent subjection to the wage-earning power of men; this subjection, far from removing women from the circuits of capitalism, sacrifices women to the never-ending compulsion to (re)produce labor power, to take care of the household.[9] Dickinson's marriage poems are so politically loaded because they target the affective complex through which reproductive labor comes to appear as nothing but an act of love. "I gave Myself to Him" offers a name for this ideological sleight of hand: "Sweet Debt of Life." The life of a wife is a life of debt. It's a life split from itself—a life split not only from libidinal fulfillment but also from survival or subsistence—insofar as the conditions of the housewife depend on the husband as creditor. If both partners appear at first glance to share the risk of the marriage venture equally, it's only the wife whose life is on credit, only the wife who is under the scrutiny of a "great Purchaser." This semantic asymmetry contradicts the syntactical parallelism of the poem's opening lines; it transforms the wife from business partner into commodity and, in doing so, it makes explicit the connections between compulsory heterosexuality and the capitalist regime of private property. Becoming-wife means giving oneself over to "The Daily Own—of Love," to love as a practice of ownership. It implies conscription into a system of reproduction in which love is a labor, care is a duty, and the husband's satisfaction the ultimate object.

"I gave Myself to Him" demonstrates not merely the chance that marriage might end in ruin but, more important, the structural inequality of marriage understood as a patriarchal and heteronormative institution. This inequality makes itself felt subtly in the poem's first lines, with the innocent "mistake" of a reflexive pronoun ("himself") where, grammatically speaking, there should be a simple object pronoun ("him"): "I gave Myself to Him/And took Himself, for Pay—" Although this substitution might seem insignificant, it actually homes in on the specific object of the poem's critique, namely, the affective economy of the household. "Himself" designates less the person than the person's relation to himself (the conjunction of the "him" and the "self"). It marks the exchange of vows as the entry point into a field of relations in which the circulation of global capital links up with emotions in the household. These relations include interpersonal relations, as well as relations to oneself, but they exceed and undermine the psychological subject. Discussions of interpersonal relations and emotion tend to presume a preconstituted individual whose interior domain constitutes a reserve of true feeling. They rely on an idea of personhood whose genealogy stretches back to ancient and early modern concepts of legal culpability and citizenship. In other words, they depend on presuppositions connected to the concept of sovereignty and to the desire to monopolize political power in the form of the state.[10] In contrast, Dickinson's marriage poems do not presume the figures of husband and wife, they rehearse their production. They push aside fictions of the autonomous subject in favor of unrolling an intricate fabric of preindividual relations and forces. Husband and wife are neither cause nor origin of this assemblage but effects of it; they are arrangements of material sensations and the ideas of these sensations in the historically specific situation of capitalism.

Although I've described Dickinson's marriage poems as dissecting the political economy of marriage, they might more accurately be described as attempts to dismantle the *affective* economy of marriage. It's not so much that Dickinson lacks the conceptual terminology of political economy but rather that her critique of political economy takes place on affective grounds. Ahmed defines affective economy as a process of circulation through which objects (including the subjects of capitalism) take shape as bearers of value: "Affect does not reside in an object or sign, but is an affect of the circulation between objects and signs (= the accumulation of affective value over time)."[11] Moreover, affects don't just circulate between bodies, they also generate the surfaces or contours of bodies, by making "sticky" (read: habitual) our relations to other objects in the world. In other words, the composition of social bodies depends on the repetition of encounters, as well as on the values and meanings attached to these encounters: "The accumulation of affective value shapes the surfaces of bodies and worlds."[12] Affects compose subjects over time, by orienting their material relations and encoding those relations with specific values. For example, the angel in the household—a figure of bourgeois femininity in the nineteenth century—can be parsed as an assemblage of affects including piety, devotion, and compassion. These affects designate not only emotions but also the material vectors that orient beings toward one another in specific manners. The housewife, then, might be understood as a geometrical figure composed of material vectors (affects) that sustain the household for the sake of capitalism and the nation-state.[13]

"I gave Myself to Him" shows how the affective economy of marriage transforms women into the material substrate of bourgeois satisfaction. In becoming-wife, the lyric subject of the poem receives the husband as affective creature ("Himself"), while delivering herself over to him as object. Whereas she offers herself up body and soul, he offers only gated access to his emotional life. A variant version of the poem highlights this inequality, the first two lines reading not "I gave myself to Him—/And took Himself, for Pay—" but rather "I gave Him *all* Myself/And took Himself, for Pay."[14] It is her duty to care for him, to sustain the labor power of which he is the bearer. Moreover, she must do so not as an equal partner but as the sentimental matrix that binds the household together. She must give it her "all," which is to say she must not only perform her labors but do so with a smile. Housework includes not only the obvious material chores of cooking, cleaning, and laundry but also the no less material affective labor of maintaining a happy home. The poem describes this affective order of compulsion in terms of "Vision": "Myself a poorer prove/Than this great Purchaser suspect,/The Daily Own—of Love/Depreciate the Vision." "The Daily Own—of Love" not only implies the conflation of property and sentiment but also a surveillance culture in which a wife must prove herself to her husband by maintaining the promise—"the Vision"—of happiness. It's a cycle of self-sacrifice in the name of reproducing a bourgeois fantasy of satisfaction. She not only exists for his pleasure; she exists as the material basis of his fantasy life. She's the affective medium through which he converts the future into something that can be grasped. "Vision" thus brings together the specularization of woman—her transformation into a spectacle imbued with romance and adventure—and the identification of woman with futurity, with hope. It is woman as voice of the poem that secures the unity of pleasure and futurity, transforming unpredictable risk into the measured hope of love's labors. The lyric dimension of the poem, its linguistic extravagance, cannot be separated from the bourgeois fantasy of the happy household. It is as if the poem's rhetorical flourishes were signs of the strenuous effort involved in playing wife.

In this context, happiness is more than a feeling of contentment. It is a meta-affect, a political mechanism that captures and organizes affects for the sake of social reproduction. Happiness generates social ease, the sense that things are operating smoothly. As Ahmed explains, happiness is "an orientation toward objects we come in contact with": "Things become good, or acquire their value as goods, insofar as they point toward happiness. Objects become 'happiness means.'"[15] The fantasy of domestic bliss structures the lifeworld of capitalism into a series of good and bad object choices. Happiness maps society in terms of what positively contributes to its reproduction. It also frames deviations from the pursuit of happiness as obstacles needing to be eliminated or assimilated. Insofar as happiness comes to be associated with the heteronormative family, queer life can appear only as trouble. The framework of heteronormative happiness asks (sometimes explicitly, sometimes implicitly) whether queer folks wouldn't be happier if they were straight. Alternatively, it incorporates queerness into the rituals of heteronormativity, inviting non-normative subjects to own, or own up to, some version of bourgeois satisfaction—as, for example, in the assumption that same-sex partners not only want to be able to marry one another but also that they should want to do so. Happiness is compulsory. It is a fundamental axiom of social existence, because one's not even allowed to question the value, conditions, or consequences of happiness. Happiness is more than feeling satisfied. It's the political regulation of social reproduction.

The housewife is a biopolitical technology for managing happiness. It codes women as caregivers and moral guardians, transforming femininity into the ongoing labor of maintaining capitalist society. A 1790 article from *Columbian Magazine*, "The Influence of the Female Sex on the Enjoyments of Social Life," spells out this role in detail:

> Cultivation of the female mind is of great importance, not with respect to private happiness only, but with respect to society at large. The ladies have it in their power to form the manners of the gentlemen, and they can render them virtuous and happy, or vicious and miserable. What a glorious prize is here exhibited, to be contended for by the sex![16]

Happiness and virtue are knit together. What's good *feels* good. Pleasure and virtue are the two sides of the good life, and the possibility of both depends on the "influence of the female sex," or a wife's ability to shape her husband's "manners," to absorb the stress of capitalist competition, converting it into the ease of domestic bliss. It is her responsibility to ensure that her husband is "virtuous and happy," not "vicious and miserable," and, as the exhortation of the final sentence suggests, the wife should *enjoy* this duty. She should find her happiness in the "glorious prize" of her "sex." In short, the role of the housewife entails not only the labor of satisfying others but also the requirement of being happy with one's own position as a "happiness means."

I've already suggested that the phrase "Sweet Debt of Life" gestures toward the elision of housework from the capitalist point of view, or the sleight of hand through which the labor of social reproduction comes to appear no more than an act of love. However, the phrase also describes the more general condition of the housewife as what Marx terms the "virtual pauper," a figure of subjectivity that is without value only insofar as it is also the source of value.[17] It is precisely because the housewife doesn't receive a wage, because her labor is unpaid, that she constitutes the core of capitalism. Her wagelessness subsidizes the wage, by allowing capital to save on the costs of maintaining its labor force. Federici again:

> Housework is much more than house cleaning. It is servicing the wage earners physically, emotionally, sexually, getting them ready for work day after day.... This means that behind every factory, behind every school, behind every office or mine, there is the hidden work of millions of women who have consumed their life, their labor, producing the labor power that works in those factories, schools, offices, or mines.[18]

Of course, the wagelessness of this hidden work also generates the housewife's dependency on her husband; it compels her to rely on a man for her material well-being. "Sweet Debt" describes an infinite cycle of service and subordination to capital and its flag-bearer, the husband: "Sweet Debt of Life—Each Night to owe—/ Insolvent—every Noon—" The promise of happiness is advanced as a line of affective credit, the repayment of which comes in the form of the wife's repeated sacrifice of herself to her husband. The poem alludes to the sex act, to the wife's offering her body up "Each Night," but the offering never satisfies or settles accounts. She's always left "Insolvent," as if the price of her body were only enough to pay the interest, never the principal, on her "Sweet Debt." Indeed, her insolvency is necessary to the marriage, because the impossibility of repayment implies the ceaseless renewal of the social bond. Insofar as the housewife constitutes the heart of capitalism, her endless duties guarantee its future. She is the affective-material nexus ensuring the continuity between capitalism's historical conquests and its never-ending speculations on the future.

To conclude my reading of "I gave Myself to Him" with the housewife's endless servitude would be to ignore the poem's central political gesture, namely, the passage from the housewife to the killjoy. The poem doesn't content itself with describing or representing the normative model of social reproduction. In calling attention to the pain, anxiety, and loss experienced by the housewife, it cultivates unhappiness, a sense that all is not right with the world. One hears a hint of this discontent in the line, "At least—'tis Mutual—Risk."[19] "At least" cannot help but call attention to loss, to what might have been or perhaps still could be. One might say that the poem as labor, as affective practice, calls into question the labor of social reproduction represented by the poem. It does so not by resolving the contradictions among capitalism's scales, nor by finally settling accounts with the marriage ledger, but rather by presenting the housewife's anxiety as a line of fracture immanent in social reproduction. The housewife frets under her husband's scrutiny; she worries that "the Vision" might "depreciate," that "The Wealth might disappoint—/Myself a poorer prove/Than this great Purchaser suspect." This anxiety speaks to the existential and material burden borne by the housewife. It represents an experience of suffering, deprivation, and sacrifice. However, it also suggests the possibility of insubordination. Anxiety congregates around those points where the promise of happiness is betrayed as a form of coercion. It emerges from the gap between the role of the housewife and a woman's desires, feelings, needs, and hopes. As such, anxiety traces a path toward the housewife's defection from capitalist reproduction; it draws a line from the temporality of cyclical repetition to the punctuality of political rupture. Anxiety, then, is more than worry, more than the concern that the voyage of marriage might end in a shipwreck. It *is* the shipwreck, at least potentially. Anxiety articulates in positive form an excess of desire over the promise of happiness. It marks the immanent fault lines in the capitalist reproduction of society.

Discontent, then, is not a failure on the part of Dickinson's poetry. It is its modus operandi. If the housewife is the figure that converts the labor of social reproduction into an act of love and, in doing so, sustains the social promise of happiness, then the killjoy is the figure that transforms the anxiety of marriage into the potential of political subversion. The killjoy objects to happiness. She criticizes the terms on which happiness is promised. She embodies negativity as a positive force, meaning that her negation of normative models of social reproduction involves its own pleasures and its own socialities. As Ahmed writes: "There is solidarity in recognizing our alienation from happiness, even if we do not inhabit the same place (as we do not). There can even be joy in killing joy. And kill joy, we must and we do."[20] In Dickinson, the killjoy's pleasures revolve around sarcasm, parody, and irony. It is the pleasure in watching the world burn, in laughing at the destruction of the patriarchal and heteronormative order of things. It is also the pleasure of deviant forms of syntax, of dashes that break the laws of grammar and of rhetorical figures so extravagant that they challenge common sense. Finally, Dickinson's killjoys are the figures through which an alternative sociality emerges—a commons that rejects patriarchy, nationalism, and capitalism in favor of a queer form of relationality.

Although the housewife is surely a capitalist subject, she is no less a subject of the nation-state, a figure through which the nation and its administrative apparatuses take on concrete form. The housewife is one of the crucial libidinal objects of the nation-state, because she turns allegiance into what might seem an abstract entity into an affective bond that includes affection, care, hope, and love. One might sum up what's at stake in this equation of nation-state and housewife through Lauren Berlant's concept of national sentimentality, which she defines as "a rhetoric of promise that a nation can be built across fields of social difference through channels of affective identification and empathy," as well as an "antipolitical politics," "a politics that abjures politics, made on behalf of a private life protected from the harsh realities of power."[21] If the feminist slogan "the personal is political" calls attention to the power dynamics involved in the most intimate arenas of social life, national sentimentality's slogan is "the political is personal"—a sentence that reduces politics to a narrow range of emotions ruled over by the nuclear family. Even today, the housewife—especially the housewife as mother—remains a mechanism for depoliticizing the conditions of social reproduction. Dickinson's poetry responds to national sentimentality not by replacing affect and emotion with a properly political rationality. Instead, Dickinson deploys critical affects; she mobilizes feelings of discontent that interrupt the smooth flow of identification and empathy, that mark the social contradictions embedded in national feeling, and that reorient beings toward other kinds of social relations.

The difficulty of analyzing these critical affects has to do with their relationship with parody. Most of Dickinson's marriage poems mimic the bourgeois satisfaction that they criticize, so that discontent emerges not so much from the content of the poem, nor from distinct formal elements, but from the tone of the poem, from its mood and its voice. If voice is the material trace of the act of enunciation, then the poem's mood might be understood as the feeling of voice, or, to borrow from Barthes again, as "meaning in its potential voluptuousness." Critical affects emerge from the potentiality of the poem, from its power of sensuous expression. Given that potentiality withholds itself from actuality—that, by definition, potentiality suspends what *is* in favor of what might *become*—the power of these critical affects becomes most evident in the ways in which Dickinson's marriage poems grapple with time. In other words, the killjoy's discontent appears in those moments in Dickinson's poetry when the different rhythms of social life collide. In "I gave Myself to Him," it is the disjunction between the timeline of transatlantic trade and the cycle of household reproduction that provides the occasion for considering the disappointment of the marriage bond. Unhappiness stems from the anxiety involved in bridging the gaps between these temporalities, in trying to harmonize the discrepant scales of capitalism.

Perhaps the most consistent critical affect in Dickinson's marriage poems is a sense of losing the future. The life of the wife becomes a kind of death, a living death but a death nonetheless. Her daily labors to maintain the household evoke a perpetual sameness; they imply the eclipse of change by a kind of numbness.

I'm "wife"—I've finished that—
That other state—
I'm Czar—I'm "Woman" now—
It's safer so—

How odd the Girl's life looks
Behind this soft Eclipse—
I think that Earth feels so
To folks in Heaven—now—

This being comfort—then
That other kind—was pain—

> But Why compare?
> I'm "Wife"! Stop there! (225)

Even as the present tense refrain of "I'm 'wife,'" "I'm 'Woman,'" "I'm 'Wife'" insists on marriage as an irreversible, life-changing event, the poem engages in the very act of comparison that it seems to forbid ("But Why compare?"). The kernel of the poem is the metaphor according to which marriage is not life but afterlife—a condition in which one gazes back on an earth from which one has departed. Life on earth, then, is the "pain" of the third stanza and afterlife the "comfort." The symbolic death that is marriage functions as a release of tension, a discharge of the excitement that plagues the living. The poem even ends on a note of cessation, the iambic foot of the last line leaving the reader with an abrupt halt: "I'm 'Wife'! Stop there!" The exclamation point, with its downward stroke, visualizes the cutting off of life, like a fence blocking woman's passage beyond the role of wife. The life of a wife is static; it has all the vitality of a corpse, or an angel.

The poem's tone, however, is less melancholy than sarcastic. The same exclamation points that seem to shut the door on a woman becoming something more than a wife mixes dissatisfaction with willful disbelief. The poem's focus is less on the metaphor of marriage as death or afterlife than on the failure of that metaphor, its inability to cover over the gap between woman and wife. "But Why compare?" gives the lie to the poem's semblance of surrender: The question is no mere rhetorical gesture but a redoubling of the poem's efforts to mark the distance between wife and woman. The poem gazes not at the life to which it's been confined but at "that other state," "that other kind." Although the poem seems to suggest a necessary path leading from a "Girl's life" to the life of a wife, the quotation marks surrounding "woman" and "wife" ironically fissure the smooth transitions from one stage of womanhood to another. These scare quotes indicate the arbitrariness, or social contingency, involved in yoking together woman, wife, and girl. The otherness of "that other state," the "odd[ness]" of a life before the wife, strikes a dissonant chord within the rhythm of social reproduction. It signals that something is missing in the life of a wife—the future. For not only does the poem "soft[ly] eclipse" the future tense, but the repetition of "now" and "so" suggest that the present is but an endless parade of social niceties. "Comfort" thus names the dreadful finitude of futurity foreclosed. It designates happiness understood as the bourgeois passion for national security, capitalist prosperity, and a woman in her proper place.

What makes Dickinson a killjoy is not simply that she calls into question the role of the housewife or the political order of marriage. It's that, in doing so, she calls attention to the possibility for another kind of social relation—another way of inhabiting the world. The feeling of losing the future, then, belongs less to melancholy than to utopian aspiration. It's synonymous with a sense that something is missing from the present.[22] In staging the eclipse of girlhood, or the annihilation of potentiality in a gendered form, Dickinson's poems become placeholders for futurity—proof that patriarchy, nationalism, heteronormativity, and capitalism are not all that is possible. Girlhood is a figure for a liberty that outrealms the American status quo. It is synonymous with Dickinson's signature "America," which is another way of saying that it calls forth a counter-nation that would "concern" not only housewives but also all of those deviant women who laugh at bourgeois propriety. In sum, Dickinson does not just reveal the way in which happiness disguises the labors of social reproduction; she also lends her voice to the occluded social potentiality of women. She gathers the subversive possibilities hidden in the household's shadows. She asks what happens when women refuse to play wife.

"Afraid to Own a Body"

The critical viewpoint of social reproduction finds one of its most concerted political expressions in the Wages for Housework movement of the 1970s. Founded in Italy by the International Feminist Collective—a group that included Selma James, Silvia Federici, and Mariarosa Dalla Costa, among others—the International Wages for Housework Campaign revised the Marxist critique of political economy by expanding its focus to include not only the exploitation of waged labor but also of unwaged labor. As it spread from Italy to the United Kingdom and the United States, the campaign asked what it would mean to take seriously the claim that housework is *work*, that so-called domestic labor is no less important to capital than factory labor.[23] Some of this position's implications have already been discussed, not least of all how it demystifies bourgeois romance. The viewpoint of social reproduction also highlights the depths to which capitalism penetrates social life, not only compelling the housewife to perform the duties of caring for the labor force but to do so with a smile. Social reproduction produces subjectivity; it organizes social relations on affective grounds, directing husband, wife, and children not simply to do this or that but to feel happy about it. To demand wages for housework, then, is only apparently a request for monetary compensation. As Federici makes clear, it's more a matter of demanding that social reproduction in general and the role of women in particular radically change: "If we start from this analysis [of the subordination of the unwaged housewife to the waged male laborer] we can see the revolutionary implications of the demand for wages for housework. *It is the demand by which our nature ends and our struggle begins because just to want wages for housework means to refuse that work as the expression of our nature*, and therefore to refuse precisely the female role that capital has invented for us."[24]

Emily Dickinson may not be a revolutionary in the conventional sense, but her poetry nonetheless resonates with the Wages for Housework movement in its refusal of capitalist social reproduction. Dickinson's poems do not simply represent social reproduction from a critical perspective; they also reckon with the implications of capitalism for the bodies of the poet, the reader, and the poem. In particular, Dickinson's poetry inquires into the ways in which the senses—including not only the five senses but also the faculty for language—have been transformed into private property watched over by the state. This inquiry often appears as an anxiety over embodiment, as, for example, when Dickinson writes in a letter to Abiah Root: "I do not care for the body, I love the timid soul . . . it hides for it is afraid, and the bold, obtrusive body."[25] This anxiety cannot be separated from the political and metaphysical framing of the sovereign subject as a masculine soul who lords over a feminine body. As numerous feminist critics have explained, women are not simply associated with bodily activity, especially sex and childbirth. They are often reduced to it by the ideological apparatuses of capital and the state. One need only consider right-wing depictions of the so-called Welfare Queen, imagined as a monstrous breeding machine who saps the nation's life. Or, alternatively, one might think about the ways in which pregnant women are surveilled in the name of the fetus's well-being. In constituting the material substrate of social reproduction under capitalism, women become nonsubjects exposed to the administrative power of the state and capital by the very fact of their embodiment.

Dickinson's anxiety over embodiment is not a general fear of physicality but rather a sense of disenchantment with the reduction of women to reproductive machinery. Given that so many of Dickinson's poems revolve around sensuous pleasures—for instance, the joyous flight of birds or the tactile luxury of the printed page—Karen Sánchez-Eppler is absolutely correct in arguing that "Dickinson's fantasy of a fleshless liberty constantly collides with the sensual desire for a fully palpable freedom."[26] Dickinson find herself caught in a double bind: To be embodied is to be in service to another—it is to surrender, or to be compelled to surrender, autonomy for the sake of the normative reproduction of society; at the same time, to be free in liberal-capitalist terms is to abandon the pleasures of the body—it is to exchange the joys of the flesh for the one-dimensional abstractions associated with wage labor and citizenship. This double bind is at the heart of liberalism, understood as a gendered and racialized philosophy for managing capitalist social relations. However, as the following poem suggests, liberalism does not really oppose the body but instead configures it as private property:

> I am afraid to own a Body—
> I am afraid to own a Soul—
> Profound—precarious Property—
> Possession, not optional—
>
> Double Estate, entailed at pleasure
> Opon [sic] an unsuspecting Heir—
> Duke in a moment of Deathlessness
> And God, for a Frontier. (1050)

The parallelism of the opening lines groups both "Body" and "Soul" under the domain of "precarious Property." This act of classification has profound consequences, for it suggests that the soul is just as material as the body. Soul and body constitute a "Double Estate"; they are twin registers of one and the same substance (property). Indeed, another poem by Dickinson compares this symmetry between body and soul to the "Tides within the Sea": "The Spirit lurks within the Flesh/Like Tides within the Sea/That make the Water live, estranged/What would the Either be?" (1627). It is not materiality or embodiment that provokes fear in Dickinson. It's the way in which materiality congeals into property, the way the body and the soul become private things—objects to transmit and inherit through patriarchal and heteronormative structures of kinship. The capitalist imperative to own ("Possession, not optional") entails not only the precarity involved in the transmission of property, including the unequal distribution of personhood (or agency), as well as goods. It also implies a form of dominance synonymous with self-sacrifice. The "moment of Deathlessness" is the apex of capitalist power; it is the telos of self-mastery, notably gendered masculine by the word "Duke." But what is "deathlessness" if not also an absence of life? What else could it be but an immunization of selfhood from the material contingency involved in living? It's as if the only way to win in the situation of capitalism were to become a vampire—an undead creature who is immortal only insofar as it does not truly live.

Like the feminists involved in the International Wages for Housework Campaign, Dickinson struggles with the way in which capitalism redefines the nature of human existence. Her fear of embodiment is actually an anxiety over how capitalist private property takes over the flesh. It's also an anxiety about poetry—about the impossibility of poetry—because of the way in which capitalism assimilates the senses to the prose of business as usual. If one can speak of the body of a poem, it is not simply because of the conventional analogy between the organic unity of the poem and the unity of the human organism. The poem also constitutes a body because it belongs to the affective economies of everyday life. The poem doesn't simply reflect the material production of subjectivity; it participates in it, redirecting emotional and libidinal energies toward new objects or new ways of being in the world. Dickinson's poems dealing with embodiment are therefore also meditations on the role of poetry—on the responsibility of poetry in respect to social life. More generally, Dickinson's poetry might be understood as an attempt to emancipate sensuous existence from "Possession, not optional."

From this perspective, lyric poetry is political therapy that cultivates a noncapitalist mode of sensuality. This is one way of reading Dickinson's well-known definition of poetry, formulated in conversation with T. W. Higginson: "If I read a book [and] it makes my whole body so cold no fire ever can warm me I know *that* is poetry. If I feel physically as if the top of my head were taken off, I know *that* is poetry. These are the only way [*sic*] I know it. Is there any other way."[27] Although it's impossible to disregard Virginia Jackson's important critique of the "faith in anatomy"—i.e., the critical desire to reach through the poem to grasp the poet incarnate—it's equally problematic to sidestep the sensuous power of poetry, especially when so much of Dickinson's poetry presupposes this power as its raison d'être. One would do well, then, to heed Jackson's warning that Dickinson's poetry should be "imaged as neither warm and capable of earnest grasping nor as a dissected and speech-producing body," while at the same time considering the ways her poetry reorganizes the affective economies of everyday life.[28] Such an approach doesn't confine itself to mining the semantic values of Dickinson's poetry, nor does it reduce the materiality of the poem to its historical context. Instead, it ponders the discrepant registers of materiality, including not only the materiality of manuscripts and historical contexts but also the materiality of affect—the composition of subjects through the linguistic circulation of preindividual relations and forces. How, then, does one distinguish poetry? One *feels* it in one's body. Poetry takes your head off; it irreversibly changes your bodily existence. For Dickinson, the truth of poetry appears only in the trace of a life radically transformed. Poetry puts an end to self-possession. It leaves the house of prose in disrepair.

Nobody's Commons

Emily Dickinson famously wrote that "'No' is the wildest word we consign to Language."[29] In respect to her marriage poems, saying "no" means transforming discontent into a refusal of social norms. It implies a flight into the wilderness that surrounds the domestic social order. It also suggests a loosening of the bodily potentials that have been harnessed and constrained by capitalist social reproduction. In short, to say "no" is as much a positive exercise of power as an act of negation: It suspends the social framework that destines women for wifehood, and, in doing so, it begins an experiment in living otherwise. In this section, I show how Dickinson recovers the commons by reinventing it as a noncapitalist commonality among women—a form of relation founded not in self-possession, or private property, but in sharing without reserve, in a mode of tactile pleasure that connects singular beings.

It's worth recalling that the history of the commons is also a history of social reproduction. The precapitalist commons consisted not only of material resources that supplemented household subsistence. It was also a space—often the woods, the banks of a river, or a meadow—in which socialization among women occurred without the scrutiny of men. It would be a mistake, however, to romanticize the commons, given that it seldom, if ever, constituted a full-blown alternative to either capitalism or feudalism. Even the precapitalist commons were usually a supplement to feudal social reproduction—a form of compensation for the shortfalls of subsistence farming. Moreover, the political valence of the commons dramatically changes following the transition into capitalism. This is the case not only because the commons becomes an object of political nostalgia. It's also the case because capitalism transforms women into the commons. Through restrictions on marriage, the criminalization of prostitution, the gendering of trade unions as masculine, and the mystification of housework as an act of love, women increasingly come to be defined as compensation for the loss of the precapitalist commons. In Federici's words: "In the new capitalist regime *women themselves became the commons*, as their work was defined as a natural resource, laying outside the sphere of market relations."[30] With the transition into capitalism, women transform into a gift from God/Nature, asking for nothing but love in return.

Dickinson's poetry doesn't take the condition of women for granted, however. It participates in what Ahmed terms a queer phenomenology—a practice of looking at things that takes neither the subject's orientation, nor their familiarity with things for granted. Indeed, the disavowal of housework—its consignment to the status of nature, rather than labor—is precisely the backgrounding of household things as if they were too self-evident to bear mention. Queer phenomenology, in contrast, looks behind things; it asks where they come from, how they go about their day, and what's going on in their material lives. In a discussion of Husserl, Ahmed conceptualizes this turn toward the background of things as a reorientation of philosophy around domesticity. The "glimpse of the domesticity of his world" "makes an impression" on Ahmed, who longs "to dwell there by lingering on the folds of the materials that surround him [Husserl]." She elaborates this longing as "a desire to read about the particularity of the objects that gather around the writer. It is also a desire to imagine philosophy as beginning here, with the pen and the paper, and with the body of the philosopher, who writes insofar as he is 'at home' and insofar as home provides a space in which he does his work."[31] Dickinson's lyric practice can be understood in exactly these terms. Her language lingers over those things—domestic matters, the stuff of everyday life—that the dominant traditions in philosophy relegate to the background. She does so not in order to suspend philosophical speculation but in order to give it a queer turn, to send it slantwise toward what lies behind things. And what lies behind things is labor: the labor of reproducing a household, of making time and space for writing poetry or for thinking about the world. Of course, belonging to a bourgeois family—a family of politicians, landowners, and entrepreneurs—Dickinson seldom had to perform her own household chores; she could rely on the labor of her family's Irish servants.[32] Her critique of the affective economy of domesticity would seem to speak less to her own social condition than to the more general condition of women in the nineteenth-century United States.

Dickinson's queer speculations turn, however, on a desire for concealment and retreat—a desire that suggests that even for well-provisioned women, domestic space still involves suffocation, claustrophobia, or alienation. Although social class certainly structures capitalist social reproduction, Dickinson's critique of marriage calls attention to the ways in which women are positioned *beneath* class, pressed into the service of social reproduction insofar as they are supposedly delivered from the hierarchies of labor. In other words, no matter their estate, women find themselves under the eyes of a "great Purchaser." They are a capitalist and patriarchal commons—a priceless commodity. Dickinson responds to this situation not by escaping domestic interiority but by changing the terms on which it's lived. It's well known that Dickinson spent a great deal of her life secluded in her Amherst home. Less discussed is the fact that, it being the residence of an eminent politician, this home was far from quiet, a parade of guests constantly shuffling through its ground-floor rooms. Dickinson would often keep herself out of sight, writing poetry in her bedroom or perhaps gazing out of the house's cupola onto the nearby Holyoke mountains. Diana Fuss argues that this seclusion shouldn't be understood in terms of repression or marginalization but as a kind of lyric freedom: "Dickinson lay claim to poetic authority by transforming herself into a voice. . . . Dickinson lyricizes space, recreating in the domestic interior the very condition of poetic address and response. If so many of Dickinson's lyrics resemble miniature domestic interiors, the domestic interior functions for the poet something like a lyre—an instrument of sound."[33] I've already argued that the voice of the poem is also the site of social reproduction, that insofar as voice is the material trace of the act of enunciation, it constitutes a source of futurity, a potential for social difference. Fuss suggests that Dickinson's voice is also a disappearing act—a way of leaving an audible trace without letting oneself be seen. In other words, Dickinson's retreat from sight constitutes a manner of making herself heard; her poetry queers domesticity by making poetry of it. It evades the scrutiny of the patriarch, and, in doing so, it crafts another commons, one in which the poetic voice abandons self-possession for the sake of a touching without propriety, property, or reserve.

Of course, domesticity includes not only the architecture of a home but also the familial and marital relations filling it. In "Title divine is mine," Dickinson rehearses marriage once again, but, in contrast to "I gave Myself to Him," this one begins not from within the marriage bond but from the other side of its threshold:

> Title divine—is mine!
> The Wife—without the Sign!
> Acute Degree—conferred on me—
> Empress of Cavalry!
> Royal—all but the Crown!
> Betrothed—without the swoon
> God sends us Women—
> When you—hold—Garnet to Garnet—
> Gold—to Gold—
> Born—Bridalled—Shrouded—

In a Day—
"My Husband"—women say—
Stroking the Melody—
Is *this*—the way?³⁴

The difficulty of interpreting this poem lies in the apparent contradiction between the voice's claim to divine title and its identification with unsanctioned wifehood. How does one lay claim to divine title—to the ratification of a relationship under the eyes of God—without going through the proper channels of marriage? What does it mean to inhabit the social role of wife without complying with the domestic destiny of women? The poem reminds its readers that in the New England Puritan context, marriage brings together not only husband and wife but also bride, groom, and God. It's not only the father who gives away the bride but also the Lord above: "God sends us Women." That women are sent by God, a divine gift, implies that women are born into the role of wife, destined eventually to say, "My Husband." Everything else is waiting for "the Sign." The proper woman is the woman who has been wed, and thus every other event in her life is but a prelude to marriage. The poem suggests the tragic constraints of this situation in what might be thought of as a biography in miniature: "Born—Bridalled—Shrouded—" There is no sign that a woman lives between birth and death, except marriage. In other words, a woman does not live without "the Sign"; she does not enjoy social recognition, unless she's harnessed ("Bridalled") by a husband. To exist unmarried is, then, a kind of social death. The poem presents an ugly paradox: She becomes a woman, an adult, only by becoming a beast of burden, a creature ensuring the reproduction of the domestic sphere. "The Sign" not only fails to guarantee personhood, it forecloses it.

To be a "Wife—without the Sign" would seem to entail a double lack of recognition. Not only does this voice exist outside of marriage. She also exists outside of the entire normative framework of gender (and, one might add, of humanity insofar as humanity is gendered).³⁵ If woman is always already wife, or at least on the road to becoming one, then the sign of wifehood attaches itself to the feminine regardless of whether or not vows have been exchanged. To be "without the Sign," then, constitutes a refusal—it's not that the subject of this poem is not yet a wife but that she occupies wifehood without the proper seal. She lives a life that does not fit into the teleology of "Born—Bridalled—Shrouded—" However, this without-ness—this being on the outside of things—is not entirely negative. The poem hovers between positivity and negativity, visibility and invisibility, for not only is she "without the Sign," she's also "Empress of Cavalry! / Royal—all but the Crown." The voice of the poem asserts her sovereign power, but it is a rule without sanction, an autonomy without propriety. It is, in short, a sort of anarchy. The line "Betrothed—without the swoon" confirms this lawless power by opening up a space in which coupling occurs without the passivity of the swoon or the dependency of the "bridal."

"Title divine—is mine" is an immanent critique of marriage. It mines the latter's ceremonies for a social potentiality exceeding heteronormativity, patriarchy, and capitalism. The last line of the poem ("Is *this*—the way?") epitomizes this combination of salvage operation and critique. The italicized deictic, *this*, cleaves the actual conditions of marriage from the possibility of some other arrangement; it introduces a gap between "the way" things are and "the way" things could be. The poem thus concludes with a rejection of fatalism, with a denial that a woman's normal course through life ("Born—Bridalled—Shrouded—") is the only course. Indeed, the last line retroactively reframes the entire poem as a polemical traversal of marriage—an inhabitance of marriage that reveals its fissures. In this light, the dashes falling vertically down the center of the poem are visual markers of marriage's contradictions. In interrupting the rhythmic flow of the poem, they dilate the time and space separating the positive ("The Wife," "Royal," "Betrothed") from the negative ("without the Sign," "all but the Crown," "without the swoon"). The dashes conduct a horizontal passage of ink from the enunciation of social position to the unworking of social position—the hollowing out of the normative dimensions of a social role by the "without" and the "but."[36] More generally, with their snarky imitation of women who lovingly cherish the words, "My Husband," the last lines of the poem demonstrate Dickinson's strategy of parody—her knack for withdrawing the voice of the poem from the content of the poem. Dickinson does not sanction the marital routines her poem describes; she mocks them. She doesn't present "the Sign"; she undermines it. Indeed, the poem parodies the traditional sonnet, its fourteen lines upending the genre's usual celebration of love in order to call into question the kinds of hierarchy and mastery involved in heteronormative visions of romance. If the last lines of a sonnet typically offer a reversal of perspective—a retrospective twist on a theme or motif—then Dickinson is quite faithful to the genre. The only difference is that her poem's concluding reversal upends the heteronormative bedrock on which the sonnet so often rests.

"Title divine—is mine" queers marriage by parodying its sanctions and signs. It doesn't so much abandon marriage as turn toward all of those things—all of those *potentials*—that the institution wishes it could do without. This queerness implies sexual orientation, but sexual orientation is always already social orientation—a certain direction or movement in respect to the things that make up a life with others. The poem's eroticism, the pleasure it derives from "Stroking the Melody" with its tongue, participates in Dickinson's general critique of capitalist social reproduction insofar as these pleasures become available only by straying from the normative course of coupling. Although I've alluded to it, it's worth explicitly remarking on the fact that marriage does the work of producing straightness, that the affective economy of marriage involves what Ahmed refers to as "straightening devices"—mechanisms for aligning sexual desire toward certain objects and practices, while occluding others.[37] That the labor of straightening out desire involves an entire political economy might be gleaned from the way the poem "I gave Myself to Him" maps the course of marriage along the trade routes leading to "the Isles of spice": Marriage is a libidinal trap, an extension and a consecration of the means of assimilating desire to the capitalist mode of reproduction. Dickinson queers marriage by interrogating it in such a way that it becomes unhinged from its presuppositions, becomes itself "without the Sign." In other words, she questions the "nature"—the reproductive grounds—on which marriage is planted. Elizabeth Maddock Dillon argues that "Dickinson's queering of marriage, then, asks us to rethink the public role of titles by placing desire—heterosexual or homosexual—in a radical and unknowable space: eroticism is signified as absent, not as present, as generated through figurative rather than literal or ontological grounds of entitlement."[38] Dickinson's poetry abolishes the liberal organization of the public and private, generating a "third space, between public and private."[39] The concept of the commons is one way of naming and articulating this third space, and what remains to be seen is how Dickinson transforms it from an abstract placeholder into the concrete social potential for another world.

Dickinson's queering of marriage goes hand in hand with the construction of another kind of sociality—a relationality whose traits include anarchy, autonomy, egalitarianism, solidarity, and concealment. It is a commons, but it is an altogether different commons from Whitman's brash song for the people or Burroughs's cowboy counter-nation. Dickinson *hides* utopia; she cultivates a zone of opacity in which queer relations, pleasures, and communications appear only to disappear. In this way, Dickinson resonates with lyric poetry's propensity toward obscurity—what Daniel Tiffany describes as "a kind of naked hermeticism." Tiffany explains that "obscurity is a way of making things disappear with words. At the same time, disappearance becomes a legible, material event through the verbal craft of obscurity. Indeed, crafting obscurity in a poem perfects the palpable art of disappearance."[40] Dickinson disappears from the family household—she takes flight from capitalist social reproduction—but she can do so only by making a spectacle of it, by flaunting tropes, conceits, and rhetorical figures that betray her secret desires. In other words, Dickinson's poem is an open secret; it's a linguistic body that shelters and conceals queer tendencies only on the condition of leaving a trace, like a firefly whose periodic flashes reveal its presence in the night.[41]

Perhaps the best example of Dickinson's queer fugitivity can be found in her poem "I'm Nobody! Who are you?" The poem articulates an anonymous and secretive community—one might even call it a secret society—in which relation is predicated on dispossession of the self. The poem pushes the concept of the commons to its limit by refusing to make what is shared a possession.[42] It models a society in which one shares a life in common without for all that *holding* some*thing* in common. What would it mean, the poem asks, to abandon ownership—even collective ownership—in favor of another way of touching things?

> I'm Nobody! Who are you?
> Are you—Nobody—too?
> Then there's a pair of us!
> Dont [sic] tell! they'd advertise—you know!
>
> How dreary—to be—Somebody!
> How public—like a Frog—
> To tell one's name—the livelong June—
> To an admiring Bog! [260]

In "I gave Myself to Him," the reader witnesses a housewife anxiously fretting over the possibility of being reduced to nothing, or nobody: "The Wealth might disappoint—/Myself a poorer prove." In contrast, this poem seems to embrace poverty, to deny the value-form associated with the affective economies of patriarchal capitalism. "I'm Nobody!" signifies in respect to capitalist social reproduction as a negation of the housewife—a suspension of the subject position through which women matter to capital. At the same time, even though it's contracted into the subject, the copula that makes a "Nobody" out of an "I" defies any simple opposition between wealth and poverty, or surplus and lack. Indeed, the word "Nobody" is itself ambiguous, suggesting not nonexistence but a certain kind of existence: negation as positive material element or valuelessness as positive ontological trait. To be a nobody is not to be without body but to be a body without worth—an uncounted presence that nonetheless makes itself heard. The "no" in "nobody" does not therefore translate to *not*-X but to *un*-X, which is to say that it suspends the phenomenological and ontological grounds of liberal personhood by allowing negativity to become difference in itself. And difference in itself is not identity but multiplicity: a plurality with no underlying unity; a relationality that doesn't presume shared attributes. In sum, Dickinson introduces a figure of nonidentity that blurs the distinctions between positivity and negativity, wealth and poverty, presence and absence.

The nonidentity of the "Nobody" presents a problem for interpretation, namely, the problem of how to grasp, or even identify, an object in retreat—a being whose essence consists in disappearing. It's tempting to solve this problem by reading the paradox of the "Nobody" as an experience of failure or depression. Doesn't the colloquial expression, "I'm nobody," suggest either that one hasn't lived up to expectations, hasn't proved one's worth, or that one is down in the dumps, incapable of feeling pleasure or perhaps anything at all? There is a way of reading this poem symptomatically, of analyzing the poem's shuttling back and forth between presence and absence, as an effect of homophobia. In this case, the lyric extravagance of the poem is a kind of contortion, rhetorical somersaults designed to evade the social censorship of nonnormative desires. Poetry would seem to serve as a substitute for the positive expression of queer desire. This approach solves the problem, however, only by misrecognizing the poem's tone. The poem doesn't lament the failure to be "Somebody." After all, being "Somebody" is "dreary." To be somebody—to be the wife *with* the sign—is to inhabit one's social role without friction or conflict; it means allowing capitalist social reproduction to follow its course without interruption The smooth flow of social reproduction cannot help but be experienced as the boredom of repetition. Each day is like the next when you're Somebody. In contrast, to be "Nobody" is exciting: the poem's abundant exclamation points; its irregular rhythm, which skips playfully from dash to dash; its loose rhyming—these formal features suggest a pleasure that oscillates between languor and ecstasy, between the dissolution of the self and its shattering. In speaking as nobody, the voice of the poem doesn't mourn a lost object of desire. She enters into a conversation that is itself an object of desire; she disappears into the poem, which has become a kind of erogenous zone—an audible and tactile surface across which queer pleasures multiply.

The pleasure of this poem is ecstatic in the precise sense of the word—it is a pleasure in which, or because of which, one is beside oneself. It's an experience in which one is no longer one (with oneself) but divided—split in two (or more than two). The repetition of "Nobody" confuses the one with the other. Which nobody is which? How do you tell one nobody from another? The poem as a whole fails to support any moment of oneness, even in its direct address, which one would think referred to a unified "you." The homophonic resonance of "too" and "two," in "Are you—Nobody—too?" undermines the identity or self-cohesion of "you," as if shadowy multiplicity were the existential condition of a somebody who is really "Nobody." One is always already two, at least two, since this poem deals with two Nobodies who are both more and less than two Somebodies. The poem withdraws from the affective economies involved in capitalist social reproduction. It insists on a nameless, invaluable mode of being that is neither the one nor the other. The poem doesn't articulate a political subject position or a polemical standpoint. After all, what would it even mean to take a position as nobody? Instead, the poem scatters the lyric voice into a sociality whose defining characteristics are anonymity, multiplicity, secrecy, and joyful intensity.

What distinguishes the life of "Nobody" from the anxious poverty of the housewife is its existence in and as conversation. The poem stages a coupling of two beings by posing questions: "Who are you? / Are you—Nobody—too?" The direct address, not uncommon in lyric poetry, is loaded with implications in this context, for in asking whether "you" are "Nobody," the voice of the poem inducts you into its anonymous multiplicity. In other words, instead of positioning one in relation to the lyric voice, the poem *de*positions one—it undermines the division of the one and the other, inventing a genre of conversation that is like speaking to oneself, but only if one (or you) consisted of more than one personality, more than one way of being in the world. The mathematical convolutions of the poem—its calculated refusal of the liberal-capitalist arithmetic of personhood—are therefore synonymous with an ontological inquiry taking the form of an open question: What kind of being belongs to nobody?

"I'm Nobody! Who are you?" doesn't answer this ontological question. Instead, it leverages the disorientation introduced by its queries in order to compose a way of living together slantwise. The question becomes a mode of connection, which rather than lining up with the reproductive machinery of domestic bliss marches to the beat of its own drum. It might seem strange to call this a marriage, but the poem not only performs a coupling—though a coupling that doesn't necessarily imply just two partners—it also invents a nonnormative mode of social reproduction—a manner of subsisting that doesn't comply with the imperative to make good on the "Sweet Debt of Life."[43] The poem infiltrates marriage. It repeats its rituals only insofar as it withdraws from the values attached to them. It is a marriage in and of secrecy: "Dont tell! They'd advertise—you know! // How dreary—to be—Somebody! / How public—like a Frog—/ To tell one's name—the livelong June—/ To an admiring Bog!" The poem forsakes a dull public in favor of an exciting privacy: the first- and second-person singular opposes the third-person plural, the latter threatening to subsume the former into the amorphous "Bog" of the "Frog." In this instance, rhyme is the kind of euphony that neutralizes alterity, that converts anonymous multiplicity into identifiable oneness. Privacy can suggest a number of possibilities, one of which is, of course, the privacy of the domestic sphere—the domain of the housewife. That kind of privacy is the complement of a public sphere structured in terms of limited social recognition (i.e., a form of inclusion that depends on restricted political legibility, as well as on the exclusion of certain others). In the context of liberalism, domestic privacy is the supplement of publicly recognized identity; it is nonidentity not as such but rather as the background against which the public makes itself appear: To retreat into domestic privacy, to withdraw from the polis, is to "advertise" one's identity as an open secret that invites the gaze it pretends to ignore.[44] From this angle, "Nobody" is really a hidden "Somebody," a creature subject to interpellation by an "admiring [read: identifying, evaluating, and recruiting] Bog."

There is, however, a richer reading of the poem's privacy, one that thinks through the ontological trouble posed by the strange being of the nobody. The coupling in this poem doesn't set itself up in opposition to the public domain, because it suspends the very distinction between the public and the private. As Dillon argues, in queering marriage, Dickinson introduces a "third space between public and private." The voice of "Nobody" weaves a commonality not out of socially recognized identities but out of scattered multiplicities (beings that are not one; creatures delivered over to ecstasy). This abandonment of social recognition is also a refusal to communicate. Strictly speaking, there is no communication in this poem, because the lyric voice follows its own instruction—"Dont tell!"—and refuses to identify "Nobody." The obscure community in this poem depends on declining "to tell one's name." It depends on a willful obscurity that frustrates the transparency and clarity demanded by the liberal public forum. Nothing happens in this poem. Nothing is said. The only sound the poem makes is that of two nobodies coming into contact only to go into hiding. The poem is therefore incommunicable. It communicates nothing but its own potentiality for speech, and it does so by turning away from publicity. It gestures toward this turning away in yet another instance of homophony: The "no" in "nobody" is also a "know," so that "nobody" is a knowing body—a body *in the know*. What better way to perform this other way of knowing than as an instance of homophony, a form of verbal play that can so easily be passed over but, when noticed, suggests the most intricate folds of linguistic possibility. One is nobody only insofar as one refuses to be recognized as somebody, refuses to surrender one's name; and, insofar as one is nobody, one is in the know—in on the secret pleasures of a being that is not one.[45]

In "I'm Nobody! Who are you?" Dickinson's lyric voice disidentifies from the liberal subject of the housewife and, at the same time, constructs a new form of collectivity. However, the collectivity that emerges from the poem is not a public. Instead, it's a secret society with its own occult rituals. These are rituals in the sense of practices that cement a social bond, but they are also erotic rituals—means of attuning oneself to queer pleasures. With this in mind, the poem's occult quality, or its tendency to conceal what it reveals, has to do not only with knowledge and communication but also with sexuality. If marriage transforms a girl into "Somebody," if it engenders straight subjects by charting desire along proper lines, then this poem produces Nobodies by steering the ship off course, by entering into a vortex of occult desire. The poem models a lesbian aesthetics of existence, in which the occlusion of women from the liberal public sphere becomes the occasion for a way of being together—of pleasuring one another— that evades the social matrix of heterosexuality. From this perspective, the "admiring Bog" is not only the liberal public sphere but also the sexual gaze of the patriarch: To be "Somebody" is to appeal to a masculine public; it entails disclosing oneself before the gaze, offering oneself up as an object of visual pleasure. This act of disclosure is temporal, as well as spatial. It's no coincidence that the only explicit marker of time in the poem is "the livelong June": June is the month of marriage (Juno, the month's namesake, is the Roman goddess of marriage); it is a time of consummation sanctioned by the social and symbolic order. There is, then, a normative calendar of desire, which marks the days, months, and years leading up to the becoming-Wife of a girl. Turning away from the "admiring Bog" by not identifying oneself implies a break with this calendar; it implies a departure from what Lee Edelman terms reproductive futurism, or the march into the future dictated by the figure of the Child (the normative product of consumption).[46] To be Nobody is to be outside the family of

Man; it is to be askew from liberal-capitalist visions of progress. Indeed, a variant of the poem emphasizes Nobody's lot as an outcast: "Dont tell! they'd banish us—you know!"[47]

In this reading of the poem, the lyric voice's retreat into a community of Nobodies constitutes at one and the same time an evasion of heteronormative social structures and a symptom of them. Turning away from the public sphere acknowledges the power of its gaze, even as it opens the door to a world of queer passion. It's an interpretation that finds biographical support in T. W. Higginson's claim that the poem was written at about the same time as a letter to Mary Bowles, one of Dickinson's regular correspondents. The letter opens: "When the Best is gone—I know that other things are not of consequence—The Heart wants what it wants—or else it does not care."[48] The letter suggests a passionate commitment to love, whatever form it takes, and its preemptive dismissal of social censure ("other things are not of consequence") alludes to a queer orientation. The object of this commitment might be Mary Bowles, the letter's addressee—critics have speculated on the amorous qualities of Dickinson's attachments to both Mary and her husband, Samuel Bowles—or it might be Dickinson's sister-in-law, Sue Gilbert—the erotic nature of Dickinson and Gilbert's relationship is well established.[49] In the latter case, Mary would be a confidant, another "Nobody" in Dickinson's secret society. In any case, Dickinson's biography suggests that the poem should be interpreted as an attempt to put queer desire into language without assimilating it to the normative form of social reproduction. The poem is a closet, but only if the concept of the closet breaks from its identification with abnormality to become a shelter—the dwelling place of a society whose principles include not only secrecy and anonymity but also the sharing of oneself without reserve. It is a way of being apart from the public, together. In Dickinson's words, "All *we* are *strangers*—dear—The world is not acquainted with us, because we are not acquainted with her."[50]

At the same time, there is a difficulty one encounters in reading "I'm Nobody! Who are you?" in terms of a lesbian aesthetics of existence. If the Nobody evades identification, then how can the reader be sure of the lyric voice's gender or sexuality? Doesn't the constitutive ambiguity of the Nobody deny both gender and sexual orientation? Perhaps so, but only if one assumes an equation between gender/sexuality and identity. The poetry analyzed in this chapter suggests a different possibility, however. In the context of Dickinson's marriage poems, lesbianism names an exit from the social role of the housewife and an entry into queer social formations. On the one hand, to be a lesbian is to depart from capitalist social reproduction, to stray from the family line. With Ahmed, one might describe this deviation as a moment of disorientation—not an identification but a refusal to fall into line. Lesbianism is a covert operation, a way of disappearing from the public and its norms. On the other hand, Dickinson's queer marriages also perform a work of reorientation—"a reorientation of one's body such that other objects, those that are not reachable on the vertical and horizontal lines of straight culture, can be reached."[51] Lesbianism isn't a generic protest against heteronormativity. It describes a distinct eroticism—an ecstasy irreducible to the symbolic economy of the phallus—as well as a specific sociality—a manner of being among women. A woman becomes Nobody with other women, and, in doing so, she not only surrenders herself over to anonymous ecstasy, she also becomes another kind of being—a being for which the term *woman* is only an approximate designation.

Dickinson's lesbianism is a singular formation. It's less a discrete sexual orientation or gender than a disorientation of straight culture and a reorientation of life toward queer relations. In other words, Dickinson's lesbianism shouldn't be confused with lesbianism as such. I've emphasized the specifically lesbian dimension of Dickinson's poetry in order to map the concrete connections between Dickinson's critique of the housewife and her invention of nonnormative forms of sociality. That being said, this itinerary from critical negativity to covert affirmation suggests a more general queer potential—an anonymous potentiality immanent in the affective economy of marriage but also in excess of it.[52] Dickinson queers marriage by constructing a nonproprietary commons—a mode of social reproduction in which beings mingle without abiding by liberal or capitalist social regulations. If the "Wife—without the Sign" commits herself to another ("Betrothed—without the swoon") or if two "Nobodies" join together ("Then there's a pair of us!"), they do so neither under the sign of identity, nor by finding their proper place in the symbolic order, but by giving themselves over to impropriety. Dickinson's queer coupling always involves a straying from the course. One might call this manner of being without reserve *queer relationality*, noting that scholars such as José Esteban Muñoz, Jack Halberstam, Elizabeth Freeman, and Michael D. Snediker have challenged the idea that queerness (or queer theory) might be reducible to negativity, deviation, or transgression.[53] As Muñoz contends in an essay describing punk rock's mixture of political subversion and community: "The challenge here is to look to queerness as a mode of 'being-with' that defies social conventions and conformism and is innately heretical yet still desirous for the world, actively attempting to enact a commons that is not a pulverizing, hierarchical one bequeathed through logics and practices of exploitation."[54] We could do far worse than to think of Dickinson as punk. Instead of accepting the popular imagination of Dickinson as virgin recluse, or patron saint of homebodies, we should embrace her poetry's commitment to a commons of queer passion and radical critique.

Dickinson's marriage poems construct communities of queer passion. Community has become something of a dirty word in the critical lexicon, because it so often implies unity on the basis of an exclusive and exclusionary essence. According to this argument, community supports the sharing of a life only insofar as it bars certain folks from belonging. However, Dickinson recuperates the intimacies of community by scattering community's essence. She unworks the liberal model of citizenship, as well as the capitalist model of labor power, by constructing a commons in which belonging doesn't suppose self-possession but rather a fundamental relationality. For Dickinson, one is together with another only insofar as one is not one. Relationality neither presupposes nor reinforces individuality. Instead, it undercuts self-possession; it exposes one to an otherness that is immanent in oneself. To think of this kind of relationality as a scattering of community, or as a community that reproduces itself on the condition of being scattered, is to conceive of relationality as an unfolding of interiority onto the outside.[55] Despite assertions to the contrary, Dickinson's poems are not models of psychic depth but rather linguistic assemblages in which emotion, feeling, and thought are always already collective matters. "I'm Nobody! Who are you?" is a perfect example. Nobody's queer passions do not belong to her; they reconstitute her as more than one, as a being that is simultaneously singular and plural. To be Nobody not only implies a refusal to identify or be identified; it's also a way of keeping company—a way of sharing one's life without reserve.

Dickinson articulates this kind of community in a letter to her love, Sue Gilbert. In the letter, community is a tactile affair, a touching that reconfigures selfhood as being-with.

> Sweet Sue—
> There is no first, or last, in Forever—It is Centre, there, all the time—
> To believe—is enough, and the right of supposing—
> Take back that "Bee" and "Buttercup"—I have no Field for them, though for the Woman whom I prefer, Here is Festival—Where my Hands are cut, Her fingers will be found inside—

> Our beautiful Neighbor "moved" in May—It leaves an
> Unimportance.
> Take the Key to the Lily, now, and I will lock the Rose—[56]

This letter writes community as a touching between two hands that are neither separate, nor intertwined, but inside one another. Interrelation becomes *infra*relation. Love is not the joining of two discrete identities, or the becoming one of two, but the unfolding of a flesh that is singular and plural (or that is common only insofar as it is multiple). There's no room for propriety, no space for the discrete partitioning of heteronormative models of coupling. To touch is to expose one's insides to otherness, to become other than oneself with another. The violence of this image is not sadistic. It speaks, instead, to a disruption of social identity—a "cut[ting]" open of the roles assigned to a married woman (Sue is married to Dickinson's brother, Austin) and an unattached daughter (Dickinson never did formally marry). Community is the gift of "Festival": "I have no field for them, though for the Woman whom I prefer, Here is Festival—" A festival is a recurring break with daily rhythms, a carnivalesque reversal of the order of things in which up is down, down is up—or in which the erotic love between two women is not a perversion of marriage but its consummation in ecstasy. The regular deviations of the festival are complicated, however, by the oddness of the word "preference" in the letter. To prefer someone ("for the Woman whom I prefer") does not imply that that other belongs to oneself but rather something more contingent: a *liking*—a process of attraction, a nearness without propriety, an inclination. Preference doesn't come at a preordained time but simply when it happens to occur; it is always doubled by its intimate other—to prefer not to. In other words, preference presupposes the absolute contingency of the chance encounter. Love as preference is love as "Festival," a surplus of potentiality over the normal course of things, an interruption of the calendar in the name of a being together that just happens to be.

The love expressed in this letter is not fated. It is instead an intense but contingent sharing without reserve—a singular community of pleasure. Dickinson has "no field" for the "Bee" or the "Buttercup," for in the act of writing, everything goes (in)to Sue. This isn't to say that the singular relation between the two is solitary in a privative sense. It does not exclude the outside. Other singularities pass through, including "our beautiful Neighbor [who] 'moved' in May." If the description of the neighbor's departure as an "Unimportance" seems to suggest the neighbor's simple exteriority to the letter's community ("It leaves an Unimportance"), it is nevertheless only as exteriority—only through the traffic between Dickinson's house and Sue Gilbert's house next door—that their love takes place. In other words, the queer relationship in this letter is a composition of contingent elements, a manner of keeping company sustained by passion. It is preference that turns the contingent relations among things into a commons, which is to say that the commons emerges from a liking that holds beings together without assimilating them into an identity. Emily is not Sue, Sue is not Emily, but through a "Festival" of feeling, they become a commons—a singular way of moving through the world together.

Dickinson's queer passion takes place within the domestic economies of the nation, even as it exceeds them in a singular fashion. Whereas capitalist social reproduction commodifies time and space, securing the future by conscripting women into the role of housewife, the queer forms of social reproduction discussed in this section imply a kind of contingent community. As happenings, such contingent communities lack guarantees, but they gain the intensity of a commonality whose existence is completely immersed in its manner of being. In other words, community becomes nothing more and nothing less than contact with another through one's own otherness: "Where my Hands are cut, Her Fingers will be found inside—" The dash ending this sentence could be read in performative terms as a linguistic emission that touches the reader, or at least tries to do so, but which is also a gesture—a way of signaling toward something beyond the horizon. Indeed, in the letter above, the dashes all appear elliptical, implying a wealth of knowledge and feeling that the letter invokes without disclosing. The dash, then, is the emblem of Dickinson's queer communities, the sign of her festival of feelings.

Dickinson's dashes are odd creatures—strange forms of punctuation that produce more questions than answers. Each dash fragments the landscape of the poem, restructuring the poem so that its semantic units are less individual lines than islands of language that happen to fall between the dashes. Cristanne Miller writes, "The dashes correspond to pauses for breath or deliberation, or to signs of an impatient eagerness that cannot be bothered with the formalities of standard punctuation. Dickinson's dashes operate rhetorically more than syntactically."[57] Miller suggests that the dash generates a confusion between patience and haste, as if time contracted into the length of the line, allowing one to recapitulate the entirety of the poem in an instant, to view the language surrounding the dash from this angle and then that angle in an endless play of reflection. In enabling such reflection, "Dickinson's punctuation, like her poetry, teaches the reader to trust the play of the mind."[58]

To speak of the dashes as rhetorical, associating them by proxy with linguistic tropes, is to suggest that the dashes are turns of phrase that do not secure a linear flow of meaning (as one might expect syntax to do) but produce semantic twists, not all of which can be subsumed in a single act of interpretation. Paul Crumbley takes this line of thought a step further, arguing that these suspended moments—these contracted eternities—are also markers of dialogism. Dickinson's poetry is not the monologue of a single lyric voice but a "dialogic heterogeneity," a revelation of the "interplay of speakers' voices and the mix of discourses."[59] The dash is more than a "play of the mind," for in Crumbley's words, it

> liberates meaning from syntax that would ordinarily narrow the field of reference for specific words; at the same time it alerts readers to the role they play in expanding these fields of reference. In this sense, the poems trigger imaginative responses to conservative, centripetal impulses within language that aim to stabilize meaning, so that readers personally experience the explosion of centrifugal force.[60]

The dashes generate plural subject formations—voices meeting together to form a new collective entity, like the "pair" of "Nobodies" or "the Wife—without the Sign"—but these formations are contingent; they come and they go, dissipating into the polyphony of Dickinson's poetry. More than a "play of the mind," the dashes are crucial operators in a process of subjectivization, of which a particular state of mind is merely an effect. They are the constitutive signs of a specific genre of lyric personhood, one which replaces the Romantic ideal of organic unity with what might be called a singular plurality.

Dickinson's dashes are also part of the anatomy of her poem. They not only inflect her poetry's representation of embodied life; they also constitute something like the limbs of the poem's body. There is a bodiliness to punctuation, a certain palpability, which Dickinson's dashes intensify because of the strangeness of their presence. Their length (longer than her periods, shorter than her exclamation points or question marks); their tendency to point sometimes upward, sometimes downward; and their irregular patterning or placement are all traits drawing attention to the materiality of Dickinson's poetic language. One might even say that the dashes are points of fascination—traps that catch a reader's eye—forcing the reader to become aware of the material situation of reading and writing. However, this capture of attention does not put an end to the poem's meaning-making, even if it generates an instant of suspense in which language becomes senseless (the dashes mean nothing in themselves). Instead,

Dickinson's dash functions like a caesura: a pregnant pause that interrupts and joins, that promises words to come, even as it insists on the space between words. Of course, Dickinson's dash is not a caesura, not in the strictest sense. Giorgio Agamben writes of the caesura that it is "the element that gives a halting blow to the metrical flow of the voice, it's nothing other than thought." He adds that the poem's rhythm hinges upon this halting "emptiness"—"it is this emptiness that the caesura thinks and holds in suspense, as *pure speech*, for the brief instant in which it halts the horse of poetry."[61] Like the caesura, Dickinson's dashes halt the horse of poetry, breaking with the measured stride of meter to allow for exponential leaps in thought. The dashes are not voids or empty spaces, however. If they contract the time of the poem into an instant, they do so only by way of their graphic plenitude. Whereas caesurae may go nude, may abandon the clothing of a comma, and stand in their full splendor as "pure speech," the dash is nothing but the clothing of the mark, an absorption of thought into the material trait of writing. The dash is thought *embodied*.

Dickinson's dashes are a form of touching: They bring the poem into contact with the reader; they press upon the reader, but they also produce contact between the singular figures of the poem (the Nobodies, the wives without the sign). Indeed, the dash that ends "Where my Hands are cut, Her fingers will be found inside—" suggests how literal the dash's touch may become: In touching upon the eye, the dash moves us, and, in this case, moves Dickinson and Sue, in their common attraction, their preference for one another. Dickinson's dashes are constitutive of the commons that emerges from her marriage poems; they are elemental devices through which the social capacity of language (communicability as such) is brought to a queer pitch, where the identities capitalist society holds dear come undone, and where new possibilities appear as singular preferences. The dashes happen—they happen to happen: There is no necessity to their existence; they are never wholly determined by the rhythm of the poem, nor even by the sense of the poem. They just happen. Which is not to say that they are insignificant. They do make a difference, for they act as the condition of possibility for communities of interpretation: The suspense of the dash enables the reader to exercise her preference in constructing the sense of the poem; it allows readers to share in the making of the poem, to absorb themselves in the festival of the commons. If Dickinson's dashes are the trait by which one recognizes her singularity as a poet, it is not because they secure the grounds of a proper stylistic signature, but because they are the material trace of queer propensities—scraps of writing with which, through which, one might stitch together a life in common.

"A fairer House than Prose"

In the poem "I dwell in Possibility," Dickinson draws a contrast between prose and poetry through an extended metaphor of domesticity. Whereas prose is a cramped house, poetry—which Dickinson calls "Possibility"—multiplies expanses. Despite the narrow figure its stanzas cut, the lyric poem is "More numerous of Windows—/ Superior—for Doors—" (466). Indeed, Dickinson turns the metaphysical architecture of the house inside out: The house of poetry has the sky for a roof ("And for an everlasting Roof/ The Gambrels of the Sky—"); and its "Chambers" are "as the Cedars—/ Impregnable of eye—" If Dickinson valorizes poetry over prose, it is because poetry turns ontology (the House of Being) and politics (domestic economy) on its head by insisting that infinite expanses of possibility can fit into the tightest architectural corridors, or the most compact lines of verse. Poetry potentializes being; it unworks the limits of domestic economy, the constraints of what we call home, by revealing the capacity to enter into new arrangements. Of course, as I've argued, Dickinson doesn't so much exhibit potentiality as secrete it. Her poems make a spectacle not of possibility as such but of its disappearance—its retreat into the shelter of the poem. The concluding lines of "I dwell in Possibility" allude to poetry's role in sheltering utopian possibility: "The spreading wide my narrow Hands/ To gather Paradise—" (466).

It is no coincidence that when Dickinson goes about characterizing poetry, she does so through metaphors of domesticity and corporeality. The poem is not only a house of limitless expanses; it is also the blow that knocks the top of one's head off, the gust of wind that leaves a body forever cold. Dickinson's poetry is singular because of the seamlessness with which it combines metaphysics and domesticity: Her speculations do not transcend the house of flesh; they draw near to it—they ask what lies behind it. Likewise, the politics of Dickinson's poetry stand out because instead of following Whitman down the open road of the multitudes, Dickinson discovers a desire called America in the most intimate gestures and spaces—in a marriage ceremony, in a house in Amherst, in a touch between two women. The Killjoy and the Nobody are figures that redefine American exceptionalism by demonstrating how it shapes the rhythms of the household, how it is lived in and through the gendered reproduction of capitalist society. Dickinson outrealms liberty, but she does so from within the household. She imagines a singular America as a commons in which queer desire flashes like a firefly in the night.

Dickinson's secret society is a far cry from Whitman's and Burroughs's grander visions of insurgency and revolution, but it is this intimacy that makes Dickinson's verse so capable of responding to the contemporary status quo. For the historical present of capitalism hasn't let go of women's affections; it's only intensified and generalized their exploitation. Political activists and sociologists have come to speak of a crisis of care, which takes the form of a contradiction between capitalism's increasing demand for labor and the decrease of public support for social reproduction (exemplified by neoliberalism's devastation of state-provided social welfare services).[62] Combined with the general decline of real wages since the 1970s, this crisis results not only in the deterioration of workers' living conditions but also in the direct commodification of social reproduction. Families and individuals make up for their lack of nonwork time by purchasing commodified versions of reproductive labor, ranging from expensive childcare to pre-made meals. Although these developments represent an emancipation of women from the traditional social expectations of the nineteenth century, they neither liberate women from capitalist exploitation, nor do they eliminate gendered forms of inequality. Gendered income disparities, rampant sexual harassment and assault, and the persistence of the "second shift," all speak to patriarchy and misogyny's continuing power to compel women to sacrifice themselves for the sake of capitalist social reproduction. Despite popular images of "stay-at-home dads" or "house husbands," women still shoulder the burden of social reproduction, not only because they constitute majorities in care industries such as nursing and nonprofit social work but also because ideologies of femininity still associate women with the "Daily Own—of Love." As Ruth Rosen writes: "It is as though Americans are trapped in a time warp, still convinced that women should and will care for children, the elderly, homes and communities. But of course they can't, now that most women have entered the workforce."[63]

Emily Dickinson's poetry offers insights into the biopolitics of contemporary capitalism not only because of its critique of the affective economies of the household but also because of its utopian imagination of alternative forms of social reproduction. Dickinson's "Nobody" and her "Wife—without the Sign" are figures of life that evade the social norms of the nation-state and capitalism, while still insisting on the importance of community and care. They are less representations of individuals than linguistic vehicles for envisioning an egalitarian mode of relationality. Dickinson's marriage poems are efforts to enlarge the political imagination so that it includes struggles over the conditions of social reproduction.

In this respect, Dickinson is in dialogue with recent political practices directed at changing the conditions of social reproduction, including social unionism, universal basic income advocacy, and the 2017 International Women's Strike. These practices build on the legacy of the Wages for Housework Campaign, repeating the campaign's demystification of socially reproductive labors and revising it for a situation in which so-called women's work is seldom confined to the household. Coinciding with the International Women's Day on March 8, 2017, the purpose of the International Women's Strike was symbolic, as well as material: It asked the world to consider what a world without the labor of women might look like; it demanded consideration of how integral women are to the reproduction of society. In this way, the strike combined critique and affirmation, not only interrupting the smooth flow of capitalist social reproduction but also elucidating an egalitarian social horizon. As their platform puts it:

> The International Women's Strike is a network of women in more than 50 different countries that emerged through planning a day of action for March 8th, 2017.
>
> In the spirit of that renewed radicalism, solidarity and internationalism, the International Women's Strike US continues to be a national organizing center by and for women who have been marginalized and silenced by decades of neoliberalism directed towards the 99% of women: working women inside and outside of the home, women of color, Native women, disabled women, immigrant women, Muslim women, lesbian, CIS, queer and trans women.
>
> We see our efforts as part of a new international feminist movement that organizes resistance not just against Trump and his misogynist policies, but also against the conditions that produced Trump, namely the decades long economic inequality, criminalization and policing, racial and sexual violence, and imperial wars abroad.
>
> We aim to build relationships of solidarity between diverse organizations of women, and all those who seek to build a global feminist, working class movement.[64]

I've quoted from the platform at length, because it articulates a feminist vision in which gender equality doesn't come from buying into capitalism but from developing alternatives to it. It recognizes that the Trump era is less an epochal shift than the climax of "decades of neoliberalism." This viewpoint is so important, because it acknowledges the intensity and the depth with which capitalism has taken hold of women's lives: Neoliberalism names not only the privatization of social welfare services but also the way in which women have been burdened with picking up the state's slack by covering the gap in social care.[65] This viewpoint also suggests that the project of building "a global, feminist, working class movement" cannot conclude with the achievement of equal wages across genders, even if equal wages are a step in the right direction. It is only by reorganizing the entire fabric of social reproduction that emancipation would mean something more than a right to be exploited on equal terms. Although Emily Dickinson's poetry certainly doesn't provide a blueprint for emancipation, it does contribute elements to a feminist biopolitics of social reproduction. In particular, Dickinson's marriage poems experiment with egalitarian ways of living together and with forms of love, care, passion, and support that have no need for domination or exploitation. Outrealming liberty thus comes to mean not only refusing to play wife but also refusing the entire system of capitalist social reproduction. Dickinson imagines a queer commons—a counter-nation of Nobodies—in which America might finally live up to its Carol of Liberty.

CHAPTER 4

Idle Power: The Riot, the Commune, and Capitalist Time in Thomas Pynchon's *Against the Day*

In times like these, it's easy to despair. The rise of Donald Trump to the U.S. presidency would seem to signify a turning back of the clock of political progress. The increasing regulation of national borders; intensified policing of immigrants; federal support for unchecked police violence, especially against persons of color and the poor; financial deregulation; a return to neoconservative hawkishness; the explicit promotion of white supremacism; the rolling back of hard-won protections for queer folks and women—these political pathologies speak to a dampening, if not a foreclosure, of social movements striving for another kind of America. Occupy, Black Lives Matter, and the struggle against the Dakota access pipeline have been eclipsed by a desperate sense that electoral politics are all we have, but not nearly enough. In short, radical politics seems to exist in the past tense, and left-wing melancholy has become the new political realism. At the same time, this interpretation of political reality in the United States ignores the persistence of a genuine utopianism in American culture and politics. Not only do mass feminist protests, teacher strikes, and marches against gun violence speak to a longing for a different America, they also bear the historical memory of social movements. They are placeholders, concrete traces, of an America beyond American exceptionalism. More generally, they speak the important truth that the so-called Trump era is less a coherent historical period than a political reaction whose shape depends on the riotous social energies that it opposes: Trump is a containment strategy, an attempt to hold at bay the social forces that challenge racism, heteronormativity, misogyny, and class power. That such containment involves a parasitic dependence on its opposite can be seen not only in Trump's paranoid obsession with leftist politics but also in the way that his rallies constitute garish imitations of mass protest. Trump is a farcical repetition of revolution, clowning around with the idea of social change—"Make America Great Again"—only to maintain the status quo of neoliberal capitalism. His buffoonery betrays the survival of a singular America in excess of even the most virulent exceptionalism.

In times like these, reading Thomas Pynchon's 2006 novel *Against the Day* is a lesson in recovering the powers of social change that have been submerged by political reaction. Against the neoliberal view of America as a gigantic corporation, Pynchon suggests that America bursts with a political militance at odds with entrepreneurship. Since at least *Gravity's Rainbow* (1973), Pynchon's fiction has cultivated a sense of political hope that rests on the persistence of counter-national elements in the midst of the most vicious crackdowns on left-wing politics and culture. Reading the so-called Trump era alongside Pynchon's fiction demands a long-term perspective in which Trump symbolizes less a sudden swing toward fascism than the culmination of a long and deep fear of American utopianism—a climax, if not a conclusion, of exceptionalism's quest to tame that desire called America. In the face of this reaction, *Against the Day* recuperates anticapitalist politics by showing that there can be no truly utopian vision of America without opposition to capitalism, and, furthermore, that such opposition is a struggle over the collective organization of time. In its form and its content, *Against the Day* protests against the temporal demands of capitalism; it preaches against the imperative to extract as much profit from every moment as possible. It belongs to the genre of literature Ross Chambers terms "loiterature": a literature whose principles are inefficiency and indolence and whose central narrative devices include digression, dilation, and circumlocution.[1] The sheer length of the novel—1,085 pages of small type—lends itself to this aesthetic, but it is less length than the constant short-circuiting of plot progression that pledges Pynchon's fiction to the party of unrepentant slackers. In an essay published in the *New York Times*, Pynchon highlights the gravity of such slothful carrying on: "Sloth here was no longer so much a sin against God or spiritual good as against a particular sort of time, uniform, one-way, in general not reversible—that is, against clock time, which got everybody to bed and early to rise."[2]

Against the Day is a paean to sloth, a defense of the pleasure in doing nothing. The politics of this *dolce far niente* becomes clear when situated within the context of capitalism's insistence on the value of time as the source of financial profit—to enjoy doing nothing is to valorize the loss of profit. For Pynchon, such pleasure is social, because the possibility of doing nothing, of standing against the (working) day, depends on collective strategies for subverting capitalist command and constructing alternative material conditions. Pynchon's fiction commons time, not only in the sense that it refuses time's reduction to a means of accumulating capital but also in its commitment to time as a medium for sharing life in common. Pynchon formulates a utopian praxis in which time becomes the medium of new genres of social life. Sloth is not merely the other of clock time, it's a doorway to postcapitalist futures.

Pynchon's investment in sloth situates his work in a tradition of Marxist critical theory for which the refusal of labor implies a militant political ethos. In particular, Pynchon's fiction elaborates the thinking of the autonomist Marxists—including Mario Tronti, Antonio Negri, and Paolo Virno—for whom the refusal of labor not only entails the negation of capitalist command but also the self-valorization of workers: The break with capitalist profit-making is a collective project of intensifying social potentiality in autonomous terms. Kathi Weeks argues that acts of refusing labor involve a utopian demand: The negation of capitalist command is the reappropriation of the future in the present; it transforms the embodied subjectivities of workers from a source of labor power for capital into a site of collective self-determination. Weeks writes: "Cultivating utopian hope as a political project of remaking the world is a struggle to become not just able to think a different future but to become willing to become otherwise."[3] Autonomist (or post-autonomist) thinkers such as Weeks trace a path between biopolitics and utopia by showing that the struggle over labor is inextricable from a general political contest over time. Although Pynchon is not a Marxist in the strict sense, he shares with these thinkers a commitment to the reinvention of free time, to the recuperation of a time that is not the other of capitalist time but its abolition.

It would be a mistake, however, to reduce *Against the Day* to contemporary debates regarding the politics of labor. The political ethos of Pynchon's fiction derives in large part from its commitment to retroactive utopianism. I've argued that William Burroughs's concept of retroactive utopianism speaks to a general project in American politics and culture of recuperating the revolutionary movements of the past. Retroactive utopianism rescues alternatives to capitalism and the nation-state from the oblivion of American exceptionalism. It is, in short, a militant practice in the name of a singular America. Pynchon's version of this practice can be found in his earliest works of fiction—*V.* (1963), *The Crying of Lot 49* (1966), and *Gravity's Rainbow* (1973)—each of which constructs a countermemory in which the secret histories of cabals and conspiracies interrupt the capitalist vision of history as linear progress. More important than the particular social content of these underground organizations is the way in which their presence speaks to the heterogeneity of history: Tristero, the covert postal service in *The Crying of Lot 49*, does not exemplify revolutionary change, but it does demonstrate the nonsynchronicity of the historical present. Pynchon's more recent work, beginning with *Vineland* (1990), shifts the emphasis from conspiracies to social movements, or, more precisely, it renders the two indistinguishable, suggesting that the revolutionary elements in the United States have never stopped investing America with a hope far in excess of nationalism, capitalism, and colonialism. *Mason & Dixon* (1997) articulates this utopian energy in a memorable fashion, calling America a "Rubbish-Tip for subjunctive Hopes, for all that *may yet be true*."[4] There is in Pynchon's fiction an irrepressible, underground America—a counter-nation that not only plots revolution but also dreams up new institutions for a world to come.

Against the Day realizes what is implicit in the concept of a singular America, namely, that the utopian content of America can be salvaged only through a counterhistory of lived time. It is only insofar as utopia grounds itself in the time of the flesh that a singular America separates itself from American exceptionalism. Set during the final years of the nineteenth century and the start of the twentieth, *Against the Day* assembles a patchwork of laboring and loitering multitudes, of characters building railroads, going on strike, participating in communes, inventing time machines, conducting long cons, and engaging in any number of other zany antics. Pynchon is no Whitman, however, for he never confuses the realization of the multitude's powers with the consummation of national desire. In a way, Pynchon is closer to Dickinson, for he too imagines a singular America as a flight from the nation-state, or as the turning inside out of normative models of subjectivity. Pynchon's characters are less coy than Dickinson's "nobodies," but they're no less queer. They are oddballs and misfits dedicated to living time against the demands of the (working) day. They make sloth a creative practice—an art of revolt, as well as an art of time. As one character puts it:

> This is our own age of exploration... into that unmapped country waiting beyond the frontiers and seas of Time. We make our journeys out there in the low light of the future, and return to the bourgeois day and its mass delusion of safety, to report on what we've seen. What are any of these "utopian dreams" of ours but defective forms of time-travel? (942)

These lines gesture toward a shore on the other side of history, but, paradoxically enough, they position this temporal outside *within* the day: It is less a matter of getting outside of time than of rescuing the future from capitalist visions of progress. It is counter-redemption, a salvation immanent in material history.

Pynchon's rescue of a singular America takes the form of a political and narrative logic proceeding from escape (taking time out of the workday) through sloth (pleasure in idleness) to the time of the commons. He resurrects nineteenth-century political conducts, mining them for their latent futurity and connecting them to the social struggles of the present. First, there is the anarchist deed and the strike, understood as ways of sabotaging the working day. These do not abolish capitalist time, but they demonstrate the irreducibility of time to the rhythms of capital. They insist on the surplus time of laboring flesh. Second, there is the activity of loitering, including the practices of narrative digression and dilation that Ross Chambers attributes to loiterature. *Against the Day* wanders away from linear plot structure, preferring to meander or circumlocute, to digress into strange asides that go nowhere. In doing so, the novel translates the act of swerving from clock time into the positive form of the simulacrum—a time freed from the compulsions of originality, finality, and irreversibility. Last, there is the time of the commons, a temporality of communal pauses constituting a laboratory for experimenting with new social relations. In "A Journey into the Mind of Watts," Pynchon describes the Watts riots of 1965 as social improvisation: The event represents not social chaos, as mainstream news sources claimed, but the creation of a time unhitched from the racist pulse of capital accumulation. Although *Against the Day* doesn't emulate Watts, it does organize its characters into communes—social structures in which one lives not only *with* others but also *for* others. These are pockets of time subtracted from capitalism. They generate an enjoyment (jouissance) outside of capitalist time. They are homes for a singular America. At the end of the day, a singular America is a time after America, a time after exceptionalism, but the secret of a desire called America is that this time is now, that it has always been present in bodies living otherwise, in militants making the day their own.

Beyond the Hours of Daylight: The Working Day as Biopolitical Struggle

Near its conclusion, *Against the Day* bears witness to the final triumph of the day. It is a vision of darkness's conquest by light, as electricity exorcises the night's mysteries. It is also a vision of class struggle, of labor's defeat at the hands of the working day:

> While crossing the continent the boys ["the Chums of Chance"—the novel's parodic encapsulation of the adventure novels of the nineteenth century] had expressed wonder at how much more infected with light the night-time terrains passing below them had become—more than anyone could remember, as isolated lanterns and skeins of gas-light had given way to electric street-lighting, as if advance parties of the working-day were progressively invading and settling the unarmed hinterlands of night. But now at last, flying in over southern California and regarding the incandescence which flooded forth from suburban homes and city plazas, athletic fields, movie theatres, rail yards and depots, factory skylights, aerial beacons, streets and boulevards bearing lines of automobile headlights in constant crawl beyond any horizon, they felt themselves in uneasy witness to some final conquest, a triumph over night whose motive none could quite grasp.
>
> "It must have to do with extra work-shifts," Randolph guessed, "increasingly scheduled, that is, beyond the hours of daylight." (1032–33)

The novel does not so much represent capitalism as imagine its inevitable endpoint, namely, the total annihilation of free time as the working day stretches "beyond the hours of daylight." As Jonathan Crary explains, "An illuminated 24/7 world without shadows is the final capitalist mirage of post-history, of an exorcism of the otherness that is the motor of historical change."[5] This stalling out of history is irreducible to the quantitative extension of the working day. The becoming-24/7 of capitalism also has to do with *how* we live time. To borrow Pynchon's language, capitalist time "infects" and "invades" time; it changes the experience of time so that even leisure hours are devoted to enterprise. It makes every instant of social life a function of the process of capitalist valorization. Although the progressive illumination described by the passage would seem to imply a kind of social transparency or a revelation of historical meaning, the Chums of Chance report these circumstances in a manner that suggests increasing opacity and indistinction. It is "a triumph over night whose motive none could quite grasp." The modernization of social space, or the territorialization of the earth in capitalist terms, makes time available only insofar as it encloses it. Time is not meaningful but measurable. It is all too graspable, provided that one acquiesces to the capitalist standard of "work-shifts."

Against the Day maps the enclosure of time by capital, but it also seeks out anticapitalist rhythms of life—times that are of the working day only insofar as they stand against it. As the novel's title suggests, Pynchon doesn't satisfy himself with being an "uneasy witness to some final conquest." Instead, he constructs a countermemory in respect to capitalism and the nation-state, or, as he puts it, he tells the story of America not in the declarative but in the subjunctive, not in terms of what is but of "all that *may yet be true*." Pynchon enters into contemporary debates over the extent of capitalism's colonization of social life, but he does so at a utopian slant. He repeats Marx's deconstruction of the working day in the first volume of *Capital*—Marx's demonstration that the working day is an outcome of class struggle—but he does so from the perspective of the struggle against capital. In other words, Pynchon stages the (working) day as a biopolitical struggle over time.

In contemporary Marxist theory, especially of the (post-)autonomist tradition, this debate has taken the form of two periodizing gestures. The first involves the distinction, initially articulated by Marx, between formal subsumption and real subsumption.[6] These two concepts might be defined as follows: Whereas formal subsumption adopts non- or precapitalist forces of production and turns them toward the end of capital accumulation, real subsumption changes how production occurs, directly transforming the labor process in the name of maximizing profits. Marxist theorists, most notably Antonio Negri, have sketched the history of capitalism as a transition from formal subsumption to real subsumption, identifying a moment—usually sometime between the end of World War II and the 1980s—in which real subsumption overtakes formal subsumption. The second periodizing gesture is the social factory thesis.[7] This thesis argues that the universalization of real subsumption goes hand in hand with an abolition of the distinction between labor time and free time: All of social life becomes a factory, as capital learns how to extract surplus value from even the most mundane activities. One need only consider the monetization of social media platforms, which extract profits through the collection of data from its users.[8] Both of these periodizing gestures perform the critical function of cataloging the loss of free time and social autonomy in the face of the capitalist reorganization of social life. They are theoretical means for ascertaining the degree to which capitalism has remade the earth in its own image. At the same time, they are neither melancholy, nor defeatist, because they posit an immanent outside of capitalism—a powerful rhythm of life that is simultaneously within and against the time of capital.

Against the Day follows in the footsteps of this tradition of Marxist critique, but it complicates the latter's tendency to frame matters in binary terms. Pynchon fractures the category of living labor—the potentiality of the subjects of labor in excess of waged labor—into a series of temporal conducts challenging the rhythms of the capitalist working day. In this section, I focus on a particular genre of temporal conducts, namely, those practices that involve taking time out of the capitalist workday. These are forms of escape, if not escapism. They do not overturn the capitalist mode of production, but they do introduce a caesura within the rhythm of capital accumulation. These time-outs become apparent in contrast to their opposite— the incessant pressure of capitalist temporality. The novel's most concerted reckoning with the rush of capitalist time comes from its account of the Traverse family, especially Webb Traverse, an anarchist dynamiter, and his three sons, Kit, Reef, and Frank. Although the novel wanders from scene to scene without an obvious overarching plotline, it constantly returns to the plight of this family, as if to remind the reader of that "merciless clock-beat we all seek to escape, into the pulselessness of salvation" (558). This sense of time as "merciless," as a pressure unforgiving in its constancy and indifference, is suggested by one of the novel's central events: Webb's murder by a pair of assassins hired by Scarsdale Vibe, a corporate magnate who is the text's closest figure to an antagonist. Beyond the allegorical implications of this murder—an embodiment of labor radicalism struck down by the personification of capital—what is notable is the way in which the Traverse family narrative thread repeats this traumatic wound: Webb's sudden death haunts the lives of his sons; each son rides in the wake of Webb's life, alternating between assuming Webb's revolutionary mission ("redemption" through dynamite, or the anarchist deed as "deliverance" from the capitalist workday) and pursuing vengeance for his death. It is as if Kit, Reef, and Frank are fated to sacrifice their lives to their father's memory. There is, the novel implies, no escaping the painful history of capital.

The Traverse family line does not simply repeat the history of capital; it also fractures it, revealing the contradictions and conflicts immanent in the process of capital accumulation. Webb's death is less a cutting short of time than a transmission of labor's true power, or a reminder that the refusal of the working day depends on a surplus of social potential. In concrete terms, all three of Webb's sons inherit his anticapitalist ethos, so that despite their tendency to wander aimlessly from one corner of the globe to another, they nonetheless find themselves frequently engaged in political struggles against capitalism. The novel stages this inheritance as a gospel of labor, or a political theology of anticapitalist militancy:

> He was trying to pass on what he thought they should know, when he had a minute, though there was never the time. "Here. The most precious thing I own." He took his union card from his wallet and showed them, one by one. "These words right here"—pointing to the slogan on the back of the card—"is what it all comes down to, you won't hear it in school, maybe the Gettysburg Address, Declaration of Independence and so forth, but if you learn nothing else, learn this by heart, what it says here—"Labor produces all wealth. Wealth belongs to the producer thereof." (95)

Webb takes time out of the day to educate his sons with a slogan that, from the perspective of capitalism, appears counterfactual, if not simply wrong-headed. If, as Marx argues, labor is a matter of time, not only the time one spends at work but also the time for which the capitalist pays, wealth is nonetheless only labor in an alienated or inverted form: Capitalist regimes of labor separate the activity of labor from the commodity through the social technology of the wage; they actualize the potentiality of minds and bodies at the expense of autonomy (labor's ability to decide how to organize itself) and wealth (direct appropriation of the products of one's work). Labor may produce all wealth, but wealth is certainly not the property of labor.

But Webb's slogan—by all indications, the slogan of the Western Federation of Miners (WFM), later taken up by the International Workers of the World (the "Wobblies")—is also the vision of a singular America. It constitutes an antagonistic potentialization of America through which America diverges from itself at the very moment of its founding ("Declaration of Independence") and re-founding ("Gettysburg Address"). Exceptionalism, as codified in the sacred documents of American liberty, harbors a promise of fulfillment that is also a promise of abolition: It betrays a desire for freedom, a historical jouissance, that the nation-state and capital can neither contain, nor tame. The text highlights the divergence between American exceptionalism and a singular America, as Webb goes on to juxtapose a language of truth, or "straight talk," to "double-talking . . . like the plutes do" (93). Echoing George Orwell, Webb translates three instances of double-speak: "'Freedom,' then's the time to watch your back in particular. . . . 'Reform'? More new snouts at the trough. 'Compassion' means the population of starving, homeless, and dead is about to take another jump" (93). The force of these translations lies in the way they relay the father's divergence from the symbolic authority of the nation; these speech acts generate a hermeneutic of suspicion in which the appearance of capital is not identical with its truth or its effects. In doing so, they enable a desire for the future understood as temporal alterity: One day a political act, not reform ("more new snouts at the trough") but revolution, will actualize the potentiality of American labor, bridging the gap between the first half of the slogan ("Labor produces all wealth") and the second ("Wealth belongs to the producer thereof"). Webb's praxis echoes the autonomist theory of "self-valorization" (*autovalorizzazione*), according to which revolution is a subversive intensification of the self-determining power of labor.[9] In other words, the IWW gospel of labor does not describe the historical realities of capitalism so much as sketch a trajectory beyond the status quo, an exodus from the heteronomy of capitalist command into the autonomy of living labor. It is a subjunctive vision of America.

In place of messianic hopefulness, Webb and his sons find more immediate redemption in the anarchist deed of dynamiting. In *Against the Day*, dynamiting is a temporal conduct, a "pathology" of time, if by that one understands the unbinding of clock time in a moment that exceeds the regularity of capital accumulation. Dynamite destroys the means of production, interrupting the circuits of capitalist valorization. Put differently, the anarchist deed blasts a hole in the channels through which capital extracts time from social life. Moss Gatlin, a reverend who preaches the gospel of labor, theorizes this practice as follows:

> "For dynamite is both the miner's curse, the outward and audible sign of his enslavement to mineral extraction, and the American working man's equalizer, his agent of deliverance, if he would only dare to use it. . . . Every time a stick goes off in the service of the owners, a blast convertible at the end of some chain of accountancy to dollar sums no miner ever saw, there will have to be a corresponding entry on the other side of God's ledger, convertible to human freedom no owner is willing to grant. . . .
>
> "Think about it," when the remarks had faded some, "like Original Sin, only with exceptions. Being born into this don't automatically make you innocent. But when you reach a point in your life where you understand who is fucking who—beg pardon, Lord—who's taking it and who's not, that's when you're obliged to choose how much you'll go along with. If you are not devoting every breath of every day waking and sleeping to destroying those who slaughter the innocent as easy as

signing a check, then how innocent are you willing to call yourself? It must be negotiated with the day, from those absolute terms."

It would have been almost like being born again, except that Webb had never been particularly religious. (87)

This passage recapitulates, in an inverse manner, the Protestant doctrine of "redeeming the time," that is, the capitalist political theology in which every instant of time is an opportunity for the enterprising soul.[10] As codified by ministers and laypeople from the Reformation onward, earthly time is borrowed time, time on loan from God. As such, it must be repaid, or "redeemed," through good works and the avoidance of sloth. The urgency of Moss Gatlin's words recapitulates the Protestant-capitalist investment in every moment ("every breath of every day waking and sleeping") only to upend its eschatological framework, transforming the categories of the elect and the preterite (the saved and the damned) into class categories: "Who is fucking who—beg pardon, Lord—who's taking it and who's not." As in Puritan theorizations of grace, redemption is paradoxically always already determined and subject to examination for proof. "Innocence" is not a given—"Being born into this don't automatically make you innocent"— but a mark of class belonging achieved through works. If the good works of Protestant doctrine are typically ascetic practices, the good works of Moss's proletarian theology are class struggle: "If you are not devoting every breath of every day waking and sleeping to destroying those who slaughter the innocent as easy as signing a check, then how innocent are you willing to call yourself?" In this thinking, inquiry into working conditions leads to the prescriptive implication of a political project whose lines are drawn in the "absolute terms" of an antagonism between the haves and have-nots. Salvation means the damnation of "the plutes."

Moss's proletarian doctrine would seem to do little more than repeat, albeit in an inverted manner, the Protestant-capitalist framework of redeeming the time. Although it promises a negation of capitalist command, it nevertheless reinforces a disciplinary logic according to which time is property and property is to be cherished. However, the passage points to another reading, one that departs from the Manichaean contours of what Pynchon names "the capitalist/Christer gridwork" (1043). For if dynamite is the worker's "equalizer, his agent of deliverance," it is also a *pharmakon*, in Jacques Derrida's sense of the term, a constitutively ambiguous "non-identity, nonessence, nonsubstance," a "floating indetermination" that simultaneously guarantees and undermines the structure of the system.[11] Not just the salvation of workers, dynamite is also "the miner's curse, the outward and audible sign of his enslavement to mineral extraction." This ambiguity does not, however, entail an equivalence between the two expressions of this entity, for the pharmakon, as "the matrix of all possible opposition," instills in the system an excess of "play," an indeterminate surplus of (non-)sense that drifts through the system.[12]

This surplus of play, or potentiality, emerges in this passage through a slippage between the two sides of "God's ledger." On the side of the capitalists there is a regulated economy of calculation ("Every time a stick goes off in the service of the owners, a blast convertible at the end of some chain of accountancy to dollar sums no miner ever saw..."), but on the side of labor, the "corresponding entry" is not declarative but subjunctive, tapping into a "human freedom no owner is willing to grant." There is a constitutive asymmetry between the two classes: on the one side, the (objective) plenitude of the bourgeoisie (the plutocrats, the "plutes"), the identification of wealth with the capitalist value-form, but, on the other, the proletariat, the producer of all wealth on whom value is predicated, a (subjective) void in the ledgers of capital—an insurmountable cost but also a constitutive element. This asymmetry is the condition of possibility of an incalculable surplus of time that escapes "the day," even if, as the passage reminds us, "it must be negotiated with the day." The passage reinscribes this surplus time in Webb's experience of conversion, which takes the form of a rebirth ("It would have been almost like being born again") delinked from codified systems of value ("except that Webb had never been particularly religious"). Conversion, here, is not insertion into a regulative discourse of class but rather class as surplus potentiality, class as historical jouissance. It is the becoming-autonomous of labor, meaning not only the negation of capitalist command but also the reappropriation of life itself.

Pynchon introduces a polemical division between living labor and dead labor, or labor as subjective potential and labor as the objective property of capital. Like Whitman, he represents the emancipation of labor as immanent in the conditions of capitalism: The future of labor is already present, if only in potential. However, in contrast to Whitman, Pynchon never surrenders to the fantasy that labor could realize itself through capital. Pynchon is closer to Whitman's contemporary, Marx, for he too presents labor not from the point of view of its sheer vitality but from the perspective of struggle. Although some scholars and activists have complained that Marx's *Capital* lacks a politics, that it sacrifices militancy to the quest for a scientific analysis of capital accumulation, the tenth chapter of the first volume, "The Working Day," suggests another possibility: a scientific inquiry grounded in militancy.[13] In this chapter, Marx resituates his analysis not only within the context of specific struggles over the length of the working day but also in workers' bodies. Marx defines the working day as capital's consumption of the time of life, a process whose fundamental premise is that "the worker is nothing other than labour-power for the duration of his whole life, and that therefore all his disposable time is by nature and by right labour-time, to be devoted to the self-valorization of capital."[14] Capital confuses the time of life with the time of capital. It converts even free time into a function of accumulation, reducing nonprofitable pursuits to a minimum. Life itself becomes the object of capital.

The biopolitical aspects of this process were not lost on Marx. Marx delineates the expansion of the working day—Pynchon's invasion of night by day—as capital's using up of life:

> But in its blind and measureless drive, its insatiable appetite for surplus labour, capital oversteps not only the moral but even the merely physical limits of the working day. It usurps the time for growth, development and healthy maintenance of the body.... It is not the normal maintenance of labour-power which determines the limits of the working day here, but rather the greatest possible daily expenditure of labour-power, no matter how diseased, compulsory and painful it may be, which determines the limits of the workers' period of rest. Capital asks no questions about the length of life of labour-power. (*Capital*, 1:375–76)

Marx identifies a central contradiction of capitalism in these lines: As much as the development of capitalism entails a rationalization of labor—the invention of social technologies for measuring labor time and converting life into an efficient means for making profits—capitalism also involves recklessness and blindness, an insatiable appetite for destroying the life on which it relies. It is tempting to argue that Marx reveals the concrete experience of the working day behind the abstractions of clock time, but it is precisely the abstraction of time from which labor suffers. This is what Marx means, when he writes that capital "asks no questions." Capital accumulates knowledge of labor power as a necessary condition for its own reproduction, but this knowledge depends on a constitutive carelessness in regards to the life of labor. Capital cares for life only insofar as life takes the form of labor power—or, as Jason Read explains, "The biological reproduction of living labor is always already implicated in its political reproduction; the problem of the health of labor is inseparable from the problem of control."[15]

It would be a mistake, however, to reduce the working day to capital's conversion of life into labor time. For in Marx's analysis, the working day is a historical and political compromise between the forces of labor and capital. Discussion of the legal framework of capital gives way to considerations of struggle:

> There is therefore an antinomy, of right [capital's right as purchaser to demand more time from the worker] against right [the worker's right as seller to limit the amount of time he or she gives]. Between equal rights, force decides. Hence, in the history of capitalist production, the establishment of a norm for the working day presents itself as a struggle over the limits of that day, a struggle between collective capital, i.e. the class of capitalists, and collective labour, i.e. the working class.
> (*Capital*, 1:344)

The "normal working day" is a holding pattern between labor's desire for free time and capital's drive to reduce life to labor time. In this context, "normal" indicates the emergence of necessity from political and social contingencies, or the transformation of struggle into custom. The length of the working day only appears natural because one has forgotten the struggles that the working day memorializes, or because the "force [that] decides" between rights has disappeared behind the routines of civil society. From this perspective, class struggle is a matter of time, not only because it takes time but also because its object is time's reorganization.

The day's triumph over night is that moment when there is no longer any time outside of capital, when the "blind and measureless drive" for profit sinks so deeply into the earth that one can no longer distinguish between nature and historical circumstance. This is what Fredric Jameson means by the disappearance of nature in postmodernity: Historical consciousness wanes when the free market no longer appears to be an invention of the bourgeoisie but instead seems a natural phenomenon.[16] Capital becomes like the weather—omnipresent, inexorable, taken for granted. Whereas Jameson theorizes postmodernity from the vantage point of capitalist subjectivity, or, more specifically, from within the conditions of labor's defeat in North America following the 1960s, the Italian autonomist Mario Tronti proposes another path for thought, one premised on the ongoingness of struggle. Tronti posits the thesis of the social factory in the midst of the political struggles in Italy in the 1960s and '70s. These conflicts not only pitted labor against capital but also labor radicals against the orthodoxies of the trade unions and the socialist and communist parties. There is much one could say about this period of struggle, but, for my purposes, what matters most is the way in which the theory of labor autonomy depends on the real subsumption of capital by society. Tronti elaborates this point: "At the highest level of capitalist development, the social relation is transformed into a *moment* of the relation of production, the whole of society is turned into an *articulation* of production, that is, the whole of society lives as a function of the factory and the factory extends its exclusive domination to the whole of society."[17] The social factory reveals itself to be an intensification of real subsumption. Not only does capital refuse to settle for adopting preexisting relations of production toward capitalist ends (i.e., formal subsumption), it also refuses to settle for transforming the labor process itself (i.e., real subsumption). Instead, it expands real subsumption by transposing the logic of production onto the whole of society. Capital is no longer an element of society, labor no longer a portion of life, because social life itself becomes a "function of the factory."

The theory of the social factory would seem to leave little room for revolt. Tronti, however, argues the opposite, claiming that even though the "highest level of the development of capitalist production signals the most profound mystification of all the bourgeois social relations," it also paves the way for an absolute break with capitalism:

> Not only: the working class should materially discover itself as a part of capital if it wants to oppose the whole of capital to itself. It should recognize itself as a particular of capital if it wants to present itself as its general antagonist. The collective worker is opposed not only to the machine, as constant capital, but to labour-power itself, as variable capital. It has to reach the point of having as its enemy the whole of capital, therefore itself as a part of capital. Labour should see labour-power as its enemy, as a commodity.[18]

Integration into capital does not imply an identity between life and labor. Instead, it implies an "intimacy" (as Tronti describes it elsewhere), not unlike the way in which indigo dyes fabric blue—all of life may be structured by capitalism, but that is not to say that it is reducible to it. Opposition to capital entails a work on the self; specifically, it requires a subtraction of life from labor power, a conversion of the collective subject of labor from a source of profit into a medium of self-valorization. Labor must pass through its historical particularity as "part of capital," if it is to arrive at a politics not of reform but of general antagonism. From this perspective, the conflict is no longer between capital and labor power but between labor (as element of capital) and life itself.

For autonomists like Tronti, the errors of the parties and unions were both theoretical and practical. In refusing to acknowledge the real subsumption of society, unions and parties rendered themselves blind to the general dissemination of labor politics throughout society. They resigned themselves to collective bargaining, disowning militant tactics such as wildcat strikes and workplace sabotage. In the vocabulary of the autonomists, the unions and the parties focused on the technical composition of capital to the exclusion of the political composition; that is, they neglected how the structure of social class is itself an effect of political struggle. In contrast, the autonomists had as their aim not the negotiation of the terms of the working day but the abolition of labor as such. As Tronti writes in "The Strategy of Refusal": "What are the workers doing when they struggle against their employers? Aren't they, above all else, saying 'No' to the transformation of labour power into labour? Are they not, more than anything, refusing to *receive* work from the capitalist?"[19] This conceptual pivot from negotiation to refusal signals a biopolitical turn in Marxist theory: The object of politics is no longer labor but life, or, more precisely, life's refusal to be reduced to labor.

Pynchon and the autonomists converge in posing the working day as a matter of biopolitical struggle. The day is not neutral, and negotiation never really resolves the conflicts. However, Pynchon doesn't simply reflect the findings of autonomist Marxism. Instead, he participates in what the autonomists term "co-research" (*conricerca*): a mode of inquiry into labor conditions that is simultaneously a process of political subjectivization. Gigi Roggero elaborates on the meaning of co-research by distinguishing it from conventional theories of class consciousness:

> The production of knowledge is immediately the production of autonomy. . . . Subjectivity is a battlefield: the capitalist subjectivation is always at tension with the autonomous subjectivation. This is because capital is always an antagonistic social relationship. Therefore, the political subjectivation and organization are immanent to the materiality of the processes of life and struggle, and not in a sort of objective and transcendent class consciousness.[20]

Pynchon and the autonomists collaborate, albeit indirectly, in a production of knowledge regarding labor, and this knowledge-production is also a reorganization of the collective subject of labor. It is less knowledge *about* life than knowledge *for* life. Co-research does not, Roggero makes clear, focus so much on the actuality of labor conditions as on the potentiality of labor to break with capital: "Co-research is 'lukewarm,' or 'tepid,' rather than 'hot' inquiry. It occupies the time and place of potentiality, of tendency, of organising, of a possibility to act on and overturn a tendency."[21] To paraphrase Pynchon, co-research investigates labor in the subjunctive mode, less concerned with what labor is than what it may yet become. In times of political reaction like our own, this subjunctive mode of inquiry testifies to a resiliency that doubles as hope; it is a way of refusing the posthistorical drift of 24/7 capitalism.

In *Against the Day*, Pynchon conducts a practice of co-research that eschews the chronological periodization of labor regimes in favor of subjunctive visions of the becoming-autonomous of labor. The novel does not so much represent the labor struggles of the late nineteenth and early twentieth centuries as draw a line between the present and its antecedents. This is a line of potentiality, a thread composed not of resemblances between periods but of a shared sense of what may yet be possible. It is an ongoing recuperation of living labor's potentiality in the face of the social factory. Specifically, Pynchon salvages nineteenth-century traditions of idleness, elaborated by socialist thinkers such as Marx's son-in-law Paul Lafargue, and brings them to bear on present-day matters of political subjectivity. One can hear echoes in Pynchon's fiction of Lafargue's argument that the aims of socialist politics should include not only the collective sharing of wealth but also the reduction of labor time. For Lafargue—whose *The Right to Laziness* (1883) has numerous affinities with recent calls for a postwork society—a revolutionary politics implies the educational task of dismantling living labor's attachment to "the vice of work" and of cultivating a desire for idleness.[22] With this in mind, it becomes possible to read *Against the Day* less as a representation of labor than as an invitation to enjoy not working. The novel may not spell out the practical details involved in implementing idleness as a social program, but it does participate in a political struggle over the production of subjectivity. Pynchon develops what Kathi Weeks terms a postwork imaginary, a vision of social potentiality premised on the refusal of labor.

Pynchon connects refusals of labor in previous centuries to refusals of labor, today, constructing a transhistorical "No." The activity of dynamiting constitutes a synecdoche for this metaphysics of labor, a way of crystallizing the power of refusal in a positive form. It's important to note, however, that the utopian bent of Pynchon's fiction means that history never stabilizes itself in a secure metaphysical structure (for instance, the subject of capital versus the subject of labor) but instead remains open to systemic change. The novel's most concerted narration of one of Webb's "deeds" attests to this positive deconstruction of the metaphysics of capital by focusing not on the blast itself but on the way the explosions merge with the "dynamitic mania prevailing" on the Fourth of July (*Against the Day*,

81). Webb and his partner in political action, Veikko, consider the Fourth the "perfect day all round for some of that good Propaganda of the Deed stuff," because the sounds of dynamite blasts "would just blend right in with all the other percussion" (80). Fourth-of-July fireworks may celebrate the nation's founding, constituting an almost literal illumination of exceptionalism, but pharmakon that they are, these explosions also give presence to Webb's anarchist praxis through a kind of spectacular concealment—the anarchist deed "blends" into the rituals of exceptionalism, an act of sabotage cloaked in the robes of its enemy.

If the Fourth of July is the day when America memorializes its history, then Webb gives proof to another America in an act—the dynamiting of a railroad—that splits "the day" open:

> Four closely set blasts, cracks in the fabric of air and time, merciless, bone-strumming. Breathing seemed beside the point. Rising dirt-yellow clouds full of wood splinters, no wind to blow them anyplace. Track and trusswork went sagging into the dust-choked arroyo.
> . . . "Seen worse," Webb nodded after a while.
> "Was beautiful! What do you want, the end of the world?" [said Veikko.]
> "Sufficient unto the day," Webb shrugged. "Course."
> Veikko was pouring vodka. "Happy Fourth of July, Webb." (96).

As a target, the railroad cannot help but be an overdetermined signifier, for it has served as the literal and figurative conduit for a specific narrative of American progress—westward expansion, Manifest Destiny—one in which America rides the rails, propelled onward by flows of capital. But Webb and Veikko's "cracks in the fabric of air and time" put a momentary stop to this unfolding story, signaling the haunting insistence of another America. This singular America is paradoxically presented as simultaneously a brute absence and a spectacular presence. It is a negation of American history, one might even say a demystification of it, but it also recalls the revolutionary memory of "bombs bursting in air," so that one might read in Webb's uneasiness the impossibility of any simple distinction between American exceptionalism and a singular America. The dialogue between Veikko and Webb calls attention to the ambiguity of dynamite as social pharmakon, for not only does Veikko mimic the celebration of Independence Day as if he had simply been watching a fireworks display ("Was beautiful! . . . Happy Fourth of July, Webb"), but Webb's "Sufficient unto the day. . . . Course" can be read as either the affirmation of a break with "the day" or an admission that the blast only repeats "the day" in altered form. "The day" remains on "course." The Fourth's explosions signify America in an ambiguous fashion: The echoes of the nation's founding imply not only exceptionalism but also divergence, in the sense of both betrayal—the nation no longer living up to its promises—and utopian reprisal—a visionary rearticulation of counter-national possibility.

The ambiguity of *Against the Day* shouldn't be read as resignation to the status quo but as a commitment to immanence, to co-research as a practice that seeks out the potentiality of labor in the midst of real subsumption. One is against the day, even as one is in and of it: The emergence of a singular America, or, in this context, the becoming-autonomous of labor, occurs within the structures of American exceptionalism. This becoming-autonomous of labor can be traced through the plotlines involving Webb's sons. The sons of the Traverse family repeat the life of Webb Traverse, composing new possibilities out of his remains. As one brother says to another: "You can do the mourning . . . me and Frank will what Joe Hill calls organize" (216). Although the immediate reference of this line is revenge ("that old world o' family vengeance") the more significant connotation lies in the distinction between mourning—a repetition of the past in response to loss—and organizing—a creative, future-oriented relation to time (217). Although the brothers seek vengeance—Frank kills one of Webb's killers, Reef and Kit unsuccessfully make an attempt on Scarsdale Vibe's life—these acts come to seem almost incidental in respect to the rest of the novel. The brothers wander off to Europe, Central America, and Asia; they stumble into their own adventures. They free themselves from the biopolitics of capitalism as much by drifting off course as blowing up the means of production. Of course, the history of capitalism doesn't disappear. The day continues to govern the time of life. But in the midst of the social factory, labor discovers the possibility of autonomy—the potentiality for living otherwise. In *Against the Day*, the anarchist deed memorializes the nineteenth-century dream of idleness; it recovers missed historical opportunities, transforming them into demands on the present. Pynchon says "No" to the day, but the gesture is not purely negative, for it clears a space for the imagination of utopia—it invites one to enjoy doing nothing, nothing at all.

In Praise of Sloth

Under capitalism, Marx quips, the working day has become so complex that "an English judge, as late as 1860, needed the penetration of an interpreter of the Talmud to explain 'judicially' what was day and what was night" (*Capital*, 1:390). The day's complexities only deepen with the advent of the social factory, as the permanent illumination of 24/7 capitalism annihilates the difference between labor time and free time. The mysteries of time do not belong to capital alone, however. The anarchist deed already suggests that there's an immanent outside to the time of capital, a timelessness that serves as the condition of possibility of a new day. Yet there is a significant limit to the deed as temporal figure: Dynamite's ability to blast the working day open remains trapped within a regime of representation whose governing rule is action. The anarchist deed risks fetishizing the action-oriented mode of production it wishes to overthrow, because, to paraphrase Moss Gatlin's labor gospel, it envisions the world as a "ledger" in which each dynamite blast corresponds to a moment in the accumulation of capital. The ethos of the deed judges commitment to the cause on the basis of performance; it makes anticapitalist struggle a duty whose fulfillment can and should be measured in terms of productivity. The anarchist deed thus inverts the ends of production without dispensing with its means. It sacrifices idleness to the altar of duty, deferring the promise of a postwork world until a tomorrow that may never come.

Against the Day builds on its project of emancipating time from capital through a strategy of literary idleness. Pynchon's practice of co-research takes place on the level not only of content but also of form: the aesthetic means through which *Against the Day* separates the time of reading from the time of capital accumulation. The novel employs digression, dilation, and doubling as means of overturning the literary conventions of narrative development. It does not so much develop a story as suspend the unfolding of the story in asides, pauses, and repetitions with no obvious narrative value. *Against the Day* is Pynchon's most concerted effort at devising a method of literary sloth, a narrative strategy whose aim is not to communicate a tale so much as to waste time. This waste takes on positive form when considered from the perspective not of action but of potentiality. Sloth wastes time, but it recuperates potentiality. It short-circuits the routines through which the time of life gets reduced to labor time, indicating the surplus of potentiality over the means of production. It suggests the possibility of a means without ends, or a doing without duty.[23] There is more to life, literary sloth suggests, than getting from point A to point B.

Sloth interrupts the day. One could say that it breaks with the urgency of capital accumulation (the "merciless clock-beat we all seek to escape"), but one would have to add that sloth doesn't really *do* anything, that it strikes against the day by doing nothing at all. Pynchon complicates this point, however, in "Sloth: Nearer, My Couch, to Thee" (1993), arguing that there is a distinction to be made between sloth as refusal of labor and sloth as resource for capital. In the essay, Pynchon sketches a brief history of sloth, focusing his attention on the ways in which different media technologies represent specific kinds of idleness. After summarizing the early modern history of sloth as an object of religious censure, Pynchon constructs an opposition between, on the one hand, the likes of Benjamin Franklin, for whom sloth "was no longer so much a sin against God or spiritual good as against a particular sort of time, uniform, one-way, in general not reversible—that is, against clock time," and, on the other, Bartleby the Scrivener, hero of the "first great epic of modern Sloth," whose "terminal acedia" is less a matter of resignation than a glum refusal to conform to the demands of the day.[24] Pynchon associates the time of the novel with sloth, so that the very act of writing becomes "an offense against the economy," a means of infecting the populace with laziness: "Life in that orthogonal machine [modernity as governed by clock time] was supposed to be nonfiction." In wasting time, fiction intimates a life beyond capital.

Pynchon, however, calls into question such heroic assessments of the writer's vocation. He observes, "Idleness is often of the essence of what we [fiction writers] do. We sell our dreams. So real money actually proceeds from Sloth, although this transformation is said to be even more amazing elsewhere in the entertainment sector, where idle exercises in poolside loquacity have not infrequently generated tens of millions of dollars in revenue."[25] Pynchon suggests that there is a reversal proper to capital through which the activities of free time become labors in their own right. Idle pursuits may not always be waged, but that doesn't mean they cannot be monetized. Pynchon arrives at a conclusion similar to that of the autonomists: Capitalism's quest to convert as much of life as possible into labor time leads to an abolition of the distinction between labor and leisure. There is no time that is not, at least potentially, time for profit-making. Nor does Pynchon confine the social factory to the milieu of creative labor. "Acedia is the vernacular of everyday life," he writes, explaining that the development of a consumer society over the course of the twentieth century has resulted in the dominance of a passive kind of sloth—a sloth that is not labor's negation but resignation to the status quo. Citing "the notorious Couch potato," Pynchon diagnoses postmodernity in much the same way as Guy Debord—the consumption of spectacle involves an exchange of agency for mindless pleasure.[26] In Pynchon's phrasing, the subjects of late capitalism find themselves "Tubeside, supine, chiropractic fodder, sucking it all in, reenacting in reverse the transaction between dream and revenue that brought these colored shadows here to begin with."[27] Sloth is no longer the refusal of the capitalist imposition of labor time on life. It is, instead, the "supine" condition of capital accumulation, the means through which leisure becomes labor in service of the day.

Pynchon's account of the history of sloth is admittedly very general. There is an allegorical quality to the way in which Pynchon handles devices such as the television, the novel, and the VCR, as if they were less objects embedded in social life than figures of virtue and vice. Indeed, Pynchon sees the remnants of sloth's radical social potential in transgressions against technology:

> Perhaps the future of Sloth will lie in sinning against what now seems increasingly to define us—technology. Persisting in Luddite sorrow, despite technology's good intentions, there we'll sit with our heads in virtual reality, glumly refusing to be absorbed in its idle, disposable fantasies, even those about superheroes of Sloth back in Sloth's good old days, full of leisurely but lethal misadventures with the ruthless villains of the Acedia Squad.[28]

The almost slapstick tone of these sentences could be said to conceal the political aims of Pynchon's discourse: It is as if Pynchon were smuggling melancholy refusal into a Saturday morning cartoon. But it would be more accurate to say that Pynchon creates a zone of indistinction between glum refusal and joyful affirmation, that in allowing himself these zany verbal antics in which allegorical virtues and vices are comic book characters, he makes room for an idleness of joyful refusal—a pleasure in doing nothing. Pynchon imagines a mode of praxis that could be called idle not so much because it does nothing but because it does nothing for capital.

Against the Day is cultural education for a postwork society to come. The novel not only refuses the reduction of life to labor time. It cultivates aesthetic forms in which an experience of noncapitalist temporality becomes possible. In particular, Pynchon circulates three forms—digression, dilation, and doubling—through which the act of reading becomes a sin against the economy. The first of these forms, digression, can be witnessed in the way the novel luxuriates in excurses on esoteric subjects—for instance, the notion of the aether, an explanation for action at a distance in nineteenth-century physics. This example is only one of many subjects on which the novel discourses without advancing the plot. *Against the Day* could be said to lose itself in digressions, frequently abandoning one narrative thread for another with a tone of astonished happenstance: "Whom should he run into but old Ratty McHugh"; "Who should appear but"; "Who'd they happen to run into but Frank, Stray, and Jesse"; "Where whom should he run into but" (700, 849, 1075, 1034).²⁹ This rhetorical formula (*who/whom ... but*) allows the narrator to abandon characters and then return to them in a nonchalant manner, as if they were always waiting on the next page like products lining the shelves of a retail store. The disjunction "but" is less an indication of authorial omniscience than a sign of laziness: Pynchon's narrator refuses to present contingency as if it were necessity, or chance as if it were fate, instead calling attention to the artifice, the accident, of the plot's organization. Nor is this the only rhetorical technique through which Pynchon cobbles together the multitude of plotlines. In addition to *who/whom ... but*, the novel employs *one day* ("One day Miles Blundell ..." [250]), *meantime* ("Meantime Miles and Lindsay were off to the Fair" [21]), and many other indolent adverbial phrases to transition from one scene to another. The aesthetic effect is one of formal unruliness—an incongruity between story and presentation that has less to do with lack than excess. In the words of one reviewer, the novel "starts in the air, high-minded as a kite, and gradually flutters groundward, dragged down by subplots galore and characters thrown in willy-nilly, as if a novel's only virtue were how many characters it could stuff into a phone booth."³⁰

Paradoxically, literary sloth involves overproduction, as if the alternative to capitalist temporality were not stasis but exhaustion. The novel refuses to prune the forking paths of narrative potential for the sake of formal symmetry. The distinction between central plotline and subplot gives way to episodic seriality. The stories of the Traverse family, the Chums of Chance, the intra-European conflicts leading up to World War I, the private investigator Lew Basnight, anarchist organizations in Spain—to name only a handful of the novel's narrative threads—do not so much compete for space in the novel as share narrative time in an egalitarian manner, occasionally intersecting, often diverging, but always available through a *meantime* or a *whom ... but*. The novel socializes time, substituting a proliferation of minor characters for a hierarchical division between protagonists and side characters.³¹ The result is that if the reader profits from the novel, it is not because of an individual character or plotline but because of the totality of minor narrative threads—the collective wealth of digressions.

Against the Day wastes the reader's time with its tendency to digress, but, in doing so, it recovers a sense of temporality in excess of the day's demands. Digression's counterpart in the novel is dilation—the expansion of the instant into a moment of pure potentiality. If digression serves literary sloth by insisting on the equality of moments of narrative time, dilation does so by deferring the prospect of resolution so that the value of a given narrative moment is no longer measured against what it contributes to a final revelation. Webb and Veikko's Fourth-of-July "deed" is exemplary. The act of dynamiting the railroad separates itself into two parts (the first a handful of pages, the second a handful of paragraphs), occurring at the beginning and the end of the chapter. In between these narrative segments, the novel offers a biographical account of Webb, focusing on his political activism, so that one can read the anarchist deed not only as an interruption of the working day but also as a recuperation of time in the name of anticapitalist politics. The novel displaces the evental temporality of the explosion in favor of a ballooning of the moment, an inflation of the instant so that it encompasses past and future. Potentiality gushes out of the actual, not escaping material conditions but folding them back on themselves, so that the present finds itself traversed by what has been and what is to come. Webb and Veikko's deed does not simply blast a hole in clock time. It overloads capitalist urgency by insisting on futures past, by mining the history of anarchism for the possibility of a postcapitalist world.

The narrative strategies of dilation and digression translate the refusal of labor into the domain of literature. They break with the literary convention of good narrative pacing in favor of a doing nothing—an idling—that paradoxically implies an overabundance of happenings. *Against the Day* elaborates on this sense of surplus through the practice of doubling. The novel is littered with repetition: the repetition of phrases, character types, plot strands, and particular individuals. For example, there are two characters, Professor Renfrew and Professor Werfner, each the "so-called conjugate" of the other, who may or may not be one and the same person (719). The palindromic mirroring of their names gestures toward the series of mirrorings that structure the novel as a whole. For every type, there is a counter-type: not only a crusade but also a "counter-Crusade"; not only the philosopher's stone but also the "Anti-Stone"; the "counter-Christian"; "counter-Death"; "contra-Venezia" (437; 78; 275; 372; 587). The novel is a *"zone of dual nature"* in which the singular is always already composed of plurality, in which the original is always already a simulacrum (633). Narrative overproduction not only occurs through digression and dilation. It is also a matter of content. The text recycles narrative objects in a manner that amplifies the laziness of the plot construction. Why invent new characters, events, or phrases, when you can make already existing ones serve double duty?

It would be wrong, however, to understand *Against the Day*'s tendency to repeat itself in terms of sameness or homogeneity. Repetition is creative in Pynchon's work, because it does not recapitulate identity but transforms individuality into serial plurality. Leo Bersani articulates this point in regard to *Gravity's Rainbow*: "Pynchon's novel is a dazzling argument for shared or collective being—or, more precisely, for *the originally replicative nature of being*. Singularity is inconceivable; the original of a personality has to be counted among its simulations. Being in Pynchon is therefore not a question of substance, but rather of distribution and collection."[32] Pynchon's fiction deconstructs the metaphysics of being, according to which different forms of existence derive from a primary substance. There is no substance subtending beings in the world, only the becoming of beings, the "distribution" and "collection" of beings through the proliferation of simulacra. It makes no sense to ask whether Renfrew is a copy of Werfner, or vice versa. In fact, it makes no sense to speak of identity at all, for the text introduces difference into the core of their character(s): Werfner and Renfrew are geographers with inverse theories regarding geopolitics; they are not complementary identities but rather the double articulation of a difference that is not identical with itself.

At first glance, it may not seem that the originality of the simulacrum constitutes a problem of time. However, it is precisely the deconstruction of self-sameness that enables the narrative strategies of digression and dilation in the first place. Doubling delivers the raw material that dilation and digression transform into literary sloth; it ensures that there is always a surplus of narrative objects in respect to the plot. The text comments on the temporal significance of the simulacrum in a comic anecdote featuring a magician, Luca Zombini, who employs the mineral Iceland spar in his performance of the illusion of sawing a person in half. The mineral's ability to optically double appearances makes it so that "instead of two different pieces of one body, there are now two complete individuals walking around, who are identical in every way" (355). However, Zombini finds that he cannot reunite the doubles, because from the very moment of division their lives begin to diverge. He laments:

> I thought it would be completely reversible. But according to Professor Vanderjuice up at Yale, I forgot the element of time, it didn't happen all at once, so there was this short couple of seconds where time went on, irreversible processes of one kind and another, this sort of gap opened up a little, and that was enough to make it impossible to get back exactly where we'd been. (*Against the Day*, 355)

On the one hand, it's the irreversibility of time that foils the successful resolution of Zombini's performance. If the goal of the illusionist is to construct a spectacle of appearances, while maintaining the substance of things intact, Zombini fails because he's too effective—he changes not only the appearance of things but also their essence. On the other hand, it becomes difficult to speak of the essence of things, when divergence comes to be framed not as incompletion but excess. Zombini does not so much fracture lives as multiply them, making the internal heterogeneity of subjects serve as the basis for the production of new life. Division does not reduce life to identity, just as repetition does not institute sameness. Instead, it generates a seriality in which multiplicity takes the place of identity, or, as the text concludes: "By now these subjects had gone on for too long with their lives, no longer twinned so much as divergent . . . they would have gone on to meet attractive strangers, court, marry, have babies, change jobs, move to other places, it would be like trying to put smoke back into a cigar even to find them anymore" (572). In substituting "divergent" for "twinned," the text doesn't simply emphasize the irreducibility of simulacra to identity. It also highlights that the swerve from identity should be understood in positive terms as a wealth of potentiality. Digression is the multiplication of possibilities for life.

The tale of Zombini can be read as a parable instructing readers in a counter-redemption of time. If the capitalist-Protestant tradition of redeeming the time enjoins subjects to profit from each and every instant as if it were their last, Pynchon's literary sloth does more to inspire loitering—wasting time to see what the day may bring. From the perspective of "the capitalist/Christer gridwork," such inaction can only be interpreted as a corruption of time, a squandering of the generativity whose point of origin is God.[33] In secular or utilitarian terms, the premise of temporal finitude comes to imply that efficiency is an unimpeachable virtue—clock time demands the most efficient alignment of means with ends. *Against the Day* suggests an alternative to such discipline in its recuperation of idleness. The smoke may be irreversibly out of the cigar, but irreversibility is only one aspect of time. The narrative strategies of digression, dilation, and doubling show that temporality can involve a surplus of potentiality in respect to the progress of plot, a liberation of means from ends. Pynchon transposes Bartleby's glum refusal ("I would prefer not to") onto the form of the novel itself. He makes the very experience of reading into a protest against the day, as if to suggest that there's nothing lazier than enjoying fiction. The refusal to labor for the day is not simply a flight from capitalist discipline, for it is also the transformation of time into a commonwealth. Pynchon stages his utopian praxis at the nexus of temporality, subjectivity, and politics, so that utopia is not so much another place but another time—a different way of passing the day.

Time for the Commons: From the Riot to the Commune

Pynchon transforms the working day into a utopian site through a commoning of time. It is not simply that *Against the Day* breaks the link between the passage of time and the accumulation of capital. It is also that the novel discovers in time the potential for a life in common. Utopia comes to name the becoming-autonomous of time in egalitarian terms. One can articulate this utopian praxis as a logical and political sequence, one which passes from negativity (the anarchist deed) through idleness (literary sloth) to the commons: the communization, or de-privatization, of the rhythms of the flesh. Pynchon recovers what Anne-Lise François terms "unenclosed time": a "determinate openness" with "differing degrees of looseness, responsiveness to seasonal cues, plurality, and autonomy," irreducible not only to clock time but also to the flexibility of contemporary capitalism.[34] Unenclosed time confounds oppositions between rule and custom, regularity and chance, sanctioned activity and theft; it implies a form of social reproduction without state or corporate intervention, in which the cyclical rhythm of survival remains open to aleatory encounters. It is a temporality of making do that includes traces of utopian potential. Unenclosed time anticipates a world in which getting by no longer depends on state and capitalist institutions.

If Pynchon's literary sloth recovers an experience of unenclosed time from the working day, the time of the commons transforms this experience into a concrete political alternative. The time of the commons challenges political convention, not only troubling the liberal fetishization of representational politics but also disputing the socialist valorization of the party and the organic intellectual. Pynchon positions the commons as an alternative to politics proper; the commons constitutes a social site in which the division between delegate and constituency gives way to a new unity between theory and practice. More specifically, Pynchon recuperates the eighteenth- and nineteenth-century political traditions of the riot (the unsanctioned, seemingly spontaneous uprising of the dispossessed) and the commune (the self-governing, egalitarian, and radically democratic social enclave). These are traditions that combine the invention of egalitarian forms of social life with the refusal of the status quo. As Joshua Clover argues, such traditions have become timely once again, because they are forms of political expression through which surplus life—populations excluded from the circuits of capitalist valorization—create new conditions of social reproduction.[35] Surplus populations are proliferating and expanding in contemporary capitalism, because the realization of profit has increasingly migrated into the realm of circulation through financialization and logistics.[36] For many of capitalism's subjects, exploitation no longer involves the lengthening of the working day but the replacement of regular labor by intermittent gigs and unpaid work. Such precarity is not unenclosed time, because, in this context, surplus time means exposure to the contingencies of capital; exclusion from regular waged labor transforms life into an endless struggle to make ends meet—a qualitative, if not quantitative, poverty of time. In contrast, the riot and the commune transform the desperate conditions of poverty, precarity, and exclusion into chances for another world. They do not negotiate over the working day but instead couple a radical refusal of labor with a promotion of egalitarian social relations. They are utopian resources in a world in which labor seems to have little, if any, future.

Pynchon's essay "A Journey into the Mind of Watts" traces a path between aesthetics and the riot, suggesting that the time of the commons involves an art of political improvisation.[37] Written in 1966, a year after the Watts riots, the essay examines the "terrible vitality" of Watts, where "the poor, the defeated, the criminal, the desperate" are inventing new urban practices for the sake of survival. The condition of Watts is one of invisibility, a racialized positioning of bodies into a place that does not count, at least not within the white supremacist matrix of post–World War II American life: "Watts is country which lies, psychologically, uncounted miles further than most whites seem at present willing to travel." At the same time, it's also a place where "no one can afford the luxury of illusion," because poverty and policing make existence itself a struggle. Pynchon describes how simply walking from one point to another in Watts becomes a trial, due to the "L.A. poverty war's keep-them-out-of-the-streets effort." In this situation, refusal becomes a positive act, even an art:

> August's riot is being remembered less as chaos and more as art. Some talk now of a balletic quality to it, a coordinated and graceful drawing of cops away from the center of the action, a scattering of the Man's power, either with real incidents or false alarms. Others remember it in terms of music; through much of the rioting seemed to run, they say, a remarkable empathy, or whatever it is that jazz musicians feel on certain nights; everybody knowing what to do and when to do it without needing a word or a signal.

Pynchon's description of the artfulness of the Watts rebellions contests the mainstream representation of the riots as pure chaos or irrational acting out. Drawing on James Bogg and Ruth Wilson Gilmore, among others, Clover argues that the riot has come to be cast as a formless release of energy in contrast not only to the antiblack racism of the state but also to the whiteness of the strike (or the whiteness of state-sanctioned labor politics).[38] Along with Clover, Pynchon recognizes that rioting isn't a negation of form but an insistence on formal surplus, or the irreducibility of social life to civil order. In the riot, the refusal of police commands becomes a communal music composed of bodies in movement. This movement is not unthinking but coordinated, thoughtful, and communicative. Pynchon hesitates to use the term "empathy" in explaining this coordination ("a remarkable empathy, or whatever it is that jazz musicians feel on certain nights; everybody knowing what to do and when to do it without needing a word or a signal"), because this harmony in dissent is not merely about feeling for the other. It's about transformation. The virtuosity of the riot lies in its reinvention of sociality beyond not only the state but also bourgeois civil society. The riot is biopolitical, because it abolishes the distinction between public and private, politics proper and everyday life, locating political struggle in the daily conditions of bodies, in the struggles of the dispossessed to survive. As Clover puts it, "The riot is an instance of black life in its exclusions and at the same time in its character as surplus, cordoned into the noisy sphere of circulation, forced there to defend itself against the social and bodily death on offer. A surplus rebellion."[39] Clover's description suggests the utopianism of the riot, the way it brings together utter negativity—the abjection of racialized bodies—and future-oriented positivity—survival not as maintenance of the status quo but as social improvisation. The riot doesn't simply recover unenclosed time, it reinvents it as the basis for another kind of collective life. The riot is on the time of the commons.

The theory of the riot suggests a way of thinking about the commons that respects its embeddedness in socioeconomic conditions without dissolving political contention. The riot is a struggle over the working day, after the latter has generalized itself in the form of the social factory. It is a revolt against dispossession, against the impoverishment of time at the heart of capital accumulation. Riots interrupt the circulation of capital, but they also improvise new forms of cooperation. Rioting stitches together a commonality out of singular bodies, without ever reducing the plurality of bodies in struggle to a homogenous mass. The riot falls under the more general category of the assembly, which Judith Butler has analyzed as a mode of political action that makes a virtue of vulnerability. Assembly introduces a corporeal performativity through which physical presence—

the exposure of bodies protesting in the streets—conjures up new genres of public life.[40] It's tempting to classify the riot as a destructive form of the assembly, given that riots typically involve destruction of private property. However, such classification confuses an aspect of the riot for the whole, concealing the creative dimension of rioting. It is more precise to say that the riot is an assembly of the dispossessed, one which does not seek recognition from the state but longs for another social system, another mode of governance. In this framework, the commune names the fulfillment of the riot, its endurance beyond momentary rupture through the institutionalization of a commons.

The riot and the commune are not only particular political practices but genres of theory and practice that expand the political imaginary beyond the dichotomies of the public and the private, collective and individual, revolution and reform, the social and economic. Pynchon's essay on Watts should be understood as an artistic and political manifesto as much as an account of events and conditions. It implies that understanding the politics of artistic practices entails a revision of what one means by politics, an expansion of politics to include the quotidian and illicit practices that all too often pass under the radar of mainstream and academic analyses. Watts constitutes the historical jouissance, or utopian foundation, of the Pynchonian aesthetic. One cannot reduce the politics of his fiction to this kernel of radical potentiality, but reading his fiction with Watts in mind does bring to light the specific consistency of his politics—what one might call Pynchon's riotous ballet. This view offers a corrective to one of the dominant readings of Pynchon's fiction, which interprets its politics as a Romantic commitment to resistance against the corruption of Power.[41] From this perspective, Pynchon is less interested in grappling with the concrete realities of political struggle than in escaping from politics into a realm of cultural authenticity, in which experiences of sex, drugs, and rock and roll substitute for political conflict. The proliferation of subterranean organizations such as Trystero (*The Crying of Lot 49*), the Kunoichi Sisterhood (*Vineland*), and the anarchists in *Against the Day* are not an alternative politics but an alternative to politics. This reading depends, however, on a reductive view of politics, one which measures political potential solely in terms of state recognition. It mistakes Pynchon's rejection of state and corporate power for a naïve rejection of power as such. It is an anti-utopian view, for it assumes that liberal democracy and capitalism exhaust politics and, in doing so, forecloses the imagination of other worlds. In contrast, reading Pynchon in good faith means allowing the experimental and zany qualities of his aesthetic to revise the meaning of politics.[42] It means remembering Watts.

Against the Day revises the political not only through anarchist deeds and literary sloth but also through its utopian figurations of the commons. These figurations are not always riots, in the strict sense, but they involve a riotous energy—a surplus of futurity that is quotidian, fugitive, and revolutionary. Even though Pynchon's fiction builds on the encyclopedic ambitions of the Whitmanian merge—the desire to realize the world in a book—the narrative and representational strategies of *Against the Day* eschew that genre of universality. Instead of predicating utopia on a preexisting, molecular, and universal vitality (Whitman's version of the common), Pynchon imagines a dissident, patchwork solidarity: a cobbling together of universality through a series of irreducible social experiments and political struggles. Pynchon's utopian figuration is akin to Dickinson's practice of subtracting sociality from the institution of marriage, but whereas Dickinson's poetics insist on anonymity and seclusion, Pynchon's formal strategies convert the margins into a vast underground, a parallel universe with respect to authorized politics. To borrow Pynchon's metaphor, it is as if the night were winning its autonomy from the working day, free time no longer a coda to labor but a world of its own.

The Chums of Chance—a crew of boys plucked from the dime-store adventure novels of the nineteenth century—are the most obvious utopian figures in the novel. Their skyship, *The Inconvenience*, constitutes a refuge from the world below, as well as a site of libidinal excess: The Chums go on fantastic adventures, visiting faraway lands and participating in all manner of capers; they float above the historical conditions of the world below, living in a timeless time in which they never age (their boyishness seemingly eternal) and in which there is always another adventure on the horizon. In this context, utopianism doesn't necessarily connote emancipatory potential but instead a pleasure based on the suspension of worldliness. This unworldliness is a complicated affair, however, for the Chums blur the line between complicity and detachment. In fact, when the reader first encounters the Chums, they are performing surveillance at the Chicago World's Fair, an activity that garners them comparison to the notorious Pinkerton Agency, whose private investigators and security details were often employed to crack down on labor activism (25). The novel positions the Chums as an antidote to anarchist insurgency: They are hired to prevent riots and acts of sabotage by monitoring social life on the ground from the air. They are essentially freelance counterterrorist agents, their aerial freedom funded and circumscribed by the state and corporate institutions that keep them in business.

At the same time, there is a tonal and ontological levity to the Chums of Chance. This levity comes in the first place from their association with dime-store adventure novels, the text attributing the Chums' adventures to a series of published novels: "The more scientific among my young readers may recall the boys' earlier adventures (*The Chums of Chance at Krakatoa, The Chums of Chance Search for Atlantis*)"; "For details of their exploits, see *The Chums of Chance in Old Mexico*" (6; 7). The Chums belong to this world but are not quite of it.[43] Their presence creates a zone of indistinction between realism and fantasy, an outer margin in which the quotidian stuff of nineteenth-century realist fiction gives way to the fantastic material of the pulps (time travel, exotic lands, alien visitors). This outer margin is utopian not because it rectifies the social ills of the present but because it offers libidinal compensation for them: The timeless time of the Chums does not so much negate the daily grind as suspend it, providing an amusing diversion from the dreariness of everyday life under capitalism. The novel describes this detachment ambivalently as "the terms of the long unspoken contract between the boys and their fate—as if, long ago, having learned to fly, in soaring free from enfoldment by the indicative world below, they had paid with a waiver of allegiance to it and all that would occur down on the Surface" (1023).

The Chums of Chance are contradictory figures, for they not only embody the ideological dimensions of the dime-store adventure novel but also gesture toward a genuine utopian commitment to noncapitalist forms of solidarity. On the one hand, the Chums' adventures do more to supplement capitalism and state rule than to challenge them. Beyond their participation in surveillance and security, their travels to strange and exotic lands reproduce a colonial epistemology that transforms non-Western territories into inviting spaces of fantasy. Their encounters with social difference—whether it be cultural and ethnic difference or the political difference of anarchism—reinforce and expand the purview of imperial control. Difference becomes subordinated to identity, as the Chums' aerial surveys convert the unknown into the codified knowledge of state and capitalist governance. In this context, the riot can signify only criminality, its novelty seen as little more than destructive fanaticism.

On the other hand, as much as the Chums of Chance serve as a counterpoint to the anarchist ethos of *Against the Day*, they also constitute a reserve of utopian hope—a figure of sociality irreducible to capitalist exchange or national belonging. It's not simply that the Chums cross national boundaries with little concern for the rule of law but also that they commit themselves to "the supranational idea," a vision of belonging unmediated by state institutions (1083). The novel consecrates this utopianism through marriage, joining the Chums of Chance with an "Aetherist sorority" in "a domesticity of escape and rejection" (1030). Although one can certainly criticize Pynchon's reliance on heterosexual coupling as a social alternative, the text insists on the egalitarian and communal qualities of the arrangement, noting that the women agree "to join their fortunes with those of *Inconvenience*, only on the understanding that they would always operate independently" (1083). This unity of autonomy and collectivity is the condition of possibility for a utopianism that no longer reproduces a fear of difference.

> Never sleeping, clamorous as a nonstop feast day, *Inconvenience*, once a vehicle of sky-pilgrimage, has transformed into its own destination, where any wish that can be made is at least addressed, if not always granted. For every wish to come true would mean that in the known Creation, good unsought and uncompensated would have evolved somehow, to become at least more accessible to us. No one aboard *Inconvenience* has yet observed any sign of this. They know—Miles is certain—it is there, like an approaching rainstorm, but invisible. Soon they will see the pressure-gauge begin to fall. They will feel the turn in the wind. They will put on smoked goggles for the glory of what is coming to part the sky. They fly toward grace. (1085)

The utopianism in these sentences blends messianism with pragmatism, making the practices of everyday life into conduits of a speculative futurity. This futurity is both already present and to come; it is here and now in the "clamor" of a "nonstop feast day," yet it is also then and there in "the glory of what is coming to part the sky." It's a form of unenclosed time, which is to say that the Chums replace clock time with the nonlinear temporality of wish fulfillment—a time guided by the ebb and flow of libidinal urges or the improvisational zigzag of social experimentation. The Chums enter into what might be called a democratic state of exception: an ongoing suspension of the rules in response to the desires of the crew. The skyship no longer needs a destination, because the space of the ship has itself become open to social change. This is the exception of "grace," of a communal experience in which the Chums' chumminess—their boyish solidarity—gives way to a transcendence of the world below.

The Chums of Chance are a figure of the commune without the riot. They embody a utopian commitment to social experimentation, but they do so in a manner that leaves questions of social conditions and political strategy to the side. There are, of course, historical traditions of communal experiments with little relationship to the riot. Nineteenth-century experiments in communal living such as Brook Farm and the Oneida Community challenged social mores regarding the gendering of labor, the sanctity of marriage, private property, and education.[44] At the same time, they were seldom connected to social movements aiming at large-scale change. Instead, they functioned as enclaves—pockets of noncapitalist, non-statist social life supplementing the institutions of modern life, without subverting them.[45] Absent the riot, the commune becomes a refuge for alternative forms of social life, but it concedes the social totality to the status quo. The grace toward which the Chums fly cannot help but signal a retreat from politics, even as it preserves belief in a noncapitalist, nonsovereign polity. The Chums thus constitute an example of what Ernst Bloch terms abstract utopianism—a wishfulness that serves as a placeholder for utopian praxis but which does not manage to root itself in the concrete futurity inhabiting the present.[46]

Against the Day brings the riot and the commune together in a utopianism whose object is not transcendence but radical poverty. In this context, poverty has less to do with a lack of income than with a refusal of private property. This conception of poverty has roots in premodern Christianity, especially the Franciscan tradition, which espoused "the highest poverty" as a form of life rejecting the rule of property. In place of property, the Franciscans valorized *use*: a mode of relation and activity premised on the inappropriability of the world. Use invents a commonality that is without sanction, whose norms of conduct coincide with life itself. Giorgio Agamben has written extensively on this subject, arguing that the Franciscan tradition does not simply intimate the possibility of a communism without the state but also illuminates an entirely different ontology from Western metaphysics—one in which essence and existence, life and form, potentiality and actuality are indistinguishable.[47] The Franciscan monks devoted themselves so wholly to the gospel of Christ, Agamben explains, that there was no room in their lives for the rule of law (including property rights). Put differently, the only rule they obeyed was the rule of their hearts. Paradoxically, then, despite the meticulous discipline of prayer schedules, the time of the Franciscans was wholly their own: The rhythm of their social life was unenclosed not simply because of the absence of the profit imperative but also because of the indistinction between individual and collective temporalities. Radical poverty thus has less to do with the absence of

Idle Power

material goods than with one's mode of existence. It names a subjective destitution, in which the stripping away of attachments to private property paves the way for social reinvention. It's not another kind of sovereignty but a complete refusal of command. This concept of poverty implies utopian praxis, for it extracts the greatest social and political potentiality—the possibility of life without property, of life without law—from the negation of the status quo.

Poverty takes many forms in *Against the Day*, some more literal than others. The novel features miners who lose their jobs for going on strike; soldiers of the Mexican Revolution on a nomadic circuit through the countryside; refugees from the violence of World War I; and, of course, anarchists pledged to the destruction of capitalism. Even the Chums of Chance embody a form of poverty, their withdrawal from worldly affairs resembling nothing so much as a strange monasticism. However, the tradition of radical poverty distinguishes itself from the monastic isolation of the Chums of Chance by linking subjective destitution to earthly, especially erotic, pleasures. Pynchon associates the negation of property with the ecstasy of sexual relations. It's as if the only thing stopping the world from erupting into an orgy were the restrictions of property rights. The distinction, here, is not simply one between transcendence and immanence—the boyish innocence of the Chums versus the worldly knowledge of the poor—but between economies of difference. Whereas the Chums' devotion to grace involves an orderliness exemplified by marriage, radical poverty brings together the riot and the commune, queering sociality in the process. Difference is no longer subordinated to identity, no longer incorporated into civil society by way of state recognition. Instead, difference becomes anarchic, life rioting against the imposition of law and property. The poor of Pynchon's fiction have little use for grace, preferring that unenclosed time in which pleasure makes the day its own.

Although *Against the Day*'s figures of radical poverty are irreducible to one another, the romantic triangle between the characters Cyprian Latewood, Yashmeen Halfcourt, and Reef Traverse serves as an exemplary instance because of the way it fuses social experimentation, political commitment, scientific curiosity, espionage, eroticism, and nomadism. These characters are, respectively, a spy working for the British who finds himself in love with a woman (an uncharacteristic turn of events, as Cyprian usually prefers the company of men); a brilliant mathematician known for her hypnotic beauty (to which Cyprian succumbs); and the son of Webb Traverse, a gambler and class warrior (who also falls for Yashmeen). Cyprian, Yashmeen, and Reef represent the underground realms of espionage, mathematics and physics (the non-Newtonian heresies of the late nineteenth and early twentieth centuries), and anarchism. In bringing these together, the novel constructs a parallel universe in which governments, corporations, and even natural laws give way to experiments in living otherwise. Moreover, all three characters are in exile in some manner: Reef running aimlessly from his father's legacy; Yashmeen caught up for unknown reasons in power struggles among rival national factions; and Cyprian betraying the intelligence agencies of several nation-states. These characters combine singularity and disidentification—each becomes singular by disidentifying with state, capitalist, and sexual institutions. The proximity of singularity and disidentification is a feature of the novel as a whole, almost every major character entering into a process of self-transformation by breaking with the institutions that define him or her. These disidentifications are the verb form of the ontological condition of poverty in the novel; they translate what might seem like deprivation into a power of exodus—the improvisation of new forms of life through an ongoing rejection of property and propriety.[48] There's a queerness to poverty, as the destitution of normality opens onto the perverse pleasures of surplus potentiality.

In *Against the Day*, disidentification doesn't simply establish singularity. It also produces a commons—a dense corporeal knot in which relationality and individuality mutually constitute one another. The novel dramatizes this production of commonality at the moment when the relationship between Cyprian, Reef, and Yashmeen goes from being solely mediated by Yashmeen—a heteronormative triangle with only two sides—to transpiring equally among all three of them. This transformation emerges from the situation of a riot, specifically, "the secret counter-Carnevale known as Carnesalve," which, in contrast to Lent, constitutes "not a farewell but an enthusiastic welcome to flesh in all its promise. As object of desire, as food, as temple, as gateway to conditions beyond immediate knowledge" (880). Whereas the sanctioned Carnevale preceding this perverse double amounts to an outlet for repressed desires, counter-Carnevale interrupts the dialectic between the law and its transgression.[49] In qualifying the counter-Carnevale as "an enthusiastic welcome to flesh in all its promise," the text amplifies the rebellious pleasures and desires of the flesh. The body "in all its promise" is utopian, for it is no longer simply a thing in extended space, like the Cartesian body, but a rich nexus for experimenting with different forms of life. This processual fleshiness realizes the body and transforms it. If "counter-Carnevale" implies the extrication of a subversive corporeality from a dominant form of subjection, "Carnesalve" suggests a repair of the body—its restoration to its full powers. It is as if the only way that the body could satisfy itself, could make itself whole, were to change utterly, to become another body.

The "enthusiasm" involved in Carnesalve implies the breakdown of the possessive individual, a process of social interference in which the individual gets caught up in a movement of becoming common. It is a movement explicitly associated with the underground energies of espionage, revolution, anarchism, and the riot.

> With no interference from authority, church or civic, all this bounded world here succumbed to a masked imperative, all hold on verbatim identities loosening until lost altogether in the delirium. Eventually, after a day or two, there would emerge the certainty that there had always existed separately a world in which masks were the real, everyday faces, faces with their own rules of expression, which knew and understand one another—a secret life of Masks.... At Carnevale, masks had suggested a privileged indifference to the world of flesh, which one was after all bidding farewell to. But here at Carnesalve, as in espionage, or some revolutionary project, the Mask's desire was to be invisible, unthreatening, transparent yet mercilessly deceptive, as beneath its dark authority danger ruled and all was transgressed. (880)

The passage defines autonomy against "authority, church or civic," but it also distinguishes it from the modern concept of personal autonomy, or that notion of self-reliance according to which the subject's independence and individuality depend on ownership of one's body. Here, autonomy is neither self-identity nor independence from the other. Carnesalve eschews the propriety of the modern subject, valorizing instead a blurring of the self and other, as well as the literal and figurative—"all hold on verbatim identities loosening until lost altogether in the delirium." As "delirium" suggests, life in Carnesalve is life besides itself, caught up in an ecstasy that renders one *not* one, that breaks with oneness in favor of a plurality that is both more than one (multiple, rather than unitary) and less than one (irreducible to self-closure). The passage reinforces this sense of multiplicity by emphasizing deception not as a covering up—the Mask concealing psychological depth—but as a positive conception of simulacra that cannot be contained by transcendental unification. Appearances ("transparent yet mercilessly deceptive") are everything; they "have their own rules of expression." These rules constitute another idea of autonomy: autonomy as the negation of authority in and through relations with others.

The anarchy of Carnesalve is not the end of sociality but the reconstitution of the social as a commons. The break with the ruling order occurs not through a transcendence of the flesh in which the individual finally becomes authentically himself or herself but through the multiplication and modification of the flesh in a becoming permeable to others. This process constitutes a radical perversion of the Pauline doctrine of the circumcision of the heart—a major touchstone for contemporary critical theory grappling with the question of how to imagine a nonexclusionary, nonessentialist genre of universality.[50] Whereas Paul predicates universality on overcoming the differences of the flesh through commitment to the singular figure of Christ, Carnesalve's logic of Masks predicates commonality on the promiscuous connections among singular forms of flesh. Carnesalve's utopian content is inextricable from the body's becoming common; it is a leveling movement in which an egalitarian logic of shared bodily contact reigns. If universality is at stake in this manifestation of the riot, it's a universality delivered over to singularity and plurality—a universality entirely immanent in the messiness of embodied life.

The triangulation of erotic desire between Cyprian, Yashmeen, and Reef exemplifies the anarchy of Carnesalve. Their romance doesn't exhaust the social potentiality of the event, but it does demonstrate a mode of subject production in which singularity, plurality, and commonality operate in tandem. Whereas prior to Carnesalve heteronormative logic dictates that only Yashmeen has access to every partner in the relationship, Carnesalve interrupts this closure by opening up contact between Reef and Cyprian, the text narrating Cyprian performing fellatio on Reef, as well as the two engaging in anal sex: "They had never been all together quite like this till now, the proceeding has been limited to the two heterosexual legs of the triangle" (881). Cyprian becomes a "little go-between," the diminutive in this instance suggesting not so much that Cyprian is a mere means but rather a sense of intimacy and a bent toward troublemaking (883). As mediating body, Cyprian isn't neutral, for he troubles the proprietary erotic relations between bodies with an indiscriminate play of pleasures that is no less differentiated for running against the grain of the heterosexual matrix. The text is full of graphic detail describing the "biomechanics" of their bodies and the flow of their vestments: "Cyprian sank to his knees in a rustling of silk taffeta . . ."; "having aroused herself with kidgloved fingers busy at clitoral bud . . ." (882). Pynchon writes sexual relation as texture, as a play of vibrating and rustling surfaces untethered by identity or depth. This is not the annihilation of difference in mystical communion but a queering of the economy of difference—an abolition of propriety in favor of the use of bodies. As Agamben argues, the use of bodies doesn't involve appropriation, or, if it does, it does so only as a parody of propriety and property.[51]

Instead, use begins and ends in impropriety. It takes the messy commingling of human and nonhuman bodies as a point of departure—not only silk taffeta, leather gloves, and fleshy members but also the anarchy of Carnesalve, the unruly press of bodies in a democratic state of exception. Cyprian, Yashmeen, and Reef invent a sexual commons, or an erotic economy in which the normative split between heterosexuality and deviance gives way to an unruly process of differentiation. Sexuality becomes anarchism.

Pynchon's literary-political thinking of bodies in love, lust, and riot rhymes with Agamben's philosophy of anarchy. Agamben's *Homo Sacer* series conducts an archaeology of sovereign power whose ultimate object is not sovereignty but rather anarchic human potentiality. At first glance, Agamben's investigations into power strike a grim note. His analysis of how sovereign power relies on the sacrifice of bare life seems to imply a politics devoid of hope. The thesis that the concentration camp is "the hidden matrix and *nomos* of the political space in which we are still living" lends itself to an apocalyptic vision in which the only way out of sovereign power's hold is either total ruination or the coming of the messiah.[52] Contrary to appearances, however, Agamben's archaeology actually revolves around freedom, understood as human potentiality or, really, *im*potentiality. Agamben explains that the essence of potentiality is not the ability to do this or that but the ability *not to*, and, as such, freedom has less to do with positive capacity than with the possibility of suspending action. "Here it is possible to see how the root of freedom is to be found in the abyss of potentiality. To be free is not simply to have the power to do this or that thing. To be free is . . . *to be capable of one's own impotentiality*, to be in relation to one's own privation."[53] Freedom is a kind of poverty, a process of privation or destitution that transforms the exercise of a capacity—say, the right to vote—into a contingency. One is not free when democracy gets conflated with the right to vote, because not only does such a rights-based definition of freedom occlude other kinds of political action, but it also converts contingency into necessity, or freedom into duty. For Agamben, what's at stake in excavating the operations of sovereign power is not the protection of human rights but instead the power—the *potentiality*—to turn participation into refusal. Freedom involves the radical poverty that Agamben associates with the Franciscan concept of use. Or, as Pynchon might put it, the truth of freedom is neither labor, nor duty, but sloth.

Pynchon and Agamben share a sense that political freedom comes down to the power to say *no*. They are inheritors of Melville's Bartleby, and like Bartleby, they construct a circuit running from philosophy and literature to willful idleness. In contrast to Melville, however, they locate the culmination of refusal not in death but in the living of life. The gerund *living* gestures toward a modal and processual understanding of life that Agamben names *form-of-life*.

> By the term *form-of-life* ... I mean a life that can never be separated from its form, a life in which it is never possible to isolate something such as naked life. A life that cannot be separated from its form is a life for which what is at stake in its way of living is living itself.... It defines a life—human life—in which the single ways, acts, and processes of living are never simple *facts* but always and above all *possibilities* of life, always and above all power [*potenza*: potentiality].[54]

This is a material, and materialist, paradox: Life becomes a positive force only insofar as it founds itself not on positive properties (the "*facts*" of life) but on the process of living (the "*possibilities*" of life)—and process always involves negativity, a suspension of being in the name of becoming, a preference *not to*. More precisely, *form-of-life* renders the distinction between positivity and negativity inoperable, just as it does the division between *bios* (social and political life) and *zoe* (animal life).

Agamben's love for the term *inoperable* has everything to do with the way it combines a sense of unworkability and dysfunction with a sense of flow and potentiality. To render inoperable is not to reach some final conclusion. It is instead to idle away, to linger in one's own (im)potentiality:

> If thought, the arts, poetry, and human practices generally have any interest, it is because they bring about an archaeological idling of the machine and the works of life, language, and the economy, and society, in order that in them the becoming human of the human being will never be achieved once and for all, will never cease to happen.[55]

One could, of course, complain that Agamben reduces freedom to a human property, but we might do better to acknowledge what even the most subtle thinkers of posthumanism often ignore, namely, that the only freedom worth fighting for implies idleness, that the only exodus from state and capitalist forms of governance entails a rendering inoperable of the work(s) to which we've consigned ourselves. It is this unworkable truth that makes Agamben's writing a philosophy of anarchy.[56]

Owing as much to Marx and the Wobblies as to Saint Francis, Pynchon offers less a correction to Agamben's philosophy than a useful addendum: Freedom is the living of labor's refusal. Freedom is sloth. Freedom is riot. Pynchon performs an epistemological shift, which makes it so that the truth of anarchy reveals itself from the standpoint of labor politics. *Against the Day* is the demonstration of this truth in the form of a riotous ballet, an artistic improvisation on willful idleness. The sexual commons in which Yashmeen, Reef, and Cyprian participate belongs to this general riot. It is a singular instantiation of the commons in erotic terms. It's a form of radical impoverishment, stripping away property and propriety not in order to get at some putative truth of sexuality but so as to learn new uses for bodies. One could say that their romantic triangle is a microcosm of the commune, a figure for the general project of reinventing social life. The distinction is one of degree, rather than kind.

Against the Day offers a scaled-up model of the commune through "the Anarchist spa of Yz-les-Bains," into which Yashmeen, Cyprian, and Reef wander near the end of the novel, discovering a reprieve from the intensifying conflicts of the European states. Indeed, the name of the commune suggests the relaxation (easing, or "Yz"-ing) of temporal constraints, the classification of the commune as a spa signifying not bourgeois indolence but what Kristin Ross in reference to the Paris Commune terms "communal luxury": a generalization of artistic practice and aesthetic experience so that society becomes a collectively authored work of art, a democratic oeuvre.[57] Communal luxury is the "transvaluation of abundance"; it transforms surplus from the substance of private property into a communal wealth from which everyone benefits and to which everyone contributes. In *Against the Day*, Yz-les-Bains and the romance of Reef, Cyprian, and Yashmeen don't simply represent communal luxury, they cultivate it, acting as moments of literary indulgence, distractions from the serious business of capitalist labor. These figures of the commune constitute the determinate negation of the social factory, or the concrete sabotage of real subsumption, as well as the invention of unenclosed time. They are utopian not only because they delineate an alternative social space but also because they draw the reader into an experience of time in excess of the working day.

Yz-les-Bains constitutes another iteration of the enclave, a pocket of social life serving as an alternative to the dominant political and economic orders. However, the earthbound condition of the commune, as well as its embrace of political exiles, implies an immanence distinct from the Chums of Chance's pursuit of grace. The cooperative commonwealth is "hidden near the foothills of the Pyrenees, among steep hillsides covered with late-ripening vines, whose shoots were kept away from the early frosts by supports that looked like garlanded crucifixes" (931). It is accessible only by way of "a secret path" (933). The language in this description, with its vague spiritual allusions and naturalistic imagery, gestures toward a recovery of earthly paradise, a return to a state of nature before financial and political corruption. The novel's depiction of Yz-les-Bains is almost Rousseauian in its identification of social experimentation with natural innocence. At the same time, the text qualifies the isolation of Yz-les-Bains by emphasizing its openness to dissidents and exiles:

> Veterans of the Cataluñan struggle, former residents of Montjuich, hasheesh devotees enroute to Tangier, refugees from as far away as the U.S. and Russia, all could find lodging at this venerable oasis without charge, though in practice even those against the commoditizing of human shelter were often able to come up with modest sums in a dozen currencies and leave them with Lucien the concierge. (931)

The commune depends not only on a subtraction from the status quo but also on a complicity in political and socioeconomic matters. It can only decommoditize social life (shelter, food, sex, recreation, etc.) through the redistribution of foreign currencies, which is to say that it can invent post-capitalist relations only through the inclusive exclusion of money, a troping on finance that changes money's purpose from the accumulation of wealth to collective well-being. Money doesn't evaporate into the aether, just as society and history do not simply disappear in the advent of a new Eden. Instead, utopia becomes a process that makes use of the same worldly elements it is dedicated to overcoming. It is a utopianism of the commons, not only in the sense that it dedicates itself to abolishing property and instituting a commonwealth but also in the sense that it replaces subtraction from the quotidian with social promiscuity.

There's no better encapsulation of the utopian ethos of Yz-les-Bains than "the Anarchists' golf course," a recreational practice that blends together art, rebellion, and social experimentation. The novel describes the sport as

> a craze currently sweeping the civilized world, in which there is no fixed sequence—in fact, no fixed *number*—of holes, with distances flexible as well, some holes being only putter-distance apart, others uncounted hundreds of yards and requiring a map and a compass to locate. Many players had been known to come there at night and dig new ones. Parties were likely to ask, "Do you mind if we *don't* play through?'" then just go and whack balls at any time and in any direction they liked. (934)

Anarchist golf suspends the sport's well-known class content. It removes the financial obstacles—green fees, expensive clubs, etc.—insulating the sport from the poor. It replaces the orderliness of bourgeois custom, the well-regulated rituals of the green, with carnivalesque chaos. At the same time, it doesn't so much destroy the sport as loosen its rules in a creative manner. Chaos is not pure disorder but the multiplication of possibilities, every hole dug in the middle of night tracing a new virtual itinerary for the players. Moreover, instead of valorizing individual prowess, the sport puts the accent on collaboration—the ongoing design and revision of the course—and social mixing—the intersection of distinct games during play. Finally, the indeterminacy not only of the sequence but also the number of holes speaks to *Against the Day*'s more general preoccupation with the nexus of pleasure, experimentation, and holes. It's as if surplus potentiality can appear only with the multiplication of orifices, as if new social relations can only secrete themselves from cracks in the ruling order. Anarchist golf is thus another figure through which Pynchon articulates the riot in positive terms, demonstrating that revolt has its own social consistency.

Anarchist golf allegorizes the general commitment of Yz-les-Bains to communal luxury. It testifies to the possibility of a form of collective life in which autonomy, equality, and solidarity reinforce one another in a virtuous cycle. In doing so, it also tracks the conversion of the riot into the commune, or the transformation of radical poverty into the commonwealth. This conversion of social life is as much a temporal as a spatial affair, for the freedom of the commune implies its own version of sloth—a playful refusal to make good time, exemplified by the nonlinear and indefinite process of anarchist golf. The commune makes room for another kind of time. This temporal clearing operation has as its correlative a "limitless faith that History could be helped to keep its promises, including someday a commonwealth of the oppressed" (942). The novel ascribes this faith to Yashmeen, noting that she "was the one who shared most deeply the Anarchist beliefs around here" and contrasting this commitment to Reef's unreflexive "class hostility" and Cyprian's cynicism ("if it couldn't be turned into a quip, it wasn't worth considering") (942).

> It was her old need for some kind of transcendence—the fourth dimension, the Riemann problem, complex analysis, all had presented themselves as routes of escape from a world whose terms she could not accept, where she had preferred that even erotic desire have no consequences, at least none as weighty as the desires for a husband and children and so forth seemed to be for other young women of the day. (942)

The commune marks the point at which escape becomes escape *into* instead of escape *from*. Yashmeen finds the company of anarchists so satisfying less because of the absence of rules than because of the new dimensions they bring to social life. The commune queers sociality, showing how access to surplus—surplus wealth, surplus pleasure, surplus potentiality—need not be regulated by restrictive norms but can instead circulate in an egalitarian fashion as a commons.

Yashmeen's desire for escape returns the riot and the commune to the erotics of social life. It frames revolt as a biopolitical and utopian matter, a question of cultivating new kinds of embodied life through encounters with temporal alterity. Yashmeen elaborates an anarchist erotics when she states that, in regard to the romantic triangle of Cyprian, Reef, and herself, "The rule . . . is that there are no rules" (943). This declaration serves as prelude to a sex scene in which Cyprian once again comes on to Reef's "appealing bottom":

> And Reef stalked out, not nearly as annoyed as he was pretending to be. For Yash was right, of course. No rules. They were who they were, was all. For a while now, anytime he and Yash happened to be fucking face-to-face, she would manage to reach around and get a finger, hell, maybe even two sometimes, up in there, and he guessed it wasn't always that bad. And to be honest he did wonder now and then how it might be if Cyprian fucked him for a change. Sure. Not that it had to happen, but then again . . . it was shooting pool, he supposed, you had the straight shots, and cuts and English that went with that, but around these two you also had to expect caroms, and massés, and surprise balls out the corner of your eye coming back at you to collide at unforeseen angles, off of cushions sometimes you hadn't even thought about, heading for pockets you'd never've called. (943)

The passage generates a zone of indistinction between singularity and commonality, as well as presence and futurity. The seemingly tautological statement, "They were who they were," doesn't so much insist on self-authenticity as admit social and sexual experimentation into the production of subjectivity. Pynchon deploys the image of billiards—a well-known figure in the history of philosophy, usually an example of deterministic causality—to highlight the aleatory dimensions of the sexual encounter. Anal penetration becomes analogized to a billiard ball that deviates from the "straight shots" in favor of "unforeseen angles." Reef's "wonder" at the pleasure of being penetrated is a forgetting of propriety, a loosening of the norms governing sexual orientation and a negation of time's enclosure. That the event of penetration may or may not occur, that it remains suspended as a question ("Not that it had to happen, but then again . . ."), only intensifies the utopianism of this erotic exposition: Penetration is a contingency, not an act that defines a sexuality; it is a play of bodies, not an expression of sexual identity. It is, as Agamben might have it, the freedom of impotentiality. This break with teleology marks the advent of a time that "you hadn't even thought about," that "you'd never've called." That the textual appearance of radical novelty coincides with anal pleasure should come as no surprise. The novel consistently associates queerness with futurity, antinormativity with the arrival of another world. More specifically, the commons doesn't emerge as a simple realization of bodily potentials, for it requires a loosening of convention, an impoverishment of the body through which propriety gives way to promiscuous affection. There is no other world, except for that which comes from the otherness in this world, from the immanence of a queer futurity.

Pynchon's project of commoning time is, at its core, a queer one. *Against the Day* queers politics in a double sense: It not only challenges the status quo through representations of queer sexual encounters; it also changes the dimensions of the political by opening it to the fugitive practices of everyday life. The vast underground universe of anarchism, espionage, and quantum physics opens the door for institutions of the commons, which are not simply alternative institutions—different ways of organizing the same sorts of social life—but different genres of social existence. Textual figures of the riot and the commune show how antinormativity achieves positive consistency, as well as how unenclosed time takes on queer rhythms. Instead of reconciling autonomy and solidarity, as if they were contraries, Pynchon suggests that the true meaning of those terms appears only through their mutual imbrication. Singularity realizes itself only through commonality, and vice versa. This reciprocity between singularity and commonality is the fundamental premise of the commoning of time, for it is only by way of shared, yet distinct, experiences of time that one can take leave of capitalist temporality. The commoning of time doesn't merely reappropriate time, it transforms time into a commonwealth. Time becomes a medium of life in common. It becomes free time, irreducible to the working day. The commoning of time combines the refusal of labor with idle pleasure, so that the day no longer names the governance of life by capital but flesh's experiments in queer rhythms. It is Pynchon's riotous ballet, which sees in revolt not formless chaos but the shape of another world.

"The Last Corner of the U.S. Map"

What if instead of understanding the Trump era in terms of the foreclosure of the riot, we understood it as a symptom of it? What if we're not living in the Trump era but the Ferguson or the Oakland era? More generally, what if the years since the early 1970s are not the period of labor's defeat but the reinvention of labor politics as an informal insurgency of the dispossessed? What if ours is a time of riots? This is the possibility toward which Pynchon's fiction gestures. *Against the Day* offers a hermeneutics of the riot and the commune. It asks its readers to see America not for what it is but for what it might become, or, in Pynchon's phrasing, it reads America in the subjunctive instead of the declarative. It recovers the freedom of saying *no*, of refusing labor, by constructing a genealogy of social struggles from the nineteenth century to the present, cultivating a pleasure in anarchy. Every time the Trump administration rolls back labor protections for federal employees, excludes queer folks from employment, blocks immigrants from entering the country, or condones police violence against persons of color, we might look for the riotous energy seething beneath the nation-state and capitalism, the many acts of dissent that cross the boundaries of what passes as propriety. This approach doesn't ask for a return to normalcy, or a restoration of the liberal order. Instead, it searches for the imaginative social alternatives that emerge from the practices of people struggling day to day.

Given the expansive global geography of *Against the Day* it's tempting to associate the hermeneutics of the riot with postnationalist or antinationalist commitments. However, much like the protests of Occupy, Black Lives Matter, and the Women's March, Pynchon's fiction cultivates a counternational politics—an unworking of the nation-state and the invention of a counter-nation. The novel makes this political distinction apparent in the way that it pulls many of its characters (including the Traverse brothers and the Chums of Chance) back to the United States, but only so that they can experiment with new forms of life. The following description of Reef's motives holds true for the novel as a whole: "They headed west, Reef propelled by his old faith in the westward vector, in finding some place, some deep penultimate town the capitalist/Christer gridwork hadn't got to quite yet" (1075). Pynchon associates westward motion with the subjunctive mode ("all that *may yet be true*"). In doing so, he reproduces a version of American exceptionalism that sees in westward expansion not merely novelty but also jouissance—libidinal intensity in excess of the status quo. *Against the Day* gravitates toward that which in America is more than America, its surplus potentiality or promise. The novel longs for a singular America. It's in the commoning of time, in the queer rhythm of the flesh, that a singular America takes flight from exceptionalism. It's less about territory than about ways of moving through the world. A singular

America is how American exceptionalism departs from itself, how it takes leave of empire through the invention of new forms of life.

That there's a danger in Pynchon's attraction to America is undeniable. The characters' paths reduplicate Manifest Destiny in a parodic manner, zigzagging east and then west, searching after sites of queer possibility on the frontier. The text situates itself between American exceptionalism and its critique, borrowing the libidinal energies of empire in order to turn them toward emancipation. The novel knows this longing isn't innocent, but it can't manage to abandon it. A scene in which Jesse, Reef's son, brings home an assignment from school, "an essay on What It Means To Be American," exemplifies the push and pull between American exceptionalism and a singular America. Jesse's response to the assignment is short and to the point: "*It* [being American] *means do what they tell you and take what they give you and don't go on strike or their soldiers will shoot you down*" (1076). Jesse channels his grandfather, Webb, in these words, abandoning the exceptionalist fantasy of a land of plenty in favor of a lucid account of "who is fucking who." The Traverses, however, choose not to secede from America, even though Yashmeen entertains the idea of "start[ing] our own little republic" (ibid.). Instead, they continue experimenting with new ways of living together, carving out autonomous spaces—counter-nations—on the nation's margins.

For Pynchon, the departure from America remains immanent in America; it's a movement not antinational but counter-national. This is another way of saying that the refusal to be American doesn't so much negate America as mutate it. Pynchon recognizes that it is difficult, if not downright impossible, to surrender that desire called America; he realizes that oppositional criticism can never fully exorcise the dream that one day America might make good on its promises, if only by becoming something other than itself. In times like these, when it's easy to be embarrassed by Americanness, when political reaction makes revolution seem like a fairy tale, we could do much worse than to reclaim the commitment to all that is riotous in America. We might start by saying no to work, by protesting in the street, or by constructing a commune. However we choose to riot, one thing is certain: Freedom begins in refusal, in saying no to the merciless pressures of the day in the name of all that may yet be true.

CODA

Assembling the Future

There is no redeeming America. To travel with America is to be haunted by the ghosts of its origins: settler colonialism, slavery, systemic racism, heteropatriarchy—one could easily continue. These ghosts are double, however. They are ghosts of the future, as well as the past, specters of what might have been, as well as what has come to pass. They are the missed opportunities cited by Burroughs; the subjunctive America in Pynchon's novels; and the optative mood that F. O. Matthiessen identified as what is American in American literature. They are so many moments of historical jouissance, conjuring up a singular America. Reading Emerson, Stanley Cavell remarks that one only turns toward America by turning away from it, that a drama of attraction and repulsion emerges from the fundamental unapproachability of America, from the way in which America not only promises more than it can deliver but always seems to teeter on the edge of its own abolition.[1] This is a counter-national version of Foucault's sense of curiosity. For Foucault, curiosity is a will to know that emancipates subjectivity from subjection; it describes an encounter with alterity as the becoming-other of the self. In short, curiosity "enables one to get free of oneself."[2] Each of the writers on whom I have focused makes literature a dwelling place for curiosity, and each does so in the name of America, even or especially when naming "America" means overcoming America. A singular America, I've argued, is not the simple rejection of exceptionalism. Instead, it pushes exceptionalism to its breaking point; it consummates that desire called America only insofar as it radically changes what it means to be American.

The concept of a singular America recuperates speculation on America without assuming a post- or anticritical stance. It asks what kinds of life emerge in the excluded middle between American exceptionalism and its critique. A singular America takes the place of the culture of redemption dissected by Leo Bersani; it replaces the project of recovering America's good name with the experience of historical jouissance.[3] This is the invention of another politics—an affirmative biopolitics—through encounters with a surplus of social potentiality. The crossing of biopolitics and utopianism suggests a response to the postcritical turn in the humanities.[4] It is sympathetic to the plea for more affirmative modes of reading, but rather than associate affirmation with strict literality or pure positivity, it revels in mixtures of the literal and the figurative, as well as combinations of positivity and negativity. Instead of getting over critique, the concept of a singular America traces an itinerary through which critique converges with hope. As Chris Castiglia argues, we don't so much need to do away with critique as develop "the active potential of critical hopefulness."[5] Critical hopefulness insists on the power of the imaginary and the not-yet real to transform the present; it expands our sense of the world by measuring the present against the ideal. In this context, literature isn't just an object. It is a "model," a supplementary reality that not only troubles the limits of the present but also plays out alternative scenarios, envisions different figures of life.[6] The task of criticism, then, is not to step back from the literary work in the name of analytical objectivity but to participate in it, to become complicit with it, in the hopes that one might discover other ways of inhabiting the world. Criticism demands curiosity more than knowingness.

The literary commons that I've articulated in this book is a way of practicing critical hopefulness. To read a singular America as a literary commons means modeling a counter-nation. Not only does it involve locating figures of the commons in poetry by Dickinson or fiction by Burroughs. It also demands that one turn literature into a commons. One could call this the dismantling of the canon, but it is a particular manner of doing so, one that does not so much pose an alternative to American literature as elaborate on how American literature is already an alternative to itself. In other words, commoning American literature entails de-exceptionalizing American exceptionalism by pushing it to its limit, by exposing it to the explosive surplus of potentiality that is at its heart. The production of a literary commons exceeds academic territory insofar as one understands this literature to include the many ways of figuring life beyond the status quo. What would it mean to read assemblies such as Occupy encampments or the Women's Marches as figures of a singular America in their own right? How can we read the poetry—that is, the play of form and potentiality—that traverses Whitman's writings on America and indigenous protests against oil pipelines? What kind of commonalities link Pynchon's rioters to Black Lives Matter's protests against racial capitalism?[7] The point of these questions is not to ask how scholarly work might explain social movements, nor is it to seek validation for criticism in the vitality of movements. It is, instead, to ask how these different practices share the project of commoning America. It isn't a matter of theory versus practice but of the diverse social genres through which critical hopefulness works on this world for the sake of another world.

In times like these, it is difficult to feel hopeful. Call it the Anthropocene, neoliberalism, or the Trump era, the climate of politics today is apocalyptic. It is a time of endings, not beginnings, of disaster, not repair. However, utopia often thrives in the midst of disaster. It takes on a renewed urgency when the world itself is at risk. As Rebecca Solnit puts it: "How do we get back to the struggle over the future? I think you have to hope, and hope in this sense is not a prize or a gift, but something you earn through study, through resisting the ease of despair."[8] In times like these, utopian figures of politics proliferate as signs of hope and resistance: Black Lives Matter, indigenous ecological activism, the Women's Marches—each of these is a figure not only in the sense of making an injustice legible but also in the sense of making a home for the future in the present. They acknowledge the particularity of an injustice, the way in which systems of oppression and exploitation target specific populations for injury and death, poverty and exile. At the same time, they insist that what's needed is another world, one without racism, petrocapitalism, patriarchy, misogyny, transphobia, or heteronormativity. These movements make demands. They demand that America live up to its promise. They seek repair and restitution, not restoration, which is to say (with Fred Moten) that the repair for which they long is inseparable from (re)making the world.[9] They demand nothing less than everything—everything that has been stolen, everything that might come to pass. They demand the conditions for a livable life, which isn't the same as mere survival. They demand no less of themselves. They are curious about what new kinds of life might appear in the interval between this broken world and a world to come. Even as they struggle to repair injuries, to make life livable, they make a commons out of their bodies and their voices. They do not wait for the future of America, they invent it in the here and now; they compose a singular America out of the disavowed surplus potentiality at the heart of American exceptionalism. They assemble figures of that which in America is so much more than America.

ACKNOWLEDGMENTS

I began this book nearly a decade ago, during a presidential administration that campaigned on hope. For many on the left, the task in the Obama years was to make sure liberals didn't become too complacent. President Obama promised change, but the change was relatively minor. We were still at war; persons of color living in the United States were still more likely to be shot by the police; and economic inequality remained extreme. Meanwhile, I was writing about utopia. I was trying to distinguish something like radical hope from what passes for the American Dream. I was convinced that social justice and political change are impossible without concrete visions of a better future. Fast-forward to the present, and things look bleak. With Trump in office, it's easy to be nostalgic for Obama, to dream wistfully of the procedural regularity of liberal democracy. However, I remain convinced that we need utopianism—ways of imagining the future as something more than just a return to normalcy. A return to the frustrated hopes of the Obama years won't cut it, not least because the neoliberal status quo has a way of conjuring up the worst of worlds. We can't afford to lose hope. We can't afford to forget utopia. We need to imagine a better world, and we need to fight for it.

    I wouldn't have been able to sustain this hope, nor would I have known how to write about it, without a number of teachers, mentors, colleagues, friends, and family members. Hope, it turns out, requires its own commons. I remain immensely thankful for the guidance and support of Cesare Casarino, who pushed me to think and write as rigorously as possible. Just as important, he regularly reminded me that my passion for politics and philosophy need not be separated from my passion for literature. Richard Leppert and Tony C. Brown offered invaluable advice on the structure of the book and scholarly publishing. They taught me a great deal about how to survive the material conditions of academic labor without surrendering my intellectual commitments. Last but not least, Phillip Wegner introduced me to the utopian tradition, as well as to Marxist critical theory. In many respects, he sent me down the path that led to writing this book.

A number of friends also made this book possible. "Business Lunches" with Tom Cannavino and Ben Stork reminded me that there is little point in writing Marxist critical theory if one didn't also enjoy time away from work. Aly Pennucci and Ricardo Rebolledo always reminded me what's what. Robert St. Clair is a startlingly brilliant comrade and one of my favorite individuals with whom to drink scotch. Andrea Gyenge was always excellent and intellectually stimulating company, especially over burgers. Nathan Snaza continues to be a remarkably generous interlocutor. Jessamyn Abel, Jonathan Abel, Jennifer Boittin, Samuel Frederick, Courtney Gildersleeve, Jens-Uwe Guettel, Brendan McGillicuddy, Sean Nye, Benjamin Schreier, Gabe Shapiro, Julietta Singh, Anita Starosta, Matt Stoddard, Matt Tierney, and Sarah J. Townsend are all brilliant scholars and good friends.

I've been fortunate to learn much from colleagues at my former institution Dartmouth College. Donald Pease has been an indispensable mentor and interlocutor. The sharpness of his intellect is matched only by his generosity. My fellow Americanists—Michael Chaney, Ivy Schweitzer, Colleen Boggs, Sam Moodie—have provided much needed support. Andrew McCann, Aden Evens, George Edmondson, Jeff Sharlet, Meli Zeiger, Tommy O'Malley, Vievee Francis, Alexander Chee, Mary Coffey, Will Cheng, Eng-Beng Lim, and Bethany Moreton have been and continue to be incredibly supportive colleagues. I cannot express enough gratitude for my fellow junior colleagues in English at Dartmouth—in particular, Alysia Garrison, Azeen Khan, and Patricia Stuelke. Last but not least, though Aimee Bahng and Bill Boyer departed New Hampshire for sunnier climes, they remain irreplaceable friends, colleagues, and family.

I've been fortunate to participate in the Futures of American Studies Institute as a faculty member for the past several years. I've learned a great deal from a number of scholars at the Institute, and although there are too many to list, I would be doing an injustice if I didn't at least mention some of them: Russ Castronovo, Soyica Diggs Colbert, Elizabeth Maddock Dillon, Duncan Faherty, Winfried Fluck, Donatella Izzo, Cindi Katz, Eric Lott, Lisa Lowe, Dana Luciano, Annie McClanahan, Dana Nelson, Caleb Smith, Hortense Spillers, Ivy Wilson, and Lynda Zwinger. The Leslie Humanities Center at Dartmouth College provided material support in the form of its Manuscript Review Program. This support brought Branka Arsić and Leerom Medovoi to the College to offer feedback on an early draft of the manuscript. Branka and Lee, as well as George Edmondson and Don Pease, provided invaluable advice regarding the book's arguments and analyses. Everything that's compelling in this book is at least in part because of them, while the faults are certainly my own.

Acknowledgments

I've accumulated an immense number of intellectual debts scattered across the United States and elsewhere. Andrew Knighton and Emilio Sauri brought me to Cal State (Los Angeles) and the University of Massachusetts (Boston), respectively, to present pieces of my manuscript. I've also benefited a great deal from conversations over the years with Jason Berger, Michael Boyden, Chris Castiglia, Joshua Clover, Claire Colebrook, Nan Z. Da, Jeffrey R. Di Leo, James Duesterberg, Cristie Ellis, Meredith Farmer, Kevin Floyd, Sean Grattan, Susan Hegeman, Peter Hitchcock, Liam Kennedy, Kiarina Kordela, Anna Kornbluh, Leigh Claire La Berge, Sophia McClennen, Mark Noble, Jasbir Puar, Jordy Rosenberg, Kyla Schuller, Stephen Shapiro, William V. Spanos, and Angie Willey. Renée Bergland and Jonathan Abel deserve special mention for the advice they gave me on the publication process. Christopher Breu is a remarkable comrade, and our intellectual exchanges regarding biopolitics, capitalism, and much else are reflected in numerous ways in these pages. I want to thank Richard Morrison, my editor at Fordham University Press, for seeing the potential in this book and leading me through the publication process. I also want to acknowledge the work of John Garza, Eric Newman, and Teresa Jesionowski in preparing, copyediting, and otherwise shepherding my manuscript into print.

Family is a queer thing, or at least it should be. I've been lucky enough to have the support of an extended family full of loving oddballs and misfits. My grandmother, Nicoletta "Letty" Bruno, was the first person I knew who completed a college degree. Her expectations for her grandchildren were only exceeded by the affection with which she showered us. She continues to live in my thoughts. My mother, Donna Haines, passed as I was writing this book. She was a published author and a pagan priestess. She paid little heed to social expectations, but she was always there for those in need. I owe to her the courage to follow my convictions and so much more. This book is dedicated to her. I began working with my father, John Haines, in boatyards around the age of thirteen. I not only learned my work ethic from him but also my commitment to speaking truth in the face of power. He taught me that being a worker doesn't always mean saying yes to bosses. My sister, Erica Haines, and my nephew, Gavin, are two of the most charming and funny people I know. They always put a smile on my face. Finally, Tracy Rutler and Beatrice Strelow became a part of my family (or I became a part of theirs) nearly ten years ago. I cannot begin to describe how much joy, strength, and hope I receive from them. Beatrice is more than any parent could possible ask for—a brilliant, funny artist whose confidence always impresses me. Tracy is my best friend, my partner, and a brilliant scholar. I've learned so much from her over the years, not least of all that a militant commitment to equality is inseparable from a deep care for the world. Tracy convinces me every day that, in times like these, it's more important than ever to imagine utopia.

NOTES

INTRODUCTION: IMPOSSIBLY AMERICAN

1. See Jeff Sharlet, "Donald Trump, American Preacher," *New York Times Magazine*, April 12, 2016.

2. Stuart Hall, "The Great Moving Right Show," *Marxism Today* (January 1979): 15.

3. On the mutually supporting tendencies of neoliberalism and neoconservatism, see especially Wendy Brown, "American Nightmare: Neoliberalism, Neoconservatism, and De-Democratization," *Political Theory* 34, no. 6 (2006): 690–714; and Melinda Cooper, *Family Values: Between Neoliberalism and the New Social Conservatism* (New York: Zone Books, 2017).

4. Thomas Paine, *The Rights of Man and Common Sense*, ed. Peter Linebaugh (New York: Verso, 2009), 50.

5. See John Locke, *The Second Treatise of Government* and *A Letter Concerning Toleration* (New York: Dover Thrift Editions, 2002); and G. W. F. Hegel, *Introduction to the Philosophy of History: With Selections from the Philosophy of Right*, trans. Leo Rauch (Indianapolis: Hackett Classics, 1988).

6. On the modern production of "Man," see Michel Foucault, *The Order of Things: An Archaeology of the Human Sciences* (New York: Vintage, 1994), chaps. 9, 10; and Sylvia Wynter, "Unsettling the Coloniality of Being/Power/Truth/Freedom: Towards the Human, After Man, Its Overrepresentation—An Argument," *CR: The New Centennial Review* 3, no. 3 (2003): 257–337.

7. See Denise Ferreira da Silva's critique of the racialized universality of "Man" and "the human" in *Toward a Global Idea of Race* (Minneapolis: University of Minnesota Press, 2007).

8. Robyn Wiegman, "The Ends of New Americanism," *New Literary History* 42, no. 3 (2011): 391.

9. See Christopher Castiglia, *The Practices of Hope: Literary Criticism in Disenchanted Times* (New York: New York University Press, 2017).

10. The biopolitical turn in American studies begins in the early 2000s with the publication of Cesare Casarino's *Modernity at Sea: Melville, Marx, and Conrad in Crisis* (2002), Donald Pease's "The Global Homeland State:

Bush's Biopolitical Settlement" (2003), and Judith Butler's *Precarious Life: The Powers of Mourning and Violence* (2004). The choice of these texts is to some degree arbitrary, but it seems, at least retrospectively, that a threshold was crossed at this moment. Work dealing explicitly with biopolitics in American studies begins to proliferate in the 2000s and continues to do so. Moreover, the works that appear under the aegis of biopolitics between 2003 and now are arguably works that have redefined the field. Some notable examples include Jasbir Puar's *Terrorist Assemblages: Homonationalism in Queer Times* and Dana Luciano's *Arranging Grief: Sacred Time and the Body in Nineteenth-Century America* (both published in 2007), as well as Pease's *The New American Exceptionalism* (2008), Lauren Berlant's *Cruel Optimism* (2011), Mel Chen's *Animacies: Biopolitics, Racial Mattering, and Queer Affect* (2012), Christopher Breu's *Insistence of the Material: Literature in the Age of Biopolitics* (2014), and Kyla Schuller's *The Biopolitics of Feeling: Race, Sex, and Science in the Nineteenth Century* (2017). This list is by no means exhaustive.

11. Wald's address was published the following year in *American Quarterly*. Priscilla Wald, "American Studies and the Politics of Life," *American Quarterly* 64, no. 2 (2012): 186.

12. Susan Hegeman offers an excellent account of this disavowal of "America" in "Culture, Patriotism, and the Habitus of a Discipline; or, What Happens to American Studies in a Moment of Globalization?" *Genre* 38 (Winter 2005): 443–66. I don't have the space to reckon with the transnational and hemispheric turns in American studies. However, I would suggest that more often than not they commit to what can be called (riffing on David Harvey) a spatial fix—an attempt to displace the ontological problem of "America" through an enlargement of scale beyond the limits of the nation. Comparativism becomes a way of bypassing, rather than thinking through, the libidinal attachments of political subjects to that desire called America. For a notable exception—one that manages to combine attention to transnational dynamics with a concern for the ontological dimension of America—see Lisa Lowe, *The Intimacies of Four Continents* (Durham, N.C.: Duke University Press, 2015).

13. William V. Spanos, "American Studies in the 'Age of the World Picture': Thinking the Question of Language," in *The Futures of American Studies*, ed. Donald E. Pease and Robyn Wiegman (Durham, N.C.: Duke University Press, 2002), 388–89. See also William V. Spanos, *Redeeming Nation in the Interregnum: An Untimely Meditation on the American Vocation* (New York: Fordham University Press, 2016), chap. 3.

14. See especially Jacques Lacan, *Seminar XI: The Four Fundamental Concepts of Psychoanalysis*, trans. Alan Sheridan (New York: W. W. Norton, 1998).

15. Ibid., 178–80.

16. Lacan never offers a strict definition of *jouissance*. Instead, he characterizes it in terms of "inaccessibility," "obscurity," and "opacity," distinguishing it as a painful pleasure that exceeds and refuses the pleasure principle. In positive terms, it is a crossing of the limit (of the symbolic order) or a tarrying with the death drive. Lacan also elaborates *jouissance* in terms of a good—the highest good, as it were—that overturns the moral distinction between good and evil. See especially Jacques Lacan, *The Ethics of Psychoanalysis, 1959–1960*, ed. Jacques-Alain Miller, trans. Dennis Porter (New York: W. W. Norton, 1992), 194–203, 319–24. Dylan Evans offers a useful catalogue of Lacan's uses of the term in *An Introductory Dictionary of Lacanian Psychoanalysis* (New York: Routledge, 1996), 93–94.

17. Gilles Deleuze and Félix Guattari, *What Is Philosophy?*, trans. Hugh Tomlinson and Graham Burchell (New York: Columbia University Press, 1994), 21–34.

18. Ibid., 216–18.

19. Cesare Casarino, *Modernity at Sea: Melville, Marx, and Conrad in Crisis* (Minneapolis: University of Minnesota Press, 2002), xxvi.

20. It's worth noting that my use of the term *singularity* differs from its use within deconstruction. In contrast to, for instance, Derek Attridge's analyses in *The Singularity of Literature* (New York: Routledge, 2004), I'm not interested in the distinctive event of literature, however impure its materials or sources, but rather in the sociality of literature, the ways in which literary practices activate a political alternative to the status quo.

21. Jacques Lacan, *The Seminar of Jacques Lacan, Book VII: The Ethics of Psychoanalysis*, ed. Jacques-Alain Miller, trans. Dennis Porter (New York: W. W. Norton, 1992), 319.

22. Michel Foucault, *The Use of Pleasure: The History of Sexuality*, vol. 2, trans. Robert Hurley (New York: Vintage, 1990), 8.

23. Michel Foucault, "The Subject and Power," trans. Leslie Sawyer, *Critical Inquiry* 8, no. 4 (1982): 785.

24. Indeed, even those approaches to biopolitics that are irreducible to Foucault's contributions tend to take Foucault as their point of departure. I am thinking, for instance, of work by Jasbir Puar, Alexander Weheliye, and Sylvia Wynter, which calls attention to the reductiveness of Foucault's treatment of race in order to elaborate more expansive accounts of racialization in modernity. See especially Jasbir Puar, *Terrorist Assemblages: Homonationalism in Queer Times* (Durham, N.C.: Duke University Press, 2007); Alexander Weheliye, *Habeus Viscus: Racializing Assemblages, Biopolitics, and Black Feminist Theories of the Human* (Durham, N.C.: Duke University Press, 2014); and Sylvia Wynter, "Unsettling the Coloniality of Being/Power/Truth/Freedom."

25. Michel Foucault, *History of Sexuality*, vol. 1, trans. Robert Hurley (New York: Vintage, 1990), 141–42.

26. Ibid., 139–40.

27. Ibid., 139.

28. On the concept of individuation, see especially, Gilbert Simondon, *L'individuation psychique et collective* (Paris: Aubier, 2007).

29. Michel Foucault, "What Is Critique?" in *The Politics of Truth*, ed. Sylvère Lotringer, trans. Lysa Hochroth and Catherine Porter (Los Angeles: Semiotext(e), 2007), 64.

30. Michel Foucault, "Nietzsche, Genealogy, and History," in *The Foucault Reader*, 78. Further citations are indicated as parentheticals in body of chapter.

31. Foucault, *Order of Things*, xviii.

32. Michel Foucault, "Les Hétérotopies," in *Le Corps Utopique, Les Hétérotopies*, ed. Daniel Defert (Paris: Nouvelles Éditions Lignes, 2009), 24–25. Translation mine.

33. Michel Foucault, "Le corps utopique," in *Le Corps Utopique, Les Hétérotopies*, 9. Translations mine.

34. Ibid., 13.

35. Ibid., 14.

36. See Ernst Bloch, *The Principle of Hope*, vol. 1, trans. Neville Plaice, Stephen Plaice, and Paul Knight (Cambridge, Mass.: MIT Press, 1986). Regarding concrete utopianism, Bloch writes: "*Concrete utopia stands on the horizon of every reality; real possibility surrounds the open dialectical tendencies and latencies to the very last*" (223).

37. Foucault, "Le corps utopique," 17

38. Michel Foucault, *The Courage of Truth: The Government of Self and Others II, Lectures at the Collège de France, 1983–1984*, trans. Graham Burchell (New York: Picador, 2011), 242.

39. Ibid., 244.

40. Ibid., 283.

41. Ibid., 287.

42. See José Esteban Muñoz, *Cruising Utopia: The Then and There of Queer Futurity* (New York: New York University Press, 2009). Regarding "assemblages," "queer asynchronies," and "the commons," see respectively Jasbir Puar, *Terrorist Assemblages*; Elizabeth Freeman, *Time Binds: Queer Temporalities, Queer Histories* (Durham, N.C.: Duke University Press, 2010); and Stefano Harney and Fred Moten, *The Undercommons: Fugitive Planning and Black Study* (Brooklyn: Minor Compositions, 2013), as well as Donald Pease, "From the Camp to the Commons: Biopolitical Alter-Geographies in Douglass and Melville," *Arizona Quarterly* 72, no. 3 (2016): 1–23.

43. Muñoz, *Cruising Utopia*, 95–96.

44. Puar, *Terrorist Assemblages*, 222.

45. Caroline Levine, *Forms: Whole, Rhythm, Hierarchy, Network* (Princeton, N.J.: Princeton University Press, 2015), 14.

46. Ibid., 18.

47. Gilles Deleuze, *Essays Critical and Clinical*, trans. Daniel W. Smith and Michael A. Greco (Minneapolis: University of Minnesota Press, 1997), 3.

48. Ibid., 5.

49. Ibid., 60.

50. Jared Hickman, *Black Prometheus: Race and Radicalism in the Age of Atlantic Slavery* (Oxford: Oxford University Press, 2016), 15.

51. Ibid., 15–16.

52. Hegel, *Introduction to the Philosophy of History*, 86.

53. Peter Linebaugh, *The Magna Carta Manifesto: Liberties and Commons for All* (Berkeley: University of California Press, 2008), 45. My historical perspective on the commons also draws from Silvia Federici's *Caliban and the Witch: Women, the Body, and Primitive Accumulation* (New York: Autonomedia, 2004).

54. Pease considers this fantasy of fusion between the sovereign and the people in *The New American Exceptionalism* (Minneapolis: University of Minnesota, 2009), Introduction, chaps. 5, 6.

55. Linebaugh, *Magna Carta Manifesto*, 216.

56. Dana Nelson, *Commons Democracy* (New York: Fordham University Press, 2016), 6–7.

57. Elizabeth Maddock Dillon, *New World Drama: The Performative Commons in the Atlantic World* (Durham, N.C.: Duke University Press, 2014), 7. On the commons as an aesthetic practice, see also Lauren Berlant, "The Commons: Infrastructures for Troubling Times," *Environment and Planning D: Society and Space* 34, no. 3 (2016): 393–419.

58. Gilles Deleuze, "Instincts and Institutions," in *Desert Islands and Other Texts, 1953–1974*, ed. David Lapoujade, trans. Michael Taormina (New York: Semiotext(e), 2004), 19.

59. Ibid., 21.

60. Adrienne Rich, "What Kind of Times Are These," *Dark Fields of the Republic* (New York: W. W. Norton, 1995).

61. For an extended analysis of Rich's poetry and its relevance for biopolitical thought, see Christian Haines, "The Impersonal Is Political: Adrienne Rich's *The Dream of a Common Language*, Feminism, and the Art of Biopolitics," *Cultural Critique* 96: "What Comes After the Subject?" (Spring 2017): 178–215.

62. Gilles Deleuze, *The Logic of Sense*, trans. Mark Lester and Charles Stivale (New York: Columbia University Press, 1990), 52.

63. Deleuze describes the concept of singularity as follows: "A singularity is the point of departure for a series which extends over all the ordinary points of the system, as far as the region of another singularity which itself gives rise to another series which may either converge or diverge from the first." Gilles Deleuze, *Difference and Repetition*, trans. Paul Patton (New York: Columbia University Press, 1994), 278

64. See Giovanni Arrighi, *The Long Twentieth Century: Money, Power, and the Origins of Our Times* (New York: Verso, 1994), chaps. 1, 4.

65. Slavoj Žižek, *In Defense of Lost Causes* (New York: Verso, 2009), 207–9.

66. On the idea of world-systems literature, see Leerom Medovoi, "'Terminal Crisis?': From the Worlding of American Literature to World-System Literature," *American Literary History* 23, no. 3 (2011): 643–59.

67. David S. Reynolds, *Beneath the American Renaissance: The Subversive Imagination in the Age of Emerson and Melville* (Cambridge, Mass.: Harvard University Press, 1989), 9.

68. Spanos, *Redeemer Nation*, chaps. 3, 4.

69. William S. Burroughs, *Cities of the Red Night* (New York: Picador, 1981), xiv.

1. A REVOLUTIONARY HAUNT: UTOPIAN FRONTIERS IN WILLIAM S. BURROUGHS'S LATE TRILOGY

1. Ronald Reagan, "Labor Day Address at Liberty State Park," September 1, 1980, http://www.americanrhetoric.com/speeches/ronaldreaganliberty park.htm.

2. See, for example, Jean Comaroff and John Comaroff, "Millennial Capitalism and the Culture of Neoliberalism," special issue of *Public Culture* 12, no. 2 (Spring 2000); Lisa Duggan, *The Twilight of Equality? Neoliberalism, Cultural Politics, and the Attack on Democracy* (Boston: Beacon Press, 2003); and David Harvey, *A Brief History of Neoliberalism* (Oxford: Oxford University Press, 2007).

3. William S. Burroughs, *Cities of the Red Night* (New York: Picador, 1981), xiv. Hereafter *Cities of the Red Night* is cited parenthetically in the body of the chapter.

4. Slavoj Žižek elaborates his own version of revolutionary mourning in *In Defense of Lost Causes* (New York: Verso, 2009).

5. Timothy S. Murphy, *Wising Up the Marks: The Amodern William S. Burroughs* (Berkeley: University of California Press, 1998), 169.

6. On the appropriation of cultural and political elements of 1960s social movements by neoliberal capitalism, see especially, Luc Boltanski and Ève Chiapello, *The New Spirit of Capitalism*, trans. Gregory Elliott (1999; New York: Verso, 2018), chap. 3: "1968: Crisis and Revival of Capitalism"; and

Paolo Virno, *Grammar of the Multitude*, trans. Isabella Bertoletti, James Cascaito, and Andrea Casson (New York: Semiotext[e], 2004), 110–11.

7. Jeffrey T. Nealon, "Periodizing the 80s: The Cultural Logic of Economic Privatization in the United States," in *A Leftist Ontology: Beyond Relativism and Identity Politics*, ed. Carsten Strathausen (Minneapolis: University of Minnesota Press, 2009), 62.

8. Burroughs's earliest works present biopolitics as a struggle with addiction. On addiction in Burroughs, see especially Eric Mottram, *William Burroughs: The Algebra of Need* (London: Marion Boyars, 1978), 13–62; and Jason Morelyle, "Speculating Freedom: Addiction, Control, and Rescriptive Subjectivity in the Work of William S. Burroughs," in *Retaking the Universe: William S. Burroughs in the Age of Globalization*, ed. Davis Schneiderman and Philip Walsh (London: Pluto Books, 2004), 74–86.

9. William S. Burroughs, *The Western Lands* (New York: Penguin Books, 1988), 34.

10. William S. Burroughs, *The Job: Interviews with William S. Burroughs* (New York: Penguin Books, 1989), 21.

11. William S. Burroughs, "Terrorism, Utopia," in *Burroughs Live: The Collected Interviews of William S. Burroughs, 1960–1997*, ed. Sylvère Lotringer(Los Angeles: Semiotext(e), 2001), 405, 404.

12. Burroughs, *Job*, 102.

13. William S. Burroughs, *The Place of Dead Roads* (New York: Picador, 1983), 171. Hereafter the text is cited parenthetically.

14. For an extended reading of retroactive utopianism in *Cities of the Red Night*, see Sean Grattan, *Hope Isn't Stupid: Utopian Affects in Contemporary American Literature* (Iowa City: Iowa University Press, 2017), chap. 1: "A Grenade with the Fuse Lit: William S. Burroughs and Retroactive Utopias."

15. This is not to say that the western doesn't have its own complexities. Richard Slotkin's work remains invaluable in this respect. See *The Fatal Environment: The Myth of the Frontier in the Age of Industrialization* (Norman: University of Oklahoma Press, 1988); and *Gunfighter Nation: Myth of the Frontier in Twentieth-Century America* (Norman: University of Oklahoma Press, 1998).

16. On the confluence of westward expansion and U.S. imperial ambitions abroad, see, for instance, Amy Kaplan, *The Anarchy of Empire in the Making of U.S. Culture* (Cambridge, Mass.: Harvard University Press, 2005); and Amy Kaplan and Donald Pease, eds., *Cultures of United States Imperialism* (Durham, N.C.: Duke University Press, 1994).

17. See, for example, Mark Rifkin, *Settler Common Sense: Queerness and Everyday Colonialism in the American Renaissance* (Minneapolis: University of Minnesota Press, 2014), xvi–xix; and Jodi Byrd, *The Transit of Empire:*

Indigenous Critiques of Colonialism (Minneapolis: University of Minnesota Press, 2011), especially chap. 1: "Is and Was: Poststructural Indians without Ancestry," and chap. 6: "Killing States: Removals, Other Americans, and the 'Pale Promise of Democracy.'"

18. Wendy Brown, *Undoing the Demos: Neoliberalism's Stealth Revolution* (New York: Zone Books, 2015), 22.

19. Burroughs thus anticipates the contemporary scholarly project of recovering the wildness of social life, as exemplified by the special issue of *South Atlantic Quarterly* 117, no. 3 (2018), ed. Jack Halberstam and Tavia Nyong'o: "Wildness."

20. See Darko Suvin, "Estrangement and Cognition," *Strange Horizons*, November 24, 2014, http://strangehorizons.com/non-fiction/articles/estrangement-and-cognition/. See also Darko Suvin, *Metamorphoses of Science Fiction: On the Poetics and History of a Literary Genre*, ed. Gerry Canavan (Bern: Peter Lang, 2016).

21. Fredric Jameson, *Archaeologies of the Future: The Desire Called Utopia and Other Science Fictions* (New York: Verso, 2005), 289.

22. Jameson describes the strategy of disruption as "restructuration and the unexpected blasting open of habits, as that lateral side-door which suddenly opens up onto a new world of transformed human beings" (ibid., 232).

23. Ibid.

24. Alex Houen writes of Burroughs's fiction, and *The Place of Dead Roads* in particular, that "characters and events are not offered as representations of the real so much as presentations of potential." *Powers of Possibility: Experimental American Writing since the 1960s* (Oxford: Oxford University Press, 2012), 132–33.

25. Nikolas Rose, *Governing the Soul: The Shaping of the Private Self* (London: Free Association Books, 1999), 257.

26. David Harvey, *The New Imperialism* (Oxford: Oxford University Press, 2005), chap. 4: "Accumulation by Dispossession."

27. William S. Burroughs, *Ah Pook Is Here, and Other Texts* (London: John Calder, 1979), 155.

28. Burroughs, *Job*, 11.

29. Burroughs's critique of the theology of the word parallels his contemporary Jacques Derrida's own deconstruction of logos. Robin Lydenberg discusses the parallels in *Word Cultures: Radical Theory and Practice in William S. Burroughs's Fiction* (Champaign: University of Illinois Press, 1987). See especially part 2.

30. This interruption of orality by writing constitutes one of the crucial formal qualities of *The Job*, in which this text is found, for the book consists of interviews with pieces of Burroughs's writing interpolated by Burroughs

during the editorial process. There are no clear boundaries indicating what text emerges from transcriptions of tape-recorded interviews and what text Burroughs wrote outside of the interview format.

31. There has been a recent turn in critical theory to discussions of species history, a turn which, I contend, is part and parcel of the more general turn to biopolitics. See, for example, Dipesh Chakrabarty, "The Climate of History: Four Theses," *Critical Inquiry* 35, no. 2 (2009): 197–222; Nick Dyer-Witheford, "Species-Being and the New Commonism: Notes on an Interrupted Cycle of Struggles," *the commoner* 11 (Spring 2006): 15–32; Jason W. Moore, *Capitalism in the Web of Life: Ecology and the Accumulation of Capital* (New York: Verso, 2015); and Neel Ahuja, *Biosecurities: Disease Interventions, Empire, and the Government of Species* (Durham, N.C.: Duke University Press, 2016).

32. On Burroughs's notion of electronic revolution, see especially "Electronic Revolution," in *Ah Pook Is Here, and Other Texts*.

33. On this subject, see also William S. Burroughs, "Technology of Writing," in *The Adding Machine: Selected Essays* (New York: Arcade, 1986): 32–36.

34. On Burroughs and counterfeiting, see Murphy, *Wising Up the Marks*, 169–80. Of course, William Burroughs is preceded in this inquiry into the political implications of reproducibility by Walter Benjamin in his well-known article, "Art in the Age of Mechanical Reproducibility." See also Fredric Jameson, "Video: Surrealism without the Unconscious," in *Postmodernism, or The Cultural Logic of Late Capitalism* (Durham, N.C.: Duke University Press, 1991).

35. On difference in itself, see Gilles Deleuze, *Difference and Repetition*, trans. Paul Patton (New York: Columbia University Press, 1994), especially chap. 1, pp. 4–5. In *The Job*, Burroughs produces a telling image of difference in itself (or primary nonidentity) by rewriting the creation myth, once again, but this time, with tape recorders: "I advance the theory that in the electronic revolution a virus *is* a very small unit of word and image. I have suggested how such units can be biologically activated to act as communicable virus strains. Let us start with three tape recorders in the Garden of Eden. Tape recorder one is Adam. Tape recorder two is Eve. Tape recorder three is God, who deteriorated after Hiroshima into the Ugly American" (14).

36. Burroughs, "Electronic Revolution," 153–54.

37. Many of the traits characteristic of Burroughs's writing are also defining features of postmodern fiction. Along with Timothy Murphy, however, I would argue that Burroughs replaces the ludic playfulness and ontological relativism of much postmodern fiction with a mode of linguistic experimentation grounded in collective struggles for emancipation. On Burroughs and postmodernism, see especially, Murphy, *Wising Up the Marks*, chap. 1;

Marianne DeKoven, *Utopia Limited: The Sixties and the Emergence of the Postmodern* (Durham, N.C.: Duke University Press, 2004), chap. 8; Steve Shaviro, "Burroughs's Theater of Illusion: *Cities of the Red Night*," in *William S. Burroughs: At the Front: Critical Reception, 1959–1989*, eds. Jennie Skerl and Robin Lydenberg (Carbondale: Southern Illinois University Press, 1991); and Wayne Pounds, "The Postmodern Anus: Parody and Utopia in Two Recent Novels by William Burroughs," *Poetics Today* 8, no. 3/4 (1987): 611–29.

38. Christopher Breu, *The Insistence of the Material: Literature in the Age of Biopolitics* (Minneapolis: University of Minnesota Press, 2014), 39.

39. William S. Burroughs, "The Limits of Control," in *Adding Machine*, 17.

40. Ibid.

41. Ibid.

42. On the notion of control in Burroughs, see also Murphy, *Wising Up the Marks*, 52–64, 80–85; and Nathan Moore, "Nova Law: William S. Burroughs and the Logic of Control," *Law and Literature* 19, no. 3 (2007): 435–70.

43. Burroughs, *Job*, 59.

44. Gilles Deleuze, "Control and Becoming," in *Negotiations*, trans. Martin Joughin (New York: Columbia University Press, 1995), 174.

45. Gilles Deleuze, "Postscript on Control Societies," in *Negotiations*, 178.

46. Jodi Dean, *Democracy and Other Neoliberal Fantasies: Communicative Capitalism and Left Politics* (Durham, N.C.: Duke University Press, 2009), especially chap. 1: "The Promises of Communicative Capitalism."

47. Deleuze, "Postscript on Control Societies," 179.

48. Ibid., 181. Deleuze thus comes to much the same conclusion as Luc Boltanski and Ève Chiapello in *The New Spirit of Capitalism*, at least in regard to the corporate co-optation of the values of the new left.

49. Gilles Deleuze and Félix Guattari, *A Thousand Plateaus*, trans. Brian Massumi (Minneapolis: University of Minnesota Press, 1987), 6, 152. Gilles Deleuze and Claire Parnet, *Dialogues*, trans. Hugh Tomlinson and Barbara Habberjam (New York: Columbia University Press, 1977), 10, 18.

50. See especially Duggan, *Twilight of Equality?*; and Melinda Cooper, *Family Values: Between Neoliberalism and the New Social Conservatism* (New York: Zone Books, 2017).

51. Michel Foucault, *"Society Must Be Defended": Lectures at the Collège de France, 1975–1976* (New York: Picador, 2003), chap. 11.

52. Burroughs, *Job*, 102–3; and *Adding Machine*, 120.

53. Burroughs, *Job*, 102.

54. Burroughs, *Adding Machine*, 117.

55. Marx, *Capital*, vol. 1, 342: "Capital is dead labour which, vampire-like, lives only by sucking living labour, and lives the more, the more labour it sucks." And see Burroughs, *Western Lands*, 164–65.

56. Burroughs, *Adding Machine*, 120.

57. A notable exception is Fredric Jameson, who has explicitly written about the politics of the multitude as a "new world of the Utopian masses." See "Utopia as Replication," in *Valences of the Dialectic* (New York: Verso, 2009), 425–33.

58. On this history, see especially Steve Wright, *Storming Heaven: Class Composition and Struggle in Italian Autonomist Marxism* (London: Pluto Press, 2002); and *Radical Thought in Italy: A Potential Politics*, ed. Michael Hardt and Paolo Virno (Minneapolis: University of Minnesota Press, 1996).

59. In regard to the concept of the common, see especially Michael Hardt and Antonio Negri, *Multitude: War and Democracy in the Age of Empire* (New York: Penguin, 2004), 103–27, 196–227, and *Commonwealth* (Cambridge, Mass.: Belknap Press of Harvard University Press, 2009), 280–95. See also Jason Read, *The Micropolitics of Capital: Marx and the Prehistory of the Present* (Albany: State University of New York Press, 2003), chap. 3, and Cesare Casarino, "Surplus Common," in *In Praise of the Common: A Conversation on Philosophy and Politics* (Minneapolis: University of Minnesota Press, 2008), 1–40.

60. Hardt and Negri, *Multitude*, 221. All further citations included as parentheticals in the chapter.

61. Hardt and Negri, *Commonwealth*, part 6: "Revolution," especially 325–44.

62. Michael Hardt and Antonio Negri, *Assembly* (Oxford: Oxford University Press, 2017), xv.

63. Ibid., 19.

64. Hardt and Negri, *Commonwealth*, 340.

65. Antonio Negri, *Insurgencies: Constituent Power and the Modern State*, trans. Maurizia Boscagli (Minneapolis: University of Minnesota Press, 1991), 14.

66. Ibid.

67. See, for example, Crystal Bartolovich, "Organizing The (Un)Common," *Angelaki* 12, no. 3 (2010): 81–104. For an excellent response to Hardt and Negri's critics, see Timothy S. Murphy, *Antonio Negri* (New York: Polity, 2012), 195–207.

68. On the concept of exodus as a political movement, see Paolo Virno, "Virtuosity and Revolution: The Political Theory of Exodus," in *Radical Thought in Italy: A Potential Politics*, ed. Michael Hardt and Paolo Virno (Minneapolis: University of Minnesota Press, 1996).

69. Casarino, "Surplus Common," 22–23.

70. Phillip E. Wegner, *Imaginary Communities: Utopia, the Nation, and the Spatial Histories of Modernity* (Berkeley: University of California Press, 2002), xviii.

71. Fredric Jameson, *Seeds of Time* (New York: Columbia University Press, 1996), 90.

72. Wendy Brown, "American Nightmare: Neoliberalism, Neoconservatism, and De-Democratization," *Political Theory* 34, no. 6 (December 2006): 690–714; and Cooper, *Family Values*, 18–24, 62–63.

2. THE PEOPLE AND THE PEOPLE: DEMOCRACY AND VITALISM IN WALT WHITMAN'S 1855 *LEAVES OF GRASS*

1. [Unknown]. "[Review of Leaves of Grass (1855)]." *Washington Daily National Intelligencer*, February 18, 1856, *The Walt Whitman Archive*, general editors Ed Folsom and Kenneth M. Price. http://www.whitmanarchive.org.

2. On Whitman's repurposing of biological, medical, and physiological discourses, see especially, M. Jimmie Killingsworth, *Whitman's Poetry of the Body: Sexuality, Politics, and the Text* (Chapel Hill: University of North Carolina Press, 1991); Joan Burbick, *Healing the Republic: The Language of Health and the Culture of Nationalism in Nineteenth-Century America* (Cambridge: Cambridge University Press, 1994), chap. 6: "Biodemocracy in *Leaves of Grass*," 113–36; Robert Leigh Davis, *Whitman and the Romance of Medicine* (Berkeley: University of California Press, 1997). Doubts regarding Whitman's investment in specifically medical/physiological discourses disappear with the recent discovery of Whitman's "Manly Health and Training, With Off-Hand Hints toward Their Conditions," *Walt Whitman Quarterly Review* 33, no. 3 (2016): 184–310. These writings were first published under the pseudonym Mose Veslor in *The New York Atlas* in 1858.

3. See Jane Bennett, *Vibrant Matter: A Political Ecology of Things* (Durham, N.C.: Duke University Press, 2010); Mel Y. Chen, *Animacies: Biopolitics, Racial Mattering, and Queer Affect* (Durham, N.C.: Duke University Press, 2012); and Rosi Braidotti, *The Posthuman* (Cambridge: Polity, 2013).

4. F. O. Matthiessen, *American Renaissance: Art and Expression in the Age of Emerson and Whitman* (1941; Oxford: Oxford University Press, 1968), book 4: "Whitman."

5. C. B. Macpherson, *The Political Theory of Possessive Individualism: Hobbes to Locke* (1962; Oxford: Oxford University Press, 2011), 3.

6. The notion of individuation has many sources, but my understanding of it emerges largely from the work of Gilbert Simondon, Gilles Deleuze, and Paolo Virno. See especially Gilbert Simondon, *L'individuation psychique et collective* (Paris: Aubier, 2007), part 2; Paolo Virno, *Grammar of the Multitude*, trans. Isabella Bertoletti, James Cascaito, and Andrea Casson (Los Angeles: Semiotext(e), 2004), 76–80, and "Angels and the General Intellect: Individuation in Duns Scotus and Gilbert Simondon," *parrhesia* 7 (2009): 58–67.

7. Walt Whitman, *Leaves of Grass* (1855), in *The Walt Whitman Archive*, general editors Ed Folsom and Kenneth M. Price, http://www.whitman

archive.org, 17. I have relied on the online Walt Whitman Archive's facsimiles of the first edition. Subsequent citations appear as parentheticals in the body of the chapter.

8. See Martin Heidegger, "The Age of the World Picture," trans. William Lovitt, in *The Question concerning Technology and Other Essays* (New York: Harper Perennial, 1977): 115–54.

9. Mark Noble, *American Poetic Materialism from Whitman to Stevens* (Cambridge: Cambridge University Press, 2014), 48.

10. Michael Moon describes this fluid medium in terms of specularity, arguing that its most intense expression is in the first edition of *Leaves of Grass*. See *Disseminating Whitman: Revision and Corporeality in* Leaves of Grass (Cambridge, Mass.: Harvard University Press, 1991), chap. 2: "Fluidity and Specularity in the Whitman Text."

11. A sampling of this lineage would include the work of Spinoza and Marx (especially the former's *Ethics* and the latter's early work), a certain Nietzsche, Henri Bergson, and the late work of J.-P. Sartre, the collaborations of Gilles Deleuze and Félix Guattari, and the work of Michel Foucault, Jean-Luc Nancy, Luce Irigaray, and Antonio Negri (among others). This lineage is not homogenous, and for all the continuity in terms of an axiomatic understanding of the commonality of being, there are, of course, significant differences between these thinkers.

12. Jean-Luc Nancy, *The Inoperative Community*, ed. Peter Connor, trans. Peter Connor, Lisa Garbus, Michael Holland, and Simona Sawheny (Minneapolis: University of Minnesota Press, 1991), 25.

13. Tenney Nathanson, *Whitman's Presence: Body, Voice, and Writing in* Leaves of Grass (New York: New York University Press, 1992), 8.

14. Betsy Erkkila, *Whitman: The Political Poet* (Oxford: Oxford University Press, 1989), 93. See also Donald Pease, "Walt Whitman and the Vox Populi of the American Masses," in *Visionary Compacts: American Renaissance Writings in Cultural Contexts* (Madison: University of Wisconsin Press, 1987), 108–58. For a more recent example, see Edward Whitley, "Whitman's Occasional Nationalism: 'A Broadway Pageant' and the Space of Public Poetry," *Nineteenth-Century Literature* 60, no. 4 (2006): 451–80.

15. Jason Frank, "Promiscuous Citizenship," in *A Political Companion to Walt Whitman*, ed. John E. Seery (Lexington: University of Kentucky Press, 2011), 162.

16. Spinoza, *Ethics*, trans. G. H. R. Parkinson (Oxford: Oxford University Press, 2000), book 4, proposition 36, p. 251.

17. Antonio Negri offers, perhaps, the most optimistic version of Spinozism in *The Savage Anomaly: The Power of Spinoza's Metaphysics and Politics*, trans. Michael Hardt (Minneapolis: University of Minnesota Press, 1991) and *Subversive Spinoza: (Un)Contemporary Variations*, ed. Timothy Murphy

(Manchester: Manchester University Press, 2004). Warren Montag offers a measured assessment of Spinoza's work situated in historical and material contexts in *Bodies, Masses, Power: Spinoza and His Contemporaries* (New York: Verso, 1999). For an excellent range of recent responses to Spinoza's work, see *The New Spinoza*, ed. Warren Montag and Ted Stolze (Minneapolis: University of Minnesota Press, 1997), and *Spinoza Now*, ed. Dimitris Vardoulakis (Minneapolis: University of Minnesota Press, 2011).

18. Gilles Deleuze, "Whitman," in *Essays Critical and Clinical*, trans. Daniel W. Smith and Michael A. Greco (Minneapolis: University of Minnesota Press, 1997), 59–60. Deleuze elaborates his Spinozism in *Expressionism in Philosophy: Spinoza*, trans. Martin Joughin (New York: Zone Books, 1992) and *Spinoza: Practical Philosophy*, trans. Robert Hurley (San Francisco: City Light Publishers, 1988).

19. Peter Coviello, *Intimacy in America: Dreams of Affiliation in Antebellum Literature* (Minneapolis: University of Minnesota Press, 2005), 129.

20. In addition to Foucault, see Eve Sedgwick's *Epistemology of the Closet* (Berkeley: University of California Press, 1990), intro. and chap. 1.

21. See especially Harold Aspiz, *Walt Whitman and the Body Beautiful* (Champaign: University of Illinois Press, 1980); David Reynolds, *Walt Whitman's America: A Cultural Biography* (New York: Vintage, 1996), 194–234; M. Jimmie Killingsworth, *Whitman's Poetry of the Body: Sexuality, Politics, and the Text*, esp. the intro. and chaps. 1–2; and Mark Maslan, *Whitman Possessed: Poetry, Sexuality, and Popular Authority* (Baltimore: Johns Hopkins University Press, 2001). If there was any doubt regarding Whitman's interest in the medical discourses of the body of his day, they have certainly been eliminated by the recent discovery of his treatise, *Manly Health and Training*.

22. Judith Butler's recent work, especially *Notes toward a Performative Theory of Assembly* (Cambridge, Mass.: Harvard University Press, 2015), moves in the direction of such a reconfigured concept of performativity. It not only founds performativity on a primary sociality or interdependency; it also offers up the notion of bodily performativity without speech acts. See especially chaps. 2 and 5.

23. See Robert Martin, *The Homosexual Tradition in American Poetry* (Iowa City: University of Iowa Press, 1998).

24. Michael Moon, "Solitude, Singularity, Seriality: Whitman vis-à-vis Fourier," *ELH* 73 (2006): 309, 322.

25. Ibid., 308.

26. Michael Warner, *Publics and Counterpublics* (New York: Zone Books, 2005), 269–89.

27. Jane Bennett, "The Solar Judgment of Walt Whitman," in *A Political Companion to Whitman*, 143. Branka Arsić's *Bird Relics: Grief and Vitalism in*

Thoreau (Cambridge, Mass.: Harvard University Press, 2016) offers, to my mind, a more subtle consideration of nineteenth-century American literature and culture in respect to vitalism.

28. The limits of Whitman's vitalism may also be understood as the limits of the so-called new materialism, insofar as the latter shares with Whitman a belief in the intrinsic political qualities of matter. In other words, some of the new materialists follow Whitman in affirming the democratic or egalitarian value of matter as such or in seeing in a generalized notion of animacy a solution to the pathologies of human exceptionalism. To Jane Bennett's credit she traces this move back to its origins—or, more precisely, one of its origins—in antebellum U.S. thought. Cristin Ellis offers an incisive and compelling account of the relationship between the materialist turn in critical theory and the antebellum United States in *Antebellum Posthuman: Race and Materiality in the Mid-Nineteenth Century* (New York: Fordham University Press, 2018).

29. Allen Grossman, "The Poetics of Union in Whitman and Lincoln: An Inquiry toward the Relationship of Art and Policy," in *The Long Schoolroom: Lessons in the Bitter Logic of the Poetic Principle* (Ann Arbor: University of Michigan Press, 1997), 77, 71.

30. The now classic version of the imperial argument appears in Quentin Anderson, *The Imperial Self: An Essay in American Literary and Cultural History* (New York: Knopf, 1971), especially chap. 4: "The World in the Body."

31. See Mayra Rivera, *Poetics of the Flesh* (Durham, N.C.: Duke University Press, 2015), chap. 2: "Abandoning Flesh: The Letters of Paul." See also Alain Badiou, *Saint Paul: The Foundation of Universalism*, trans. Ray Brassier (Stanford, CA: Stanford University Press, 2003), especially chap. 6.

32. Giorgio Agamben, *Homo Sacer: Sovereign Power and Bare Life*, trans. Daniel Heller-Roazen (Stanford, CA: Stanford University Press, 1998), 22.

33. Wai Chee Dimock offers the most compelling version of this argument in "Whitman, Syntax, and Political Theory," in *Breaking Bounds: Whitman and American Cultural Studies* (Oxford: Oxford University Press, 1996), 62–82.

34. Jason Frank, "'Aesthetic Democracy': Walt Whitman and the Poetry of the People," in *Constituent Moments: Enacting the People in Postrevolutionary America* (Durham, N.C.: Duke University Press, 2010), 183.

35. Ibid., 106.

36. Tom Yingling's essay on Whitman's utopianism is very compelling, but its emphasis on displacement—utopia as permanent interruption of the status quo—belongs more to the later editions of *Leaves*, especially to the "Calamus" section. See "Homosexuality and Utopian Discourse in American Poetry," in *Breaking Bounds: Whitman and American Cultural Studies* (Oxford: Oxford University Press, 1996), 135–46.

37. Notably, Whitman's investment in the New World does not necessarily entail a turning away from the Old World so much as a making good on it. In *Visionary Compacts* (Madison: University of Wisconsin Press, 1987), Donald Pease puts it as follows: "Like an image in a poem, the United States exists as a realization of desire; as the realization of Europe's wish to be a better world, America was from its origin the result of a reflection" (129). Pease argues that "America reverses the process of reflection," because as "the regeneration of the Old World," it does not reflect but rather projects worldly things (including the democratic people) into "what they can be" (ibid.).

38. There is another doubling or dividing that occurs in Whitman's relationship to the Revolution, namely, that between the Revolution as bourgeois and the Revolution as radical. Whitman sometimes represents the Revolution in the form of Founding Fathers, but his emphasis seems much more on the unruly multitudes described, for instance, by Gary B. Nash in *The Unknown American Revolution: The Unruly Birth of Democracy and the Struggle to Create America* (New York: Penguin Books, 2006).

39. Cody Marrs, "Whitman's Latencies: Hegel and the Politics of Time in Leaves of Grass," *Arizona Quarterly* 67, no. 1 (2011): 52.

40. Erkkila, *Whitman: A Political Poet*, 67.

41. David S. Reynolds, "Politics and Poetry: *Leaves of Grass* and the Social Crisis of the 1850s," in *The Cambridge Companion to Whitman*, ed. Ezra Greenspan (Cambridge: Cambridge University Press, 1995), 67.

42. Whitman often exemplified moderation. This moderate stance becomes startlingly clear in his response to the institution of slavery. Whitman opposed the spread of slavery, but he didn't always support the incorporation of Blacks into post-emancipation society. On this matter, see especially Martin Klammer, "Slavery and Race," in *A Companion to Walt Whitman*, ed. Donald Kummings (Hoboken, N.J.: Wiley-Blackwell, 2009), as well as Klammer's *Whitman, Slavery, and the Emergence of Leaves of Grass* (University Park: Penn State University Press, 1996).

43. See Sacvan Bercovitch, *The American Jeremiad* (Madison: University of Wisconsin Press, 1978).

44. Wendy Brown defines reactive politics in *States of Injury: Power and Freedom in Late Modernity* (Princeton, N.J.: Princeton University Press, 1995).

45. Andrew Lawson's *Walt Whitman and the Class Struggle* (Iowa City: University of Iowa Press, 2006) offers one of the most concerted accounts of this kind. I find myself more sympathetic to the arguments of M. Wynn Thomas and Cody Marrs, both of which attribute to Whitman a critique of capitalism. See M. Wynn Thomas, "Labor and Laborers," in *A Companion to Walt Whitman*, and "Whitman and the Dreams of Labor," in *Walt Whitman:*

the Centennial Essays, ed. Ed Folsom (Iowa City: University of Iowa Press, 1994); and Marrs, "Whitman's Latencies." See also Alan Trachtenberg, "The Politics of Labor and the Poet's Work: A Reading of 'A Song for Occupations,'" in *Walt Whitman: The Centennial Essays*; and Christian Haines, "Oscillations prolétaires: Poésie du travail, travail de la poésie chez Arthur Rimbaud et Walt Whitman," *Parade Sauvage: Revue d'études rimbaldiennes* 23 (Fall 2012): 65–101.

46. Betsy Erkkila makes a similar argument in "Whitman, Marx, and the American 1848," in *Leaves of Grass: The Sesquicentennial Essays* (Lincoln: University of Nebraska Press, 2008).

47. Karl Marx, *Capital*, vol. 1, trans. Ben Fowkes (New York: Penguin Books, 1990), 289–90.

48. Karl Marx, *Grundrisse*, trans. Martin Nicolaus (New York: Penguin Books, 1993), 272.

49. Antonio Negri, *Insurgencies: Constituent Power and the Modern State*, trans. Maurizia Boscagli (Minneapolis: University of Minnesota Press, 1999), 11.

50. Jason Stacy, *Walt Whitman's Multitudes: Labor Reform and Persona in Whitman's Journalism and the First* Leaves of Grass, *1840–1855* (Bern: Peter Lang, 2008), 118.

51. Donald Pease, "Colonial Violence and Poetic Transcendence in Whitman's 'Song of Myself,'" in *The Cambridge Companion to Nineteenth-Century American Poetry*, ed. Kerry Larson (Cambridge: Cambridge University Press, 2011), 245.

52. For additional discussions of Whitman's imperial tendencies, see especially Walter Grünzweig, "Noble Ethics and Loving Aggressiveness: The Imperialist Walt Whitman," in *An American Empire: Expansionist Cultures and Policies, 1881–1917*, ed. Serge Ricard (Ann Arbor: University of Michigan Press, 1990): 151–65, and "Imperialism," in *A Companion to Walt Whitman*, 151–63; Malini Schueller, *U.S. Orientalisms: Race, Nation, and Gender in Literature, 1790–1890* (Ann Arbor: University of Michigan Press, 1998), chap. 7: "Whitman, Columbus, and the Asian Mother," 175–98; and M. Jimmie Killingsworth, *Walt Whitman and the Earth: A Study of Ecopoetics* (Iowa City: University of Iowa Press, 2004), chap. 3: "Global and Local, Nature and Earth," 74–97.

53. See Orlando Patterson, *Slavery and Social Death: A Comparative Study* (Cambridge, Mass.: Harvard University Press, 1985).

54. On the para-ontology of blackness, see Fred Moten, *In the Break: The Aesthetics of the Black Radical Tradition* (Minneapolis: University of Minnesota Press, 2003) and *Black and Blur* (Durham, N.C.: Duke University Press, 2017); Christina Sharpe, *In the Wake: On Blackness and Being* (Durham,

N.C.: Duke University Press, 2016); and Nahum Dimitri Chandler, *X – The Problem of the Negro as a Problem for Thought* (New York: Fordham University Press, 2013).

55. On the whiteness of ontology, see, for instance, Derrida, "White Mythology: Metaphor in the Text of Philosophy," trans. F. C. T. Moore, *New Literary History* 6, no. 1 (1974): 5–74.

56. Klammer, "Slavery and Race." A number of excellent studies broach the ambiguities involved in Whitman's responses to slavery. See especially Karen Sanchez-Eppler, *Touching Liberty: Abolition, Feminism, and the Politics of the Body* (Berkeley: University of California Press, 1993), chap. 2: "To Stand Between: Walt Whitman's Poetics of Merger and Embodiment"; Dana Phillips, "Nineteenth-Century Racial Thought and Whitman's 'Democratic Ethnology of the Future,'" *Nineteenth-Century Literature* 49, no. 3 (1994): 289–320; Klammer, *Whitman, Slavery, and the Emergence of Leaves of Grass*; and Ed Folsom, "Lucifer and Ethiopia: Whitman, Race, and Poetics before the Civil War," in *A Historical Guide to Walt Whitman* (Oxford: Oxford University Press, 2000).

57. Keeanga-Yamahtta Taylor, *From #BlackLivesMatter to Black Liberation* (Chicago: Haymarket, 2016).

58. Ben Lerner, *10:04* (New York: Picador), 168, and *The Hatred of Poetry* (New York: Farrar, Straus and Giroux, 2016), 49.

3. NOBODY'S WIFE: AFFECTIVE ECONOMIES OF MARRIAGE IN EMILY DICKINSON

1. Emily Dickinson, *Letters of Emily Dickinson*, vol. 3, ed. Thomas H. Johnson (Cambridge, Mass.: Belknap Press of Harvard University Press, 1958), 882.

2. Michel Foucault, "Des espaces autres," *Architecture, Mouvement, Continuité* 5 (1984): 46–49. Translation mine.

3. For manuscript studies, see especially Marta Werner, *Emily Dickinson's Open Folios: Scenes of Reading, Surfaces of Writing* (Ann Arbor: University of Michigan Press, 1995); Virginia Dickinson, *Dickinson's Misery: A Theory of Lyric Reading* (Princeton, N.J.: Princeton University Press, 2005); and Alexandra Socarides, *Dickinson Unbound: Paper, Process, and Poetics* (Oxford: Oxford University Press, 2012). For new historicist readings, see, for example, Cristanne Miller, *Reading in Time: Emily Dickinson in the Nineteenth Century* (Amherst: University of Massachusetts Press, 2012); and Domnhall Mitchell, *Emily Dickinson: Monarch of Perception* (Amherst: University of Massachusetts Press, 2000).

4. Maya Gonzalez, "The Gendered Circuit: Reading the Arcane of Reproduction," *Viewpoint Magazine*, September 28, 2013, https://www.viewpointmag.com/2013/09/28/the-gendered-circuit-reading-the-arcane-of

-reproduction/. See also Leopoldina Fortunati, *The Arcane of Reproduction: Housework, Prostitution, Labor and Capital*, trans. Hilary Creek (Brooklyn: Autonomedia, 1995).

5. Sara Ahmed, *The Promise of Happiness* (Durham, N.C.: Duke University Press, 2010), 195.

6. Emily Dickinson, *The Poems of Emily Dickinson: Reading Edition*, ed. R. W. Franklin (Cambridge, Mass.: Belknap Press of Harvard University Pres, 1999), 857. Unless noted otherwise, quotations of Dickinson's poems come from this edition of her poetry.

7. Karl Marx, *Grundrisse*, trans. Martin Nicolaus (1857–58; New York: Penguin, 1973), 271–73, 296–97.

8. Roland Barthes, "The Grain of the Voice," in *Image Music Text*, trans. Stephen Heath (New York: Hill and Wang, 1977), 184, 188.

9. Silvia Federici, *Caliban and the Witch: Women, the Body, and Primitive Accumulation* (New York: Autonomedia, 2004), 98. See also Fortunati, *Arcane of Reproduction*; Mariarosa Dalla Costa and Selma James, *The Power of Women and the Subversion of the Community* (Bristol: Falling Wall Press, 1975); and Maria Mies, *Patriarchy and Accumulation on a World Scale: Women in the International Division of Labour*, 2nd ed. (New York: Zed Books, 1998). See also *Viewpoint Magazine*, no. 5, "Social Reproduction," October 31, 2015, https://www.viewpointmag.com/2015/11/02/issue-5-social-reproduction/

10. See especially Roberto Esposito, *Persons and Things: From the Body's Point of View*, trans. Zakiya Hanafi (Cambridge: Polity, 2015).

11. Sara Ahmed, "Affective Economies," *Social Text* 22, no. 2 (2004): 120.

12. Ibid., 121.

13. This conceptualization of affect owes a debt to Baruch Spinoza's *Ethics*. See *Ethics*, ed. and trans. G. H. R. Parkinson (Oxford: Oxford University Press, 2000), part 3: "On the Origin and Nature of the Emotions."

14. *The Poems of Emily Dickinson: Variorum Edition*, vol. 1, ed. R. W. Franklin (Cambridge, Mass.: Belknap Press of Harvard University Press, 1998), 451. Emphasis added.

15. Ahmed, *Promise of Happiness*, 32, 34.

16. Quoted in Elizabeth Maddock Dillon, *The Gender of Freedom* (Stanford, Calif.: Stanford University Press, 2004), 126.

17. Marx, *Grundrisse*, 296–300.

18. Silvia Federici, "Counterplanning from the Kitchen," in *Revolution at Point Zero: Housework, Reproduction, and Feminist Struggle* (Brooklyn: PM Press, 2012), 31.

19. On Dickinson's discontent, see Vivian Pollak, *Dickinson: The Anxiety of Gender* (Ithaca, N.Y.: Cornell University Press, 1986), especially chap. 6: "The Wife—without the Sign."

20. Ahmed, *Promise of Happiness*, 87.

21. Lauren Berlant, "The Subject of True Feeling: Pain, Privacy, and Politics," in *Feminist Consequences: Theory for the New Century* (New York: Columbia University Press, 2001), 128; and *The Queen of America Goes to Washington: Essays on Sex and Citizenship* (Durham, N.C.: Duke University Press, 1997), 11.

22. See Ernst Bloch, "Something's Missing: A Discussion between Ernst Bloch and Theodor W. Adorno on the Contradictions of Utopian Longing," in *The Utopian Function of Art and Literature*, trans. Jack Zipes and Frank Mecklenburg (Cambridge, Mass.: MIT Press, 1988), 1–17.

23. For a useful summary of the Wages for Housework Campaign, see Sarah Jaffe, "The Factory in the Family," *Nation*, March 14, 2018. See also *Wages for Housework: The New York Committee, 1972–1977: History, Theory, Documents*, ed. Silvia Federici and Arlen Austin (Brooklyn: Autonomedia, 2017).

24. Silvia Federici, "Wages against Housework," in *Revolution at Point Zero: Housework, Reproduction, and Feminist Struggle* (Brooklyn: PM Press, 2012), 18.

25. Dickinson, *Letters*, 1:103.

26. Karen Sánchez-Eppler, "At Home in the Body: The Internal Politics of Emily Dickinson's Poetry," in *Touching Liberty: Abolition, Feminism, and the Politics of the Body* (Berkeley: University of California Press, 1997), 126.

27. Dickinson, *Letters*, 2:473–74.

28. Virginia Jackson, *Dickinson's Misery: A Theory of Lyric Reading* (Princeton, N.J.: Princeton University Press, 2005), 203.

29. Dickinson, *Letters*, 2:562.

30. Federici, *Caliban and the Witch*, 97.

31. Sara Ahmed, *Queer Phenomenology: Orientations, Objects, Others* (Durham, N.C.: Duke University Press, 2006), 29.

32. Diana Fuss, "Dickinson's Eye: The Dickinson Homestead Amherst Massachusetts," in *The Sense of an Interior: Four Writers and the Rooms That Shaped Them* (New York: Routledge, 2004), 9–30.

33. Ibid., 20.

34. In this instance, I have used the earlier version of this poem, or first variant, because of its more differentiated formal structure. Franklin, *The Poems of Emily Dickinson: Variorum Edition*, 1:228.

35. There is a longer story to be told, here, one that articulates this lack of social recognition on the basis of the marriage institution with the social death of women of color (especially Black women) on the basis of chattel slavery and white supremacism. Hortense J. Spillers's "Mama's Baby, Papa's Maybe: An American Grammar Book," *Diacritics* 17, no. 2 (1987): 64–81,

remains one of the most compelling accounts of the "ungendering" and "dehumanizing" of African persons with respect to social reproduction. For more recent accounts, see especially Alexander Weheliye, *Habeus Viscus: Racializing Assemblages, Biopolitics, and Black Feminist Theories of the Human* (Durham, N.C.: Duke University Press, 2014), and Kyla Schuller, *The Biopolitics of Feeling: Race, Sex, and Science in the Nineteenth Century* (Durham, N.C.: Duke University Press, 2018).

36. In this respect, my argument resonates with that of Anne-Lise François in *Open Secrets: The Literature of Uncounted Experience* (Stanford, Calif.: Stanford University Press, 1999), chap. 3, in which she argues that Dickinson's poetry involves a "gesture of desisting."

37. Ahmed, *Queer Phenomenology*, 92, 96, 137.

38. Dillon, *Gender of Freedom*, 252.

39. Ibid., 253.

40. Daniel Tiffany, *Infidel Poetics: Riddles, Nightlife, Substance* (Chicago: University of Chicago Press, 2009), 15.

41. Again, see François, *Open Secrets*, chap. 3.

42. Paul Crumbley discusses the commons and Dickinson in terms of intellectual property rights. See "Copyright, Circulation, and the Body," in *Winds of Will: Emily Dickinson and the Sovereignty of Democratic Thought* (Tuscaloosa: University of Alabama Press, 2010).

43. Elizabeth Freeman's excellent *The Wedding Complex: Forms of Belonging in Modern American Culture* (Durham, N.C.: Duke University Press, 2002) analyzes practices or rituals that "partially or completely sunder the wedding from its legal ramifications, reveling in the expressive, theatrical, and symbolic aspects of the ritual" (4). Like Freeman, I'm interested in the nonnormative possibilities opened up by wedding rituals, but, in contrast to her focus on the event of the wedding (as opposed to the duration of marriage), I focus on the way in which the act of coupling prefigures alternative forms of marriage, understood as relations of social reproduction.

44. Dickinson, here, echoes Eve Sedgwick's now classical theorization of the "open secret" in *Epistemology of the Closet* (Berkeley: University of California Press, 2008).

45. Dickinson's combination of anonymity, commonality, multiplicity, and pleasure anticipates Luce Irigaray's theorization of feminine sexuality. However, Dickinson manages to avoid Irigaray's tendency to take heterosexuality for granted. See especially Irigaray, *This Sex Which Is Not One*, trans. Catherine Porter (Ithaca, N.Y.: Cornell University Press, 1985), 23–33, 205–18.

46. Lee Edelman has provided the most incisive critique of heteronormative concepts of temporality. See Edelman, *No Future: Queer Theory and the Death Drive* (Durham, N.C.: Duke University Press, 2004).

47. Dickinson, *Poems of Emily Dickinson: Variorum Edition*, 1:279.
48. Dickinson, *Letters*, 2:405.
49. On Dickinson's lesbianism, see Martha Nella Smith, *Rowing in Eden: Rereading Emily Dickinson* (Austin: University of Texas Press, 1992), 25–30; Ellen Louise Hart, "The Encoding of Homoerotic Desire: Emily Dickinson's Letters and Poems to Susan Dickinson," *Tulsa Studies in Women's Literature* 9, no. 2 (1990): 251–72; and Paula Bennet, "'The Pea That Duty Locks': Lesbian and Feminist-Heterosexual Readings of Emily Dickinson's Poetry," in *Lesbian Texts and Contexts: Radical Revisions*, ed. Karla Jay and Joanne Glasgow (New York: New York University Press, 1990).
50. Dickinson, *Letters*, 2:349.
51. Ahmed, *Queer Phenomenology*, 100.
52. On the queerness of Dickinson's poetry, in excess of its lesbianism, see especially H. Jordan Landry, "Animal/Insectual/Lesbian Sex: Dickinson's Queer Version of the Birds and the Bees," *Emily Dickinson Journal* 9, no. 2 (2000): 42–54; and Sylvia Henneberg, "Neither Lesbian nor Straight: Multiple Eroticisms in Emily Dickinson's Poetry," *Emily Dickinson Journal* 4, no. 2 (1995): 1–19.
53. See José Esteban Muñoz, *Cruising Utopia: The Then and There of Queer Futurity* (New York: New York University Press, 2009); Elizabeth Freeman, *Time Binds: Queer Temporalities, Queer Histories* (Durham, N.C.: Duke University Press, 2010); Michael D. Snediker, *Queer Optimism: Lyric Personhood and Other Felicitous Persuasions* (Minneapolis: University of Minnesota Press, 2008); and Jack Halberstam, *Gaga Feminism: Sex, Gender, and the End of Normal* (Boston: Beacon Press, 2013).
54. José Muñoz, "'Gimme gimme this . . . Gimme gimme that': Annihilation and Innovation in the Punk Rock Commons," *Social Text* 31, no. 3 (2013): 96.
55. I'm indebted to Giorgio Agamben for this formulation of community's scattering. See *The Coming Community*, trans. Michael Hardt (Minneapolis: University of Minnesota Press, 1993), 19.
56. Dickinson, *Letters*, 2:430.
57. Cristanne Miller, *Emily Dickinson: A Poet's Grammar* (Cambridge, Mass.: Harvard University Press, 1989), 51.
58. Ibid.
59. Paul Crumbley, "Dickinson's Dashes and the Limits of Discourse," *Emily Dickinson Journal* 1, no. 2 (1992): 14.
60. Ibid., 23.
61. Giorgio Agamben, *Idea of Prose*, trans. Michael Sullivan and Sam Whitsitt (Albany: State University of New York Press, 1995), 25–26.
62. See Ruth Rosen, "The Care Crisis," *Nation*, February 27, 2007; and Cynthia Hess, "Women and the Care Crisis: Valuing In-Home Care in

Policy and Practice," Briefing Paper for the Institute For Women's Policy Research, April 2013, https://iwpr.org/wp-content/uploads/wpallimport/ files/iwpr-export/publications/C401.pdf.

63. See also Nancy Fraser, "Crisis of Care? On the Social-Reproductive Contradictions of Contemporary Capitalism," in *Social Reproduction Theory: Remapping Class, Recentering Oppression*, ed. Tithi Bhattacharya (London: Pluto Press, 2017), 21–36.
Rosen, "Care Crisis."

64. International Women's Strike USA, "Our Platform," https://www.womenstrikeus.org.

65. On the gender dynamics of neoliberalism, see especially Melinda Cooper, *Family Values: Between Neoliberalism and the New Social Conservatism* (New York: Zone Books, 2017). Cooper's book is important for the way it dissects neoliberalism without nostalgia for the Fordist family wage.

4. IDLE POWER: THE RIOT, THE COMMUNE, AND CAPITALIST TIME IN THOMAS PYNCHON'S *AGAINST THE DAY*

1. Ross Chambers, *Loiterature* (Lincoln: University of Nebraska Press, 1999).

2. Thomas Pynchon, "Sloth: Nearer, My Couch, to Thee," *New York Times*, June 6, 1993. http://www.nytimes.com/books/97/05/18/reviews/pynchon-sloth.html. See also Pynchon, *Against the Day* (New York: Penguin, 2006). Citations of text appear parenthetically in chapter's body

3. Kathi Weeks, *The Problem with Work: Feminism, Marxism, Antiwork Politics, and Postwork Imaginaries* (Durham, N.C.: Duke University Press, 2011), 203.

4. Thomas Pynchon, *Mason & Dixon* (New York: Henry Holt, 1997), 345.

5. Jonathan Crary, *24/7: Late Capitalism and the Ends of Sleep* (New York: Verso, 2014), 9.

6. See Karl Marx, *Capital: A Critique of Political Economy*, vol. 1, trans. Ben Fowkes (New York: Penguin, 1976), 1019–38. See also Antonio Negri, *Marx beyond Marx: Lessons on the Grundrisse*, ed. Jim Fleming, trans. Harry Cleaver, Michael Ryan, and Maurizio Viano (New York: Autonomedia Press, 1992), 114, 142, 163; Michael Hardt and Antonio Negri, *Empire* (Cambridge, Mass.: Harvard University Press, 2001), 254–56, 271–72; and Jason Read, *The Micro-Politics of Capital: Marx and the Prehistory of the Present* (Albany: State University of New York Press, 2003), chap. 3.

7. The social factory thesis was most notably articulated by Mario Tronti in "Factory and Society," an essay originally published in *Quaderni Rossi* (Red Notebooks), a journal that Tronti co-founded and which was central

to Autonomist Marxism (*Operaismo*). See "La fabbrica e la società," *Quaderni Rossi* 2 (1962): 1–31. For an English translation, see "Factory and Society," *Operaismo in English*, https://operaismoinenglish.wordpress.com/2013/06/13/factory-and-society/.

8. On the monetization of digital platforms, including social media, see Nick Srnicek, *Platform Capitalism* (New York: Polity, 2016).

9. On Italian autonomism's concept of self-valorization, see especially Negri, *Marx beyond Marx*; "Domination and Sabotage," in *Autonomia: Post-Political Politics*, ed. Sylvère Lotringer and Christian Marazzi (New York: Semiotext(e), 2007): 62–71; and Harry Cleaver, "The Inversion of Class Perspective in Marxian Theory: From Valorisation to Self-Valorisation," *libcom.org*, https://libcom.org/library/inversion-class-perspective-marxian-theory-valorization-self-valorization. Self-valorization supposes the strategy of refusal as a necessary component of emancipation. See Mario Tronti, "The Strategy of Refusal," in *Autonomia*, 28–35. On the history of Italian autonomism generally, see Steve Wright, *Storming Heaven: Class Composition and Struggle in Italian Autonomist Marxism* (London: Pluto Press, 2002).

10. The Christian doctrine of redeeming the time appears regularly in sermons beginning at least during the early modern period. The relevant biblical verse is Ephesians 5:15–16 in the *King James Version*: "See then that ye walk circumspectly, not as fools, but as wise, / Redeeming the time, because the days are evil." The Anglican cleric John Wesley offers a telling example of the doctrine in his Sermon 93: "Redeeming the Time," which focuses on the regulation of sleep for the sake of piety.

11. Jacques Derrida, *Dissemination*, trans. Barbara Johnson (Chicago: University of Chicago Press, 1981), 70, 93.

12. Ibid., 203.

13. The question of whether Marx's *Capital* is political has a history too long to reproduce here. Harry Cleaver offers an excellent overview of these debates in *Reading Capital Politically* (Leeds: AK Press, 2000). See also William Clare Roberts, *Marx's Inferno: The Political Theory of Capital* (Princeton, N.J.: Princeton University Press, 2016).

14. Marx, *Capital*, 1:375. Further references are cited parenthetically in the text.

15. Read, *Micro-Politics of Capital*, 141.

16. Fredric Jameson, *The Seeds of Time* (New York: Columbia University Press, 1994), part 1.

17. Tronti, "Factory and Society."

18. Ibid.

19. Tronti, "Strategy of Refusal," 30.

20. Gigi Roggero, "Notes on Framing and Re-Inventing Co-Research," *ephemera: theory & politics in organization* 14, no. 3 (2014): 517.
21. Ibid., 518.
22. See Paul Lafargue, *The Right to Be Lazy*, ed. Bernard Marszalek, trans. Charles Kerr (Oakland, Calif.: AK Press, 2011). There is too much work theorizing the possibility of a postwork society to summarize, but, beyond the autonomist tradition, see especially the writings of André Gorz, *Paths to Paradise: On the Liberation from Work* (London: Pluto, 1985). More recently, see Peter Frase, *Four Futures: Life after Capitalism* (New York: Verso, 2016), and Paul Mason, *Postcapitalism: A Guide to Our Future* (New York: Farrar, Straus and Giroux, 2015).
23. On the notion of means without ends, see Giorgio Agamben, "Notes on Gesture," in *Means without End: Notes on Politics*, trans. Vincenzo Binetti and Cesare Casarino (Minneapolis: University of Minnesota Press, 2000), 49–62.
24. Thomas Pynchon, "Sloth: Nearer, My Couch, to Thee," *New York Times*, June 6, 1993. http://www.nytimes.com/books/97/05/18/reviews/pynchon-sloth.html.
25. Ibid.
26. See Guy Debord, *Society of the Spectacle*, trans. Donald Nicholson-Smith (New York: Zone Books, 1995).
27. Thomas Pynchon, "Sloth: Nearer, My Couch, to Thee."
28. Ibid.
29. I owe my attention to this trope to Richard Hardack's "Consciousness without Borders: Narratology in *Against the Day* and the Works of Thomas Pynchon," *Criticism* 52, no. 1 (2010): 105–6.
30. William Logan, "Back to the Future: On Thomas Pynchon's *Against the Day*," *Virginia Quarterly Review Online*, Summer 2007. http://www.vqronline.org/back-future-thomas-pynchon%E2%80%99s-against-day.
31. Alex Woloch's *The One vs. The Many: Minor Characters and the Space of the Protagonist in the Novel* (Princeton, N.J.: Princeton University Press, 2003) remains an excellent account of the structural distribution of protagonists and minor characters.
32. Leo Bersani, *The Culture of Redemption* (Cambridge, Mass.: Harvard University Press, 1990), 194.
33. On this transcendent model of time, see especially Eric Alliez, *Capital Times: Tales from the Conquest of Time* (Minneapolis: University of Minnesota Press, 1996), chaps. 3, 4.
34. Anne-Lise François, "Taking Turns on the Commons (Or Lessons in Unenclosed Time)," in *River of Fire: Commons, Crisis, and the Imagination*, ed. Cal Winslow (Arlington, Mass.: Pumping Station, 2016), 364–65.

35. Joshua Clover, *Riot. Strike. Riot: The New Era of Uprisings* (New York: Verso, 2016), chaps. 7, 8.

36. The literature on financialization and logistics is too large to recapitulate here, but, in respect to the former, see especially Greta Krippner, "The Financialization of the American Economy," *Socio-Economic Review* 3, no. 2 (2005): 173–208; and Randy Martin, *The Financialization of Daily Life* (Philadelphia: Temple University Press, 2002). On logistics as a social matter, see especially, Deborah Cowen, *The Deadly Life of Logistics: Mapping Violence in Global Trade* (Minneapolis: University of Minnesota Press, 2014).

37. Thomas Pynchon, "A Journey into the Mind of Watts," *New York Times*, June 12, 1966. Accessed online June 2, 2017.

38. Clover, *Riot. Strike. Riot.*, 109–12.

39. Ibid., 122.

40. Judith Butler, *Notes toward a Performative Theory of Assembly* (Cambridge, Mass.: Harvard University Press, 2015).

41. See, for instance, Seán Molloy, "Escaping the Politics of the Irredeemable Earth: Anarchy and Transcendence in the Novels of Thomas Pynchon," *Theory & Event* 13, no. 3 (2010).

42. For another corrective to the reading of Pynchon as non- or antipolitical, see Samuel Thomas's *Pynchon and the Political* (New York: Routledge, 2007), 11–14.

43. Pynchon's work often blurs the line between different ontologies, as well as between the fictive and the real. Brian McHale offers the classic version of this argument. See *Postmodernist Fiction* (New York: Routledge, 1987), 21–43.

44. On intentional or utopian communities in the United States, see especially Mark Holloway, *Utopian Communities in America, 1680–1880* (New York: Dover, 1966); *America's Communal Utopias*, ed. Donald Pitzer (Chapel Hill: University of North Carolina Press, 1997); and *Paradise Now: The Story of American Utopianism* (New York: Random House, 2017).

45. On the enclave as a utopian form, see Fredric Jameson, *Archaeologies of the Future: The Desire Called Utopia and Other Science Fictions* (New York: Verso, 2005), part 1, chap. 2: "The Utopian Enclave."

46. See Ernst Bloch, *The Principle of Hope*, vol. 1, trans. Neville Plaice, Stephen Plaice, and Paul Knight (Cambridge, Mass.: MIT Press, 1986).

47. On the concept of use and the tradition of radical poverty, see especially Giorgio Agamben, *The Highest Poverty: Monastic Rules and Form-of-Life*, trans. Adam Kotsko (Stanford, Calif.: Stanford University Press, 2013), and *The Use of Bodies*, trans. Adam Kotsko (Stanford, Calif.: Stanford University Press, 2016).

48. On disidentification, see especially José Muñoz, *Disidentifications: Queers of Color and the Performance of Politics* (Minneapolis: University of Minnesota Press, 1999).

49. See M. M. Bakhtin on the carnivalesque in *Rabelais and His World*, trans. Helene Iswolsky (Bloomington: Indiana University Press, 1984).

50. See especially Jakob Taubes, *The Political Theology of Paul*, trans. Dana Hollander (Stanford, Calif.: Stanford University Press, 2003); Giorgio Agamben, *The Time That Remains: A Commentary on the Letter to the Romans*, trans. Patricia Dailey (Stanford Calif.: Stanford University Press, 2005); and Alain Badiou, *Saint Paul: The Foundation of Universalism*, trans. Ray Brassier (Stanford, Calif.: Stanford University Press, 2003).

51. Agamben, *Use of Bodies*, especially part 1, chap. 8: "The Inappropriable."

52. Giorgio Agamben, *Homo Sacer: Sovereign Power and Bare Life*, trans. Daniel Heller-Roazen (Stanford, Calif.: Stanford University Press, 1998), 166.

53. "On Potentiality," in *Potentialities: Collected Essays in Philosophy*, trans. Daniel Heller-Roazen (Stanford, Calif.: Stanford University Press, 1999), 182–83.

54. Agamben, *Means without End: Notes on Politics*, 3–4.

55. Agamben, *Use of Bodies*, 208.

56. I've written a critical overview of the *Homo Sacer* series, which elaborates on the connections among politics, sociality, and aesthetics in Agamben's thought. See Christian P. Haines, "A Lyric Intensity of Thought: On the Potentiality and Limits of Giorgio Agamben's 'Homo Sacer' Project, *boundary 2 online*, August 29, 2016. http://www.boundary2.org/2016/08/christian-haines-a-lyric-intensity-of-thought-on-the-potentiality-and-limits-of-giorgio-agambens-homo-sacer-project/.

57. Kristin Ross, *Communal Luxury: The Political Imaginary of the Paris Commune* (New York: Verso, 2015), 57–65. The Paris Commune appears indirectly in the novel in the form of the Garçons de '71, a group of aethernauts who participated in the commune.

CODA: ASSEMBLING THE FUTURE

1. Stanley Cavell, This New Yet Unapproachable America: Lectures after Emerson after Wittgenstein (Albuquerque, N.M.: Living Batch Press, 1989), 91–94, 106–9.

2. Michel Foucault, The Use of Pleasure: The History of Sexuality, vol. 2, trans. Robert Hurley (New York: Vintage, 1990), 8.

3. Leo Bersani, The Culture of Redemption (Cambridge, Mass.: Harvard University Press, 1990).

4. I am referring, here, to the loose collection of work (epitomized by Rita Felski's The Limits of Critique) that has argued for moving beyond traditions of critique in favor of affirmative modes of reading. For a detailed response to the postcritical turn, see Christian P. Haines, "Eaten Alive, or

Why the Death of Theory Is Not Antitheory," in Antitheory, ed. Jeffrey Di Leo (New York: Bloomsbury Press, 2019).

5. Chris Castiglia, "Hope for Critique?" in Critique and Postcritique (Durham, N.C.: Duke University Press, 2017), 226.

6. Ibid., 218.

7. With Judith Butler, I want to understand political assemblies not only as protests against specific wrongs but also as performative practices of collective transformation. The act of assembling turns the flesh into a figure of a world to come. It converts vulnerability into possibility. See Butler, Notes toward a Performative Theory of Assembly (Cambridge, Mass.: Harvard University Press, 2015).

8. Rebecca Solnit, Hope in the Dark: Untold Histories, Wild Possibilities, 3rd ed. (Chicago: Haymarket, 2016), 142.

9. Fred Moten, Black and Blur (Durham, N.C.: Duke University Press, 2017), 168–69.

INDEX

abolitionism, 16–17, 110–11
abstract labor, 103–5, 107–8
abstract utopianism, 14, 36, 59–60, 62–63, 67, 190
activism. *See* social movements
affective economy, of marriage, 123–25
affirmative biopolitics, 206
Against the Day (Pynchon), 28, 30, 158–68, 173–83, 186–203. *See also* Pynchon, Thomas, writings of
Agamben, Giorgio, 5–6, 12, 98, 152, 190, 194–96, 201
Ahmed, Sara, 119, 124, 125, 128, 136, 140, 147
Air Traffic Controllers' Strike (1981), 34
Althusser, Louis, 83
American exceptionalism: biopolitical theory and, 5–7, 11; critique of, 4–5, 6, 19, 23–24; defined, 3; desire called America and, 8–9; impossibility of, 10–11; literary commons and, 16–22, 206–7; origin of, 3–4; Reagan on, 33–34; reversal of (*see* singular America); social movements and, 207–8; violence associated with, 108–12; Whitman on, 76–77
American literature: American exceptionalism and, 4–5, 6; biopolitical approach to, 18–19, 23, 27–31; New Americanist critique of, 26–27; singular America in, 3, 7, 9–10, 16–22, 27–31, 206–7, 215n20 (*see also* singular America)
American Revolution, 3–4, 34–35, 39, 95, 100–8
American studies: Foucault's contribution to, 11–15; history of, 4–7, 213–14n10, 214n12; utopianism and, 15–16, 26–27
American Studies Association (ASA), 6
anarchy, 166–67, 173–75, 195–96
animacy, 76, 224n2
antiglobalization protests, 37, 60
anti-utopianism, 2–3, 11, 58, 158, 186–87
Arrighi, Giovanni, 24–25
Arsić, Branka, 18
ASA (American Studies Association), 6
assemblages, 15. *See also* utopianism
Assembly (Hardt & Negri), 63
atomism, 81–82, 89–90

Attridge, Derek, 215n20
austerity, politics of, 30
authoritarian populism, 1–2
Autonomist Marxists, 30, 159, 163, 166, 170–73, 177–78, 236n7

bare life, 12
Barthes, Roland, 129, 122
"Bartleby the Scrivener" (Melville), 177, 195–96
Beneath the American Renaissance (Reynolds), 26
Bennett, Jane, 76, 93–94, 227n28
Berlant, Lauren, 26, 128
Bersani, Leo, 181, 206
biopolitical theory: about, 5–6, 11–13, 213–14n10, 214n12; affirmative, 103, 206; labor politics and, 116, 118–27, 154–56, 159–60, 162–75; language as biological weapon and, 53–59; language as system of control and, 46–53, 58–59, 220–21nn29–30, 221–22n37, 222n48; as literary approach, 18–19, 23, 27–31; on marriage, 116, 118–27, 154–56; riots as, 185–86, 200–1; utopianism and, 11–16, 35–36, 55–58, 60, 103, 112, 206, 219n8
Black Lives Matter, 3, 16–17, 157, 207–8
black Prometheus, 19
Bloch, Ernst, 14, 62, 190, 216n36
"Blood-Money" (Whitman), 101–2
Bogg, James, 185
Boltanski, Luc, 222n48
"A Boston Ballad" (Whitman), 102
Bowles, Mary, 146
Bowles, Samuel, 146
Braidotti, Rosi, 76
Brecht, Bertolt, 42–43
Breu, Christopher, 49–50
Brown, Wendy, 40, 72
Burroughs, William S., writings of, 33–73; about, 9–10, 28–29, 34–37, 70–71; on "America as a nightmare," 58–59; *Cities of the Red Night* (trilogy book 1), 28–29, 34–36, 37–39, 72–73; creation myth in, 221n35; on drug addiction, 36, 219n8; on evolution, 44–45, 47–48; future vision for America in, 72–73; *The Job*, 47, 220–

241

Burroughs, William S. *(continued)*
  21n30, 221n35; language-as-a-biological weapon theory, 53–59; language-as-system-of-control theory, 46–53, 58–59, 220–21nn29–30, 221–22n37, 222n48; "The Limits of Control," 50–51; literary forms in, 17, 54–55, 69–70, 72–73, 206; *Naked Lunch*, 35, 53; *The Place of Dead Roads* (trilogy book 2), 28–29, 34–37, 39, 41, 42–46, 55–60, 64–71, 72–73; *Port of Saints*, 35; repetition in, 69–70; *Speed*, 53; on theology, 47–48; utopianism in *(see* retroactive utopianism); *The Western Lands* (trilogy book 3), 28–29, 34–37, 39, 59, 72–73
Butler, Judith, 185–86, 214n10
Byrd, Jodi, 39–40

caesura, 152, 164
Cameron, Sharon, 18
Capital (Marx), 163, 168–70, 175–76, 222n55
capitalism. *See* American exceptionalism; labor politics; social movements; social reproduction theory
capitalist commons, 135
capitalist time, 162–64
Carter, Jimmy, 33
Casarino, Cesare, 9, 67, 213–14n10
Castiglia, Chris, 5, 206
Cavell, Stanley, 18, 205
Chambers, Ross, 158, 161
Chen, Mel Y., 76
Chiapello, Ève, 222n48
chiasmus, 14
Cities of the Red Night (Burroughs's trilogy), 28–29, 34–36, 37–39, 72–73
class conflicts: Burroughs on, 56–58; Dickinson on, 30, 116, 118–27, 132, 136–37, 154–56; of minorities, 50; Whitman on, 85, 98, 104; working day deconstruction as, 163. *See also* labor politics
Clinton, Bill, 34
Clover, Joshua, 183, 185
coercion, 51
Cold War ideology, 26–27, 33, 58
collectivity, 76, 78–79, 81–83, 100, 108
Columbian Magazine, on housewives, 125–26
commons. *See* literary commons
Commonwealth (Hardt & Negri), 63
communes, 30, 161, 183–84, 186–87, 189–91, 197–201, 202
concrete utopianism, 14, 29, 62–64, 216n36
conservative morality, 53–59
constituent power, 107–8, 110–12
control societies, 52–53
control systems, language as, 46–53, 58–59, 220–21nn29–30, 221–22n37, 222n48
Cooper, Melinda, 72, 235n65
co-research, 172–73, 175, 176

Costa, Mariarosa Dalla, 118, 131
counter-nationalism. *See* singular America
Coviello, Peter, 88
Crary, Jonathan, 162
critical hopefulness, 206
Crumbley, Paul, 151, 233n42
The Crying of Lot 49 (Pynchon), 160, 186
curiosity, in literature, 11, 205–6
cut-up method of writing, 48–49
Cynics, 14–15

dashes (punctuation), 150–53
Deleuze, Gilles, 9, 18–19, 21–22, 23, 52–53, 88, 218n63, 222n48
democracy, double voicing of, 76–79, 94–99, 107–12, 113, 224n2, 227n28
Derrida, Jacques, 167, 220n29
desire called America: about, 7–9, 11; ambiguity of, 10, 19–20; in American literature *(see* literary commons; singular America); American studies and, 6; defined, 3, 7; origin of, 3–4; temporality of, 22–24
Dickinson, Austin, 149
Dickinson, Emily, writings of, 114–56; about, 7, 9–10, 28, 116–18; affective economy of marriage, 123–25; on American exceptionalism, 114–16, 128–29, 153–56; commons as noncapitalist commodity, 135–40; commons as secret societies, 154, 233nn42,45; embodiment and, 131–35, 152–53; happiness and, 125–26; "I dwell in Possibility," 153–54; "I gave Myself to Him," 120–28, 129; "I'm Nobody! Who are you?" 116–17, 141–47, 148; "I'm 'wife,'" 129–31; killjoys and, 117–18, 119, 127–31; lesbianism and, 146–48; letters, 114–16, 132, 146, 148–50; literary forms in, 120–22, 150–53; marriage as death in, 129–31; marriage poems, 29–30, 116–48, 153–56; materialism of, 117, 132–33; "Nobody" and, 117–18, 131–35, 154–55; on poetry, 134–35, 153–54; queer passion communities in, 30, 116, 148–53; queer phenomenology of, 136–40; social reproduction theory and, 30, 116, 118–27, 132, 154–56; "Title divine is mine," 137–40; utopian inconspicuousness in, 29–30, 116–17, 131, 140–48, 154
digression, 161, 176, 178–80, 181, 182
dilation, 161, 176, 178, 179–80, 181, 182
Dillon, Elizabeth Maddock, 21, 140, 144
Dimock, Wai Chee, 99
disciplinary societies, 52, 88
disidentification, 11, 118, 145–46, 192–93, 200
disutopia, 63–64
doubling, 99–101, 176, 178, 180–82, 228n38

Index 243

drug addiction, 36, 219n8
dystopia, 63

ecstasy: of commons, 91–93; dissolution of self as, 142–45, 147, 193; of sharing, 83, 149
Edelman, Lee, 145, 233n46
Emerson, Ralph Waldo, 205
Erkkila, Betsy, 86, 101
Ethics (Spinoza), 87
"Europe: The 72nd and 73rd Years of these States" (Whitman), 102
evental democracy, 29, 76, 78–79, 94–99, 107–8, 111–12, 113
evolution, 44–45, 47–48
exceptionalism. *See* American exceptionalism

failure of political imagination, 2–3
faith in anatomy, 134–35
Federici, Silvia, 118, 122, 126, 131–32, 135
form-of-life, 196
Foucault, Michel: biopolitics theory of, 5–6, 11–13, 56, 215n24; on curiosity, 11, 205; on Cynics, 14–15; on disciplinary societies, 52, 88; *The History of Sexuality*, 11, 12, 88; on sexuality, 89; "The Subject and Power," 11; "The Utopian Body" (radio address), 13–14; utopianism and, 13–14, 116
Fourier, Charles, 92–93
François, Anne-Lise, 183, 233n36
Frank, Jason, 87, 99–100
Franklin, Benjamin, 177
Freeman, Elizabeth, 147
French Revolution, 101–2
frontiers, 37, 39, 41–42
Fuss, Diana, 137

gender inequality, 30, 116, 118–27, 132, 154–56. *See also* Dickinson, Emily, writings of
genocide, 55–59
George (king), 102
Gilbert, Sue, 146, 148–50, 152
Gilmore, Ruth Wilson, 185
"The Global Homeland State Bush's Biopolitical Settlement" (Pease), 213–14n10
Gonzalez, Maya, 118
grain of the voice, 122
Gravity's Rainbow (Pynchon), 158, 160, 181
Grossman, Allen, 94
Guattari, Félix, 9, 53

Halberstam, Jack, 147
Hall, Stuart, 1–2
Hardt, Michael, 37, 61–64
Harvey, David, 46, 24–25
Hegel, Georg Wilhelm Friedrich, 19, 20
Hegeman, Susan, 214n12

hegemony, of United States, 24–27, 29, 33–37, 39, 40–41, 58–59, 71–72, 109
Heidegger, Martin, 81
heterotopias, 13, 116–17
Hickman, Jared, 19
hieroglyphics, 48–49, 51–52
Higginson, T. W., 134, 146
historical *a priori*, 13
historical multitude, 62, 63–64
Homo Sacer (Agamben), 195
Houen, Alex, 220n24
housewives. *See* Dickinson, Emily, writings of
Husserl, Edmund, 136

idleness, 30, 159–61, 175–83
"I dwell in Possibility" (Dickinson), 153–54
"I gave Myself to Him" (Dickinson), 120–28, 129
immanent utopianism, 13–14, 29–30, 43, 64, 116
"I'm Nobody! Who are you?" (Dickinson), 116–17, 141–47, 148
"I'm 'wife'<HS>" (Dickinson), 129–31
institutionality, 22, 63, 107–8
International Feminist Collective, 131
International Wages for Housework Campaign, 131–32, 155
International Women's Strike (2017), 155
"in times like these," utopianism and, 22–31, 112–13, 157–58, 207–8
"I Sing the Body Electric" (Whitman), 83–85, 103, 109–11

Jackson, Virginia, 134
James, Selma, 118, 131
Jameson, Fredric, 43, 67, 170, 220n22, 223n57
The Job (Burroughs), 47, 220–21n30, 221n35
jouissance principle, 8–11, 27–28, 165–66, 168, 205–6, 215n16
"A Journey into the Mind of Watts" (Pynchon), 161, 184–86

Kaplan, Amy, 26
Klammer, Martin, 111
Know Nothings, 102

labor politics: biopolitical theory and, 116, 118–27, 154–56, 159–60, 162–75; gender dynamics of, 30, 116, 118–28, 132, 154–56; living labor, 103–8, 112, 164–66, 168–69, 173, 228n45; Marxism on, 122; Whitman on, 103–4
Lacan, Jacques, 8, 10, 49–50, 215n16
Lafargue, Paul, 173
language: as biological weapon, 53–59; doubling, 99–101, 176, 178, 180–82, 228n38; as expression of body, 83–85;

language (*continued*)
as expression of life, 85–88; repetition, 69–70; as system of control, 46–53, 58–59, 220–21nn29–30, 221–22n37, 222n48
Lawrence, D. H., 101
Leaves of Grass (Whitman), 28, 29, 74–78, 80–113. *See also* Whitman, Walt, poetry of
Lerner, Ben, 112
"Let's Make America Great Again" slogan, 1–2, 25, 33–34, 40–41, 71–72, 158
Levine, Caroline, 17, 21
"life itself," 12–13
"The Limits of Control" (Burroughs), 50–51
Lincoln, Abraham, 94, 112
Linebaugh, Peter, 20–21
literary commons: defined, 7, 15; as material commonwealth, 17, 76, 79–88; multitudes as, 17, 61–63, 66–71; as noncapitalist commodity, 135–40; queer sexual commons, 191–95, 197, 200–1; as secret societies, 154, 233nn42,45; singular America as, 16–22, 206–7, 215n20, 217n54; as utopian figurations, 187–90
living labor, 103–8, 112, 164–66, 168–69, 173
Locke, John, 19, 41
loiterature, 158

Macpherson, C. B., 80
Magna Carta, 20
majoritarian utopianism, 29
"Make America Great Again" slogan, 1–2, 25, 33–34, 40–41, 71–72, 158
Manifest Destiny, 17, 41, 174–75, 203
Manly Health and Training (Whitman), 224n2, 226n21
Marcuse, Herbert, 43
marriage poems, 29–30, 116–48, 153–56. *See also* Dickinson, Emily, writings of
Marrs, Cody, 101
Martin, Robert, 92
Marx, Karl, 83, 104–5, 163, 168–70, 175–76, 222n55
Marxism: Autonomist Marxists, 30, 159, 163, 166, 170–73, 177–78, 236n7; feminist, 118; on labor power, 122; on living labor, 104–5; working day deconstruction, 163
Mason & Dixon (Pynchon), 160
material commonwealth, 76, 79–88
Matthiessen, F. O., 27, 77, 205
Melville, Herman, 26, 28, 177, 195–96
militance, 9–10, 15–16, 24, 158–61, 165, 168–69
Miller, Cristanne, 150
Modernity at Sea: Melville, Marx, and Conrad in Crisis (Casarino), 213–14n10

Moon, Michael, 92–93, 225n10
morality, conservative, 53–59
Moten, Fred, 19, 111, 207
multitudes, politics of, 60–66, 223n57
Multitude: War and Democracy in the Age of Empire (Hardt & Negri), 61–63
Muñoz, José Esteban, 15–16, 147–48
Murphy, Timothy, 35, 221–22n37
mythography, 19

Naked Lunch (Burroughs), 35, 53
Nancy, Jean-Luc, 83
Nash, Gary B., 228n38
national sentimentality. *See* American exceptionalism
nature, politics of, 86–87
Nealon, Jeffrey, 35
Negri, Antonio: biopolitics theory of, 5–6, 12–13; on constituent power, 107; on Marxism, 159, 163; materialism and, 83; on politics of the multitudes, 37, 61–64; on utopianism, 66
Nelson, Dana, 21
neoliberalism: gender dynamics of, 154–56, 235n65; history of, 1–2; hope from, 158–59; language as weapon against, 54–55; retroactive utopianism and, 33–37, 40–42, 45–46, 59–61, 63, 70–71, 72–73; riots and, 201–2
The New American Exceptionalism (Pease), 217n54
New American studies: on American Renaissance literature, 26–27; on post-Vietnam War literature, 5–7, 27
Noble, Mark, 81

Obama, Barack, 34, 112
objectified labor, 104–5
objet petit a, 8
Occupy Movement, 16–17, 157
ontological multitude, 62, 63–64
Orwell, George, 165–66

Paine, Thomas, 3–4, 8
pantheism, 74–76, 78, 79–81, 86
Parnet, Claire, 53
Patterson, Orlando, 110
Pease, Donald, 26, 109, 213–14n10, 217n54, 228n37
performative commons, 21
pharmakon, 167–68, 174
philopoesis, 9
The Place of Dead Roads (Burroughs's trilogy), 28–29, 34–37, 39, 41, 42–46, 55–60, 64–71, 72–73. *See also* Burroughs, William S., writings of
Plato, 74–75, 94
Port of Saints (Burroughs), 35
positivism, 12–13, 42, 58, 64, 206
precapitalist commons, 135

Index

Precarious Life: The Powers of Mourning and Violence (Butler), 214n10
The Principle of Hope (Bloch), 62
Puar, Jasbir, 15–16, 215n24
Pynchon, Thomas, writings of, 157–203; about, 9–10, 28, 158–62, 191–92; *Against the Day*, 28, 30, 158–68, 173–83, 186–203; on American exceptionalism, 160–61, 165–66, 202–3; anarchy in, 166–67, 173–75, 195–96; capitalist time, 162–64; communes and, 30, 161, 183–84, 186–87, 189–91, 197–201, 202; *The Crying of Lot 49*, 160, 186; disidentification in, 192–93, 200; *Gravity's Rainbow*, 158, 160, 181; "A Journey into the Mind of Watts," 161, 184–86; literary forms in, 161, 176, 178–81; living labor, 164–65, 168–69; *Mason & Dixon*, 160; poverty in, 190–92; queer sexual commons in, 191–95, 197, 200–1; redeeming time, 167–68; retroactive utopianism in, 160; riots and, 30, 161, 183–87, 201–3; singularity in, 192–93, 200; sloth, in praise of, 30, 159–61, 175–83; "Sloth: Nearer, My Couch, to Thee," 176–78; time irreversibility in, 181–82; utopian figurations of the commons, 187–90; *Vineland*, 160, 186; working day as biopolitical struggle, 159–60, 162–75; work refusals, 30, 173–75

queer identity: in *Leaves of Grass*, 89, 91–93; lesbianism and, 146–48; queer erotics, 78, 79, 89–94; queer passion communities, 30, 116, 148–53; queer phenomenology, 30, 135–40; queer relationality, 30, 147–53; queer sexual commons, 191–95, 197, 200–1

race and racism, 19, 55–59, 86, 110–12, 228n42
Radway, Janice, 6
reactive politics, 103, 228n44
reactive utopianism, 33–34
Read, Jason, 169
Reagan, Ronald, 33–34. *See also* "Make America Great Again" slogan
redemption, 167–73, 236n10
refusal to work, 30, 173–75. *See also* labor politics; sloth, in praise of
reproductive futurism, 145–46
Republic (Plato), 94
"Resurgemus" (Whitman), 101–2
retroactive utopianism: about, 25, 29, 34–37, 70–71, 159–60; Burroughs's comments on, 36, 38; disutopianism and, 63–66; morality and, 55–59; multitudes as "the common" in, 17, 61–63, 66–71; politics of multitudes and, 60–63, 223n57; Potential America as, 36, 55, 77; settler colonialism and, 37–40, 57, 70; social potentiality of, 36, 40–46, 55, 59–60, 67, 77; social revolutions and, 25, 37–39; U.S. hegemony and, 25–26, 33–37, 38–39, 58–59, 71–72; war against control and, 53–59
revolutions, 3–4, 25, 34–35, 37–39, 95, 100–8
Reynolds, David, 26, 102
Rich, Adrienne, 22–23
Rifkin, Mark, 39–40
The Right to Laziness (Lafargue), 173
riots, 30, 161, 183–87, 201–3
Roggero, Gigi, 172
Root, Abiah, 132
Rose, Nikolas, 45–46
Rosen, Ruth, 154
Ross, Kristin, 197

Sánchez-Eppler, Karen, 132
Sanders, Bernie, 2
science fiction genre, 29, 37, 39, 41, 42–46, 72–73, 220n22
Seattle WTO protests (1999), 60
settler colonialism, 3–4, 19–20, 37–40, 57, 70, 109–10
sexuality: lesbianism and, 146–48; queer erotics, 78, 79, 89–94; queer passion communities, 30, 116, 148–53; queer phenomenology, 30, 135–40; queer relationality, 30, 147–53; queer sexual commons, 191–95, 197, 200–1
singular America: about, 3–7, 16, 206; defined, 3, 7; examples of, 3, 16–17, 31, 60, 157, 207–8; feminist vision of, 155–56; as the impossibility at the heart of exceptionalism, 10–11, 16 (*see also* utopianism); literary approaches to, 3, 7, 9–10, 16–22, 27–31, 206–7, 215n20 (*see also* Burroughs, William S., writings of; Dickinson, Emily, writings of; Pynchon, Thomas, writings of; Whitman, Walt, poetry of); temporality of, 22–31
singularities, 23–24, 192–93, 200, 218n63
slavery, 86, 110–12, 228n42
sloth, in praise of, 30, 159–61, 175–83
"Sloth: Nearer, My Couch, to Thee" (Pynchon), 176–78
small pox virus, 55–57
Snediker, Michael D., 147
social factory thesis, 163–64, 235–36n7
social movements: anti-utopianism and, 2–3; history of, 131–32, 157–58; retroactive utopianism and, 36, 37–39; as singular America example, 3, 16–17, 31, 60, 155, 157, 207–8
social reproduction theory, 30, 116, 118–27, 132, 154–56
Socrates, 14
Solnit, Rebecca, 207

"Song for Certain Congressmen" (Whitman), 101–2
"A Song for Occupations" (Whitman), 103–4, 105–8
"Song of Myself" (Whitman), 81–82, 96–98
Spanos, William V., 6–7, 27
Speed (Burroughs), 53
Spinoza, Baruch, 62, 74–75, 83, 87–88
Stacy, Jason, 108
subjectivity, 11, 13, 60, 80–85
Suvin, Darko, 42–43
syllabic language, 51–52

Thatcherism, 1–2
A Thousand Plateaus (Deleuze), 53
Tiffany, Daniel, 140–41
time irreversibility, 181–82
"times like these," utopianism in, 22–31, 112–13, 157–58, 207–8
TINA ("There Is No Alternative"), 63
"Title divine is mine" (Dickinson), 137–40
Todd, Mabel Loomis, 114–16
Tronti, Mario, 159, 170–72, 235–36n7
Trump, Donald, 1–2, 155–56, 157–58, 201–2, 207–8. *See also* "Make America Great Again" slogan

unions, 34
universality, 15
universal vitalism, 76–77
U.S. hegemony, 24–27, 29, 33–37, 39, 40–41, 58–59, 71–72, 109
utopian imagination, 43
utopianism: abandonment of, 2–3, 158; biopolitics of, 11–16, 35–36, 55–58, 60, 103, 112, 206, 219n8; of Burroughs (*see* retroactive utopianism); Dickinson's inconspicuousness of, 29–30, 116–17, 131, 140–48, 154; embodiment of, 3, 7, 9–10, 16–22, 206–8; Pynchon on, 30, 159–61, 175–82, 183, 187–90; of riots, 185; "in times like these," 22–31, 112–13, 157–58, 207–8; Whitman's utopian potentialism, 29, 77, 78–79, 95–102, 108, 113. *See also specific types of utopias*

Verfremdungseffekt, 42–43
Vietnam Syndrome, 39
Vietnam War, 38–39
Vineland (Pynchon), 160, 186
violence, associated with American exceptionalism, in Whitman's writings, 108–12
Virno, Paolo, 159
virus: language as, 46–53, 58–59, 220–21nn29–30, 221–22n37, 222n48; small pox virus, 55–57

vitalist democracy, 29, 76–79, 94, 98–99, 107, 109–11, 113, 224n2, 227n28

Wald, Priscilla, 6
Wallerstein, Immanuel, 24–25
Warner, Michael, 93
Washington Daily National Intelligencer, review of *Leaves of Grass*, 74–76
Watts riots (1965), 161, 184–87
Weeks, Kathi, 159, 173
Wegner, Phillip, 67
Weheliye, Alexander, 215n24
Wesley, John, 236n10
western genre, 29, 37, 39, 41–42, 72–73, 219n15
The Western Lands (Burroughs's trilogy), 28–29, 34–37, 39 59, 72–73
"What Kind of Times Are These" (Rich), 22–23
Whitman, Walt, poetry of, 74–113; about, 9–10, 28–29; on American exceptionalism, 76–77, 86–88; American Revolution and, 95, 100–8; "Blood-Money," 101–2; "A Boston Ballad," 102; collectivity expressed in, 76, 78–79, 81–83, 100, 108; double voicing of democracy in, 76–79, 94–99, 107–12, 113, 224n2, 227n28; "Europe: The 72nd and 73rd Years of these States," 102; hope and, 112–13; "I Sing the Body Electric," 83–85, 103, 109–11; on labor power, 103–8; *Leaves of Grass* (1855), 28, 29, 74–78, 80–113; *Leaves of Grass* (1855) review, 74–76; *Leaves of Grass* editions, 77–78; literary forms in, 17, 83–88, 103–6; *Manly Health and Training*, 224n2, 226n21; material commonwealth and, 76, 79–88; ontology of life in, 79–94; pantheism and, 74–76, 78, 79–81, 86; politics of nature in, 86–87; queer erotics and, 78, 79, 89–94; "Resurgemus," 101–2; on slavery, 86, 110–12, 228n42; "Song for Certain Congressmen," 101–2; "A Song for Occupations," 103–4, 105–8; "Song of Myself," 81–82, 96–98; subjectivity in, 80–85; utopian potentialism of, 29, 77, 78–79, 95–102, 108, 113
Wiegman, Robyn, 5
Women's Marches, 207–8
working day, as biopolitical struggle, 159–60, 162–75. *See also* labor politics
work refusals, 30, 173–75. *See also* labor politics
World Trade Organization protests (1999), 60
Wynter, Sylvia, 19, 215n24

Žižek, Slavoj, 25

CHRISTIAN P. HAINES is Assistant Professor of English at Penn State University. His work has appeared in journals including *Criticism*, *Genre*, *Cultural Critique*, and *boundary 2*. He serves as a contributing editor for *Angelaki: Journal of the Theoretical Humanities* and is co-editor of a special issue of *Cultural Critique*, "What Comes After the Subject?"

Printed in the USA
CPSIA information can be obtained
at www.ICGtesting.com
CBHW031743021123
1650CB00004B/60